NARRATION IN THE GERMAN NOVELLE

ANGLICA GERMANICA SERIES 2

Editors: LEONARD FORSTER, S. S. PRAWER *and* A. T. HATTO

Other books in the series

D. Prohaska: Raimund and Vienna: A Critical Study of Raimund's plays in their Viennese Setting

D. G. Mowatt: Friderich von Hûsen: Introduction, Text, Commentary and Glossary

C. Lofmark: Rennewart in Wolfram's 'Willehalm': A Study of Wolfram von Eschenbach and his Sources

A. Stephens: Rainer Maria Rilke's 'Gedichte an die Nacht'

M. Garland: Hebbel's Prose Tragedies

H. Cohn: Else Lasker-Schuler, The Broken World

NARRATION IN THE GERMAN NOVELLE

THEORY AND INTERPRETATION

JOHN M. ELLIS

Professor of German Literature
University of California, Santa Cruz

CAMBRIDGE UNIVERSITY PRESS

Published by the Syndics of the Cambridge University Press
Bentley House, 200 Euston Road, London NW1 2DB
American Branch: 32 East 57th Street, New York, N.Y.10022

© Cambridge University Press 1974

Library of Congress Catalogue Card Number: 73–82460

ISBN: 0 521 20330 9

First published 1974

Printed in Great Britain
at the University Printing House, Cambridge
(Brooke Crutchley, University Printer)

CONTENTS

PREFACE

The main body of this study is devoted to interpretative essays on individual Novellen. In one sense, the chapters are self-contained; each is devoted to the interpretation of a particular story. But in another sense, they all involve one central problem: the relation of the narrator to his story, and the importance of this relationship for its interpretation. My study is thus equally concerned with the interpretation of eight well-known German stories, and with the general theoretical question of the role of the narrator. The eight stories chosen are not a representative sample of the field, nor do I justify the choice as a historical survey: I have, for example, omitted Stifter, Gotthelf and Meyer, while including Tieck's *Der blonde Eckbert*, a story not normally discussed within the framework of German Novellen. My choice is mainly dictated by my central concern: I have chosen stories in which an adequate account of the narrator's relation to his story is unusually important for an interpretation. But another factor was a desire for variety and contrast; these eight stories use the narrator in very different ways for different purposes. Tieck's story, for example, is included because it provides an example of a narrative convention unlike that of any of the other stories chosen.

My introductory chapter is concerned with the general theory of this undertaking; and since the general frameworks within which a series of texts is discussed are always to some extent in competition, I have first of all considered the usefulness of the two most commonly employed for most of these texts: that of the genre 'Novelle', on the one hand, and that of nineteenth century Realism, on the other. The rest of the introductory chapter is then devoted to a general discussion of narration, covering both the theoretical distinctions which need to be made, and the practical range of possible uses of the narrator. Here I draw on the results of the eight interpretations to contrast the different ways in which the narrative schemes achieve thematic importance.

I must acknowledge many different kinds of debts to people and organisations who have been helpful to me. The John Simon Guggenheim Foundation very generously made it possible for me to complete this work by awarding me a Fellowship for the year 1970–1. The University of California also, in granting me sabbatical leave, has helped to provide time for my research. I am indebted to the English Goethe Society, and to the Editors of the *Germanic Review*, for permission to use again the material which largely forms the basis of my second and seventh chapters, and which originally appeared as 'Kleist's *Das Erdbeben in Chili*', *Publications of the English Goethe Society*, XXXIII (1963), 10–55, and 'Narration in Storm's *Der Schimmelreiter*', *Germanic Review*, XLIV (1969), 21–30.

It is not possible to say how much I have been helped by conversations over the years with teachers, friends and students concerning the theory and the texts discussed in this book, but I must especially thank Brian Rowley, Siegfried Puknat, and above all William Lillyman and Colin Russ, who read the manuscript and gave me many suggestions for its improvement. I cannot begin to describe the ways in which Carol Ellis helped my work to its conclusion.

J.M.E.

October 1971
Santa Cruz, California

1. INTRODUCTION:
THEORY AND INTERPRETATION

The German Novelle, always a popular field of study in German Literature, has been the subject of increasing attention in the last decade. During the 1960s another history of the Novelle appeared (by Himmel),[1] Bennett's older history was reissued, revised and brought up to date by Waidson, and Kunz began to publish a multi-volume history of the Novelle based on his earlier, shorter history.[2] A second volume of interpretations was produced by Benno von Wiese,[3] and four volumes concerned with the theory of the Novelle also appeared: one in the series 'Sammlung Metzler', by von Wiese,[4] a general discussion of Novelle theory by Malmede,[5] an important collection of essays from Wieland and Goethe to the present day in the 'Wege der Forschung' series,[6]

[1] Hellmuth Himmel, *Geschichte der deutschen Novelle* (Berne and Munich, 1963).

[2] E. K. Bennett, *A History of the German Novelle*, 2nd ed., revised and continued by H. M. Waidson (Cambridge, 1961). The first edition of this standard work appeared in 1934. Josef Kunz's original history was his contribution to *Deutsche Philologie im Aufriss*, II (Berlin, 1954), 'Geschichte der deutschen Novelle vom 18. Jahrhundert bis auf die Gegenwart'. A much revised and extended version of this is appearing as three volumes in the *Grundlagen der Germanistik* series published by the Erich Schmidt Verlag; the first two volumes have appeared: *Die deutsche Novelle zwischen Klassik und Romantik* (1966), and *Die deutsche Novelle im 19. Jahrhundert* (1970). Other standard histories of the German Novelle are those by Johannes Klein, *Geschichte der deutschen Novelle*, 4th ed. (Wiesbaden, 1960), and Fritz Lockemann, *Gestalt und Wandlungen der deutschen Novelle* (Munich, 1957).

[3] Benno von Wiese, *Die deutsche Novelle von Goethe bis Kafka: Interpretationen*, II (Düsseldorf, 1962). The first volume appeared in 1956.

[4] Benno von Wiese, *Novelle*, 3rd ed. (Stuttgart, 1967). First edition in 1963.

[5] Hans Hermann Malmede, *Wege zur Novelle. Theorie und Interpretation der Gattung Novelle in der deutschen Literaturwissenschaft* (Stuttgart/Berlin/Cologne/Mainz, 1966). Malmede's book is adversely reviewed by Karl Konrad Polheim in *Zeitschrift für deutsche Philologie*, LXXXV (1966), 615–28. Polheim regards Malmede's work as one which attacks previous Novelle theorists in a clumsy and unnecessarily personal way, while making no substantial positive contribution of its own to the field; and this view appears to me a reasonable one.

[6] *Novelle*, ed. Josef Kunz (Darmstadt, 1968). This volume is an invaluable collection of classic essays by Schlegel, Tieck, Spielhagen, Heyse, et al., together with a number of standard modern discussions by, e.g., Walzel, Pongs, Grolmann, Pabst, Schunicht, and many others. A comparable collection, including the same kind of material, has just appeared: *Theorie und Kritik der deutschen Novelle von Wieland bis Musil*, ed. Karl

and a 'Forschungsbericht' on the years 1945–64 by Polheim,[1] which is very largely a protracted discussion of theoretical issues. It is clear from this brief survey not only that there has been more writing on the Novelle in the last decade than in that which preceded it, but that the theory of the Novelle is now taking a larger place in such writing; in the 1950s histories of the Novelle and collections of interpretations appeared,[2] but no volume devoted primarily to the theory of the genre.

Throughout the nineteenth century, and right up to the present day, the most discussed question in the theory of the Novelle has been the simple one: what is a Novelle? And it is still, in the most recent work on the subject, thought to be as problematic as ever: this question, says Polheim, still in 1970 'bereitet der deutschen Literaturwissenschaft seit einiger Zeit erhebliches Kopfzerbrechen'.[3] In the discussion which follows I shall first set out the dimensions of the problem, and then suggest that it can be solved by means of modern conceptual analysis. Recent discussion takes place largely against the background of certain very well-known statements[4] made mainly in the nineteenth century, though there have been many different adaptations of these ideas. Despite a good deal of minor variation, however, there is a large area of common ground which is accepted by nearly all critics and scholars who have discussed the issue, and certainly by all the recent writers of histories of the Novelle.[5] It has been agreed that

Konrad Polheim (Tübingen, 1970). But the two collections do not cover the same ground; Kunz's collection is mainly concerned with the twentieth century, while Polheim's is exclusively concerned with the earlier periods.

[1] Karl Konrad Polheim, *Novellentheorie und Novellenforschung. Ein Forschungsbericht 1945–1964* (Stuttgart, 1965). This is, from a theoretical point of view, the most sensible contribution to Novelle literature in the last few decades.

[2] E.g., the works by Klein, Lockemann, and von Wiese mentioned above, and also Walter Silz's *Realism and Reality. Studies in the German Novelle of Poetic Realism* (Chapel Hill, 1954).

[3] Polheim, *Theorie und Kritik der deutschen Novelle*, p. xiii.

[4] These are reviewed by, for example, Bennett and Silz. Texts of these classic statements can be found in *Novelle*, ed. Kunz, or *Theorie und Kritik der deutschen Novelle*, ed. Polheim.

[5] E.g., Bennett, Klein, Himmel, Kunz, Lockemann; cf. also von Wiese, with his three volumes on the Novelle; and the excellent recent collection of texts *Deutsche Novellen von Tieck bis Hauptmann*, ed. A. P. Foulkes and E. Lohner (Boston, 1969). Two signi-

the Novelle deals with a *single* event, and one which is of a striking character (i.e., 'headlines' material). Thus, it is a realistic genre. The striking event makes for a narrative with a rather clear outline, and one which is sharply focused; this means that it is in its composition artistically concentrated. Because the event is so central, character is less important in the Novelle, and there is little or no development of character.[1]

This much is almost universally accepted. In addition, certain views about the narration of the Novelle, and also its temper, are commonly expressed. In that a striking event is related as if it had actually happened, it is asserted that the narration which is appropriate to the Novelle is objective and distanced;[2] the narrator

ficant exceptions are Polheim and von Arx, whose contributions I shall discuss below; but even the iconoclast Malmede accepts at least part of this common ground in his concentration on a certain kind of event as being the material of a Novelle.

[1] It will be useful to set out a sample of these points as formulated by some of the most representative, up-to-date, and widely read scholars. Von Wiese, *Die Deutsche Novelle*, I, 15–16: '... die Heraushebung *eines* Ereignisses, der Vorrang des Ereignisses vor den Personen, die pointierende Darstellung ...', and p. 14: 'Das Charakteristische der Novelle liegt vor allem in der Beschränkung auf *eine* Begebenheit.' His *Novelle*, p. 12, stresses that what a Novelle needs above all else is 'das novellistische Ereignis'; p. 26 of *Die deutsche Novelle*, I, speaks of '... das Profilierende, Pointierende und Herausgehobene des erzählten isolierten Falles ...', and of the Novelle as a genre which demands 'Beschränkung, Konzentration und Überraschung'. Bennett, p. 1: 'A minimum of definition, to be elaborated in the course of this survey, is the following: a Novelle is a narrative in prose, usually shorter than a novel, dealing with one particular situation, conflict, event, or aspect of a personality; it narrates something "new" in the sense of something unusual or striking.' Cf. also his pp. 18–19. Silz, p. 6: '... it must be concentrated and intensified, limited to one central event of crucial importance'. Kunz, *Novelle*, p. 22: '... trotz der Verschiedenheit, ja Gegensätzlichkeit der Novellentheorien bleibt durchgängig eine Gemeinsamkeit bestehen, die im allgemeinen nicht in Frage gestellt wird: daß sich diese Gattungsform auf ein Geschehen "ereignishafter" Art zentriert.' Cf. also Foulkes and Lohner, p. 1: 'Even today, a strict definition of the literary genre *Novelle* would tend to emphasise the structural and narrative qualities which would of necessity accompany the portrayal of a single "novel" occurrence. Most *Novellen* are distinguished by the fact that they depict a particular situation, portraying persons, things, and actions only insofar as they are directly affected by this central situation.' Klein's history elaborates this basic definition considerably, but without abandoning any of it.

[2] E.g., von Wiese, *Die deutsche Novelle*, II, 12–13. Koskimies in his recent 'Theorie der Novelle', (pp. 405–32 of *Novelle*, ed. Kunz, originally *Orbis Litterarum*, XIV, 1959, 65–88) argues that 'frame' narration is especially central to the Novelle form ('Die Ursituation der Novellenform ist also in einer vielköpfigen Gesellschaft zu Hause ...' p. 408), and then deals with the obvious objection that most Novellen are not so narrated by saying that it can simply be supplied: 'Meiner Ansicht nach hätte jeder beliebige neuzeitliche Novellist recht leicht seiner Sammlung einer Rahmenerzählung geben

will often appear as a 'frame' narrator addressing an actual audience, and his stance will always be one of presenting the event directly to his readers as something from his experience. Meanwhile the world view which emerges from this kind of narrative, it is often said, will be one that stresses chance, and the unpredictability of fate.[1]

Two formal criteria have been suggested which make concrete the idea that the Novelle must have a clear outline and be artistically concentrated. These are the suggestions (originally made by Tieck and Heyse) that there be first, a distinct turning point in the story (a 'Wendepunkt') at which the striking event takes place, and, second, that the story should have a silhouette and distinctive symbol.[2] The second of these two has provoked widespread dissent, but the first still has a number of adherents, who do, however, often caution against too rigid an application of the idea.[3] Typically, whenever the theory of the Novelle comes under any attack from a sceptic, these two ideas are the first to be abandoned, though the basic idea from which both spring (that the Novelle is a sharp and concentrated form) is not.[4]

können ... eine Rahmenerzählung vom theoretischen Standpunkt [ist] durchaus nicht notwendig, denn der ideale Rahmen läßt sich auch ohne sie klar genug feststellen und erkennen' (p. 411). But an argument which rules out all possible counter-examples by definition, is one which asserts nothing.

[1] Bennett (p. 5) says the Novelle presents chance as fate, and presupposes an irrational view of life. Cf. von Wiese, *Novelle*, p. 9; Klein, p. 5; and Foulkes and Lohner, p. 1: '... the Novelle can be regarded as the genre which deals with chance, with the arbitrariness and capriciousness of fate'. Lockemann and Kunz present more developed versions of the characteristic metaphysical content of the Novelle.

[2] The original texts have recently been reprinted, both in Kunz, *Novelle*, and Polheim, *Theorie und Kritik der deutschen Novelle*.

[3] Heyse's 'Falkentheorie' has been widely criticised, e.g., by Silz, pp. 4–5; Bennett, p. 14 ('neither very profound nor illuminating'), von Wiese, *Die deutsche Novelle*, I, 26, and many others; Theodor Storm's criticism of Heyse appears often to serve as a model for later critics. The 'Wendepunkt' is less challenged, however; Bennett accepts it (p. 18), Silz queries its *exclusive* occurrence in the Novelle, but still says that in this genre 'it stands out more starkly' (p. 9). Cf. the very recent Foulkes and Lohner, p. 1; and H. H. Remak's continued use of it as a criterion for the analysis of some stories by Keller ('Theorie und Praxis der Novelle: Gottfried Keller' in *Stoffe, Formen, Strukturen, Studien zur deutschen Literatur. Hans Heinrich Borcherdt zum 75 Geburtstag*, ed. Fuchs and Motekat, Munich, 1962).

[4] E.g., von Wiese (*Novelle*, pp. 11–12, or *Die deutsche Novelle*, I, p. 26) makes clear that while the formal requirement for 'Wendepunkt' or 'Falke' can be abandoned, the ideas underlying them cannot. Thus, when he asserts that there can be good Novellen

My own belief is that both the basic theory and its extensions are deficient in every particular, and I shall attempt briefly to demonstrate this. It will soon become apparent that all these statements which attempt to show characteristic features of the Novelle are subject to one or more of three general objections: first, some or even most Novellen do not show the feature in question; second, what is asserted is so general in scope that it concerns a feature of literature in general, not the Novelle in particular; third, the assertion is so vague that presence or absence of the feature concerned cannot be determined at all.

To take an easy example of the first kind of objection, most Novellen do not have 'frame' narrators, nor do they display as a group a characteristically Novellistic narrative stance – whether objective and distanced, or any other kind. The same range of narrative stances is found in Novellen as in any other kind of fiction; to this point I shall return in the later part of this chapter. The requirement of a striking event turns out to be too broad, on the other hand: works of literature are generally concerned with such things. Let us take Shakespeare's big four plays for some familiar examples: the murder of a king (*Macbeth*), the brutal rejection of a father by his daughters (*Lear*), jealousy drives a husband to kill his wife (*Othello*), a son avenges his father's murder by his uncle (*Hamlet*) – all of these offer striking events, which can be reduced to the striking headline formulae classically demanded of Novellen, though there seems to be no point in doing so. It might well be objected that these statements grossly reduce Shakespeare's plays, but in like manner, the required striking formulae have always reduced Novellen too; the formula 'two lovers perish because of the enmity between their families' is as injurious to Shakespeare's *Romeo and Juliet* as it is to Keller's *Romeo und Julia auf dem Dorfe*. Evidently, literature deals for the most part with material that is rather more concentrated and striking than everyday life, and this is a fact of artistic concentration in general, not Novellistic construction in particular. Equally,

without these characteristics, he is not in essence abandoning the common definition of the Novelle.

5

it is a general characteristic of literature that this artistic concentration often involves symbolism; this is neither less, nor more, the case in the Novelle that it is in literature generally. To demand that a Novelle have a 'Wendepunkt', on the other hand, seems both pointlessly trivial, and too vague a test. Presence or absence depends on an arbitrary analysis of plot structure rather than its real characteristics. Droste-Hülshoff's *Die Judenbuche*, usually taken as a classic example of the genre, illustrates this arbitrariness well. Is the turning-point the death of Brandes? Friedrich's adoption by his uncle? The death of Aaron? Friedrich's fate abroad? In *Das Erdbeben in Chili*, is the turning-point the decision to go back into the city? The priest's sermon? The earthquake itself? These questions are evidently pointless, and the decisions they require are arbitrary. For the sake of a theory about the genre 'Novelle' they ask us to give one aspect of the text an emphasis which it does not have, and so to distort it.

Similar considerations apply to any attempt to diagnose whether the text is about a single event rather than more than one; this depends on a definition of what a 'single' event is, not on any real characteristics of the plot of a particular story, and so this criterion also is too vague to be tested. Kleist's *Erdbeben*, or Keller's *Romeo und Julia*, can be *spoken* of as if they concerned one event, or a sequence of events; and so could most novels, or plays. As to character: Storm's *Der Schimmelreiter* shows great concern with the figure of Hauke Haien, Keller's *Kleider machen Leute* with the characters of Wenzel and Nettchen and their development, Grillparzer's *Der arme Spielmann* with Jakob, and so on; more examples are superfluous. Yet the error here is more logical than factual; for at bottom this alleged characteristic of the Novelle depends on a misconceived opposition of 'Character' and 'Situation'. All human situations are created by the characters involved in them, and all character is shown in the response of people to situations. When we talk of 'Character' instead of 'Situation' we are thus opposing one kind of analysis to another, not two different kinds of things. For this reason, the difference between the two terms cannot be used as a means of differentiating works of literature.[1] Naturally, some books can be more concerned with one central character than others (both novels and Novellen), and long novels offer more space for more detail, over a longer period, than does a Novelle. But they do so by providing more situations, and so this is still nothing to do with an opposition of situation and character or a different kind of relation between the two.

Even the demand that a Novelle be realistic in its material turns out to be not very helpful; if taken seriously it would mean that we should have to exclude Kafka when we talk about the Novelle, and Klein conscientiously does so. Other histories of the Novelle, though accepting the standard theory, seem instinctively to feel how foolish it would be to exclude Kafka from the series of works in German literature which include, for example, Kleist, Hoffmann, Hauptmann, and Hofmannsthal.[2] And even Klein seems to feel that Hofmannsthal's grotesque fantasy *Reitergeschichte* cannot be ignored. Again, who will feel that it makes sense to include Keller's collection of stories *Die Leute von Seldwyla*, but omit from it *Spiegel das Kätzchen*?[3] Much of Hoffmann would need to be rejected, and the absurdity of this would be emphasised by the fact that it would split his very closely knit *oeuvre* down the middle; presumably *Der Sandmann*, and *Der goldene Topf* would be excluded and *Das Fräulein von Scuderi* included, with *Rat Krespel* a query. Worst of all, that most popular Novelle, Storm's

---

[1] This distinction is most recently reasserted by von Wiese (*Novelle*, p. 5), who maintains that 'Kleists *Michael Kohlhaas* nicht eine Charakternovelle ist, wie sehr oft behauptet wurde, sondern nur vom Ereignisgeflecht und von der symbolischen Verdichtung her angemessen verstanden werden kann ...' The logic of what is being asserted is worth attention. Von Wiese cannot be arguing against the view that Kleist's Novelle is concerned with the character of Michael Kohlhaas – that would be simply to deny part of its 'Stoff' which we can all see. Logically, he can only be saying that it is not (or is not important for) the 'Gehalt', the meaning of the book. But on this interpretation, he must also be mistaken: the 'Gehalt' of any book is a product of all its characters, events, and symbolism.

[2] Lockemann (pp. 357–63), Bennett/Waidson (pp. 265–71), Himmel (pp. 425–26) and von Wiese, (*Die deutsche Novelle*, I, 325–42, and II, 319–45), discuss such blatantly unrealistic stories as *Das Urteil*, *Ein Hungerkünstler*, and *Die Verwandlung*, and so let their instincts judge their theory to be inadequate.

[3] Lockemann (p. 185), includes it, but Klein, in his ten pages (pp. 303–12) on the *Leute von Seldwyla*, does not even mention it by name.

Der Schimmelreiter, with its ghosts, might have to go if we took this requirement seriously. But there is no need to: when this kind of practical dilemma occurs with regularity, we may be sure that the tradition of Novelle writing has no strict and essential requirement of realistic material.[1] To be sure, a very special convention of unrealistic prose is identifiable (the Märchen) which is separable from the Novelle; but it is not *opposed* to the Novelle as unrealistic to realistic writing, i.e., the meaning of the two categories does not depend on each being the opposite of the other (as in the case, for example, in the opposition dark/light). Novelle and Märchen are not in binary opposition as categories, though this is frequently assumed.

Some of these weaknesses in the standard theory of the Novelle are so obvious that they have been commented on before, but until very recently these comments were only made in piecemeal fashion, never adding up to any serious challenge to the whole theory; and on occasion, the reconciliation of the theory with its evident flaws has been achieved with much ingenuity. Von Wiese accepts the common theory of the Novelle, and is even fairly sympathetic to the extensions of it which I have noted; and he deals with the fact that there are Novellen without 'Wendepunkt', 'Rahmen', etc., by warning against any dogmatic attitude to Novelle requirements.[2] Here, a negative value (dogmatism) is assigned to any consistent attitude to the definition of a Novelle, and thus also to any very close scrutiny of the accepted definition.

---

[1] I develop the much more serious theoretical argument against this criterion below, pp. 20–25.

[2] Von Wiese, *Novelle*, pp. 11–12: 'Jedem Dogmatismus in der Novellentheorie muß entgegengehalten werden, daß das spannungsreiche Verhältnis zwischen einer als objektiv wahr, neu und wirklich erzählten Begebenheit und einer indirekten, subjektiven Darstellungsform sehr verschiedene Abwandlungen erfahren kann. Verbindliche Regeln gibt es hier glücklicherweise nicht. Wir besitzen wertvolle Novellen mit und ohne "Falken", mit und ohne "Wendepunkt", mit und ohne "Rahmen", mit und ohne "Idee", ja sogar mit und ohne "Leitmotiv".' Yet von Wiese goes on to make it clear that the basic theory is not challenged here, and is for him as much a dogma as ever: 'Was jedoch die Novelle in erster Linie braucht, wird immer das novellistische Ereignis und seine jeweilige Formung sein' (p. 12). Much the same kind of attitude is found in Joachim Müller's 'Novelle und Erzählung', in *Novelle*, ed. Kunz, pp. 463–76 (originally *Etudes Germaniques*, XVI, 1961, 97–107); cf. for example, p. 465: 'Der Gattungstypus ist keine Norm, die eine absolute Erfüllung fordert...'

The much-quoted judgment of Pabst: 'Denn es gibt weder die
"romanische Urform" der Novelle noch "die Novelle" überhaupt. Es gibt nur Novellen',[1] is largely sceptical about the
possibility of a definition, yet even so has been turned to good use
as a means of preserving the standard theory; the unworkability
of the standard definition is related only to the demand for 'die
Novelle', while shifting from generic singular to a much more
unspecified plural ('Novellen') seems to allow for a variety and
so for less rigid conformity to the definition, which thus once
more survives without radical change.[2] A similar grammatical
shift is used by von Wiese when he seeks a way out of difficulties
by speaking not of 'Novelle' but of 'novellistisches Erzählen'.[3]
But this shifting of the grammatical status of the term makes no
difference to the substantive issue of the theory of the genre;
whether the term 'Novelle' is retained as noun or made into an
adjective, whether it is singular or plural, the question still
remains: What does it categorise, and where are the boundaries
of the category? Grammatical shifts are an avoidance of the issue,
and do not deal with the problems inherent in the standard theory,
giving only the illusion of having dealt with those problems.
Kunz,[4] too, tries to solve the problem by juggling with the notion

[1] Walter Pabst, *Novellentheorie und Novellendichtung. Zur Geschichte ihrer Antinomie in den romanischen Literaturen* (Hamburg, 1953). I cite from p. 324 of the 'Schlußbetrachtung' of this work as reprinted in *Novelle*, ed. Kunz, pp. 313–28.

[2] Manfred Schunicht ('Der "Falke" am "Wendpunkt"'. Zu den Novellentheorien Tiecks und Heyses', in *Novelle*, ed. Kunz, pp. 433–62, originally *Germanisch-Romanische Monatsschrift* XLI, 1960, 44–65) cites Pabst's statement with approval (p. 462), but still maintains many of the old distinctions between Novelle and novel, and allows the existence of a 'deutscher Novellentyp des 19. Jahrhunderts' (p. 460).

[3] Von Wiese, *Novelle*, p. 13. Martini agrees that von Wiese's phrase is a 'Verlegenheitslösung' (p. 351 of 'Die deutsche Novelle im "bürgerlichen Realismus"', in *Novelle*, ed. Kunz, pp. 346–84, originally *Wirkendes Wort*, X, 1960, 257–78), though his concept of the 'dominierende Intention' of the Novelle has become for other scholars (cf. Kunz, *Novelle*, p. 4 and p. 23, and Müller, 'Novelle und Erzählung', p. 465) just as useful a means of filling the gap between the standard theory and the facts.

[4] Kunz, *Novelle*, p. 22: 'Eine umfassende "Definition" der Novelle – etwa als Summe der hier einbezogenen Theorien – zu geben, ist unmöglich. Aber eines kann man den meisten von ihnen entnehmen: Von dem her, was man noch einmal mit Fritz Martini die "dominierende Intention" der Novelle nennen könnte, ist es sehr wohl möglich, die Novelle als Gattungsform zu erfassen und von anderen epischen Formen – etwa der Erzählung – zu unterscheiden.'

of definition; his view is that there can be no comprehensive definition of the Novelle, yet that we can nonetheless understand it and distinguish it from other genres. But what is an attempt to distinguish between one thing and another, if not a definition?

The point at issue is precisely: how can we distinguish the Novelle from other genres. One can perhaps generalise from these and other instances[1] that there is a fairly widespread attitude to the difficulties inherent in the accepted definition of the Novelle; it is that in spite of evident weaknesses, the definition works, some of the time at least, more or less adequately, if only one is not too strict about it. Thus one must be cautious rather than too normative or dogmatic; instead of a comprehensive definition one must be content with approximations; difficulties only arise if one seeks the abstract 'die Novelle' instead of talking about concrete examples, a kind of story-telling, or the dominant intent of the category. And yet: when all these qualifications have been made, the basic content of the definition remains unchanged. Involved are still the same features and characteristics of the accepted definition.

One of the reasons for this lack of real forward movement in Novelle theory has been that radical sceptics have never seemed to offer anything satisfying in place of the accepted definition; if one thing is to be abandoned, something else must take its place. Frequently, the destruction of some parts of the accepted definition leads only to a greater reliance on other (equally questionable) parts, instead of a really new departure. Thus Schunicht[2] analyses the contributions of Tieck and Heyse with great exactitude, and questions their theoretical validity; he then stresses the narrator's

---

[1] E.g., Silz (p. 10) concludes that 'these features [the usual Novelle criteria], though not individually indispensable, yet all have a certain validity as partial and approximate descriptions of a highly concentrated, highly artistic form of narrative literature'. Foulkes and Lohner adopt the standard definition of the Novelle in their 'Introduction', but, in their 'Preface', 'urge the student to approach these definitions with caution, even with skepticism . . .'

[2] 'Der "Falke" am "Wendepunkt"', in *Novelle*, ed. Kunz, pp. 433–62. For example, p. 454: 'Ein entschiedenes Kriterium novellistischen Erzählens liegt in dem deutlichen Bestreben des Erzählers, sich mit Hilfe zahlreicher Fiktionen von der dargestellten Begebenheit zu distanzieren.'

adopting the stance of distanced and objective reporter. This is a part of the accepted definition too, and just as vulnerable as the others to the test of empirical observation. Malmede attacks many points in the accepted theory before making his sole positive suggestion, that we replace Goethe's 'unerhörte Begebenheit' with 'zum Aufmerken veranlaßende Begebenheit',[1] which most readers will feel to be a distinction without much of a difference. Polheim, after a discussion of recent attempts to find a criterion for the Novelle in the stance of the narrator, concludes that 'das alles gilt nicht nur für die Novelle, sondern für jede erzählende Dichtung',[2] and thus complements the earlier findings of Silz, which he cites with approval. Silz had asserted that 'on closer examination, not one of the traditional criteria evolved by successive theorists appears strictly indispensable'.[3] Polheim then follows his rejection of earlier theory with the statement that 'Novelle' is distinguished from 'Erzählung' in that the former term, unlike the latter, refers to a story of artistic merit.[4] Usage does not support this view and it seems inherently implausible; would any writer have termed his story an 'Erzählung' in order to condemn it as an inferior one? But even more importantly, this and other positive statements offered by sceptics have not seemed substantial enough to be a satisfying alternative to the accepted definition.

A reasonable summary of the present state of opinion on the theory of the Novelle, then, would be as follows: there is still overwhelming acceptance of the theory which starts from the premise that the Novelle is concerned with a single, striking event and is thus a realistic genre which displays artistic concentration together with objective narrative. The extensions of this theory which project the tendency to artistic concentration into such formal features as 'Wendepunkt' or 'Falke' are more disputed,

---

[1] Malmede, p. 154. [2] Polheim, p. 104.

[3] Silz, p. 9; Polheim (p. 103) actually cites a related passage from Silz, also p. 9. That Silz tended to retreat from this degree of scepticism is shown in the statement cited above, p. 10, fn., on his immediately following page.

[4] Polheim, p. 106 ff. Von Arx' stress on length of text has also not been convincing; cf. below, pp. 18–19.

though the latter much more than the former. A very few sceptics have questioned more than those extensions, but their own positive solutions have not been convincing alternatives. In face of cogent arguments against both the basic theory and its extensions, scholars have tended first to abandon the extensions, and second to take refuge in the feeling that the accepted characteristics of the Novelle are basically the right ones, provided that they are not taken too strictly or normatively. In essence, therefore, the accepted theory continues as before. All influential books on the Novelle (i.e., all histories of the Novelle, and especially the work of scholars such as Kunz and von Wiese who are the authors of three volumes each on the subject) propound it, while two reprints of the nineteenth century texts on which it is largely based testify to the extent to which it is still in the air. And yet: it is also commonly thought to be an enigmatic area of theory too, and scepticism is on occasion recommended even as the theory is expounded. Meanwhile, as I have shown, it is by no means difficult to cast doubt on the whole theory from beginning to end, and from both a theoretical and practical point of view.[1]

When an impasse of this kind is reached in any theoretical enquiry, it is inherently likely that the persistence of inadequate solutions is based on a failure of logic; we need to examine whether we are asking the right question, not to try to find another answer to the same question. Traditionally, theorists of the Novelle have taken an approach to the definition of the Novelle which assumes a simple reference theory of meaning;[2] they have

[1] A section of Polheim's book is devoted to showing that standard Novelle theory has never facilitated interpretation and understanding of actual *Novellen*; he is no doubt correct, though he might have been more convincing had he not chosen an example to discuss at length – Brentano's *Geschichte vom braven Kasperl und dem schönen Annerl* – whose supernatural elements would exclude it from the genre according to the accepted theory. He also discusses a work which claims to use Novelle theory to interpret some of Keller's *Leute von Seldwyla* stories: H. H. Remak, 'Theorie und Praxis de Novelle: Gottfried Keller', in *Stoffe, Formen, Strukturen. Studien zur deutschen Literatur. Hans Heinrich Borcherdt zum 75. Geburtstag*, ed. Fuchs and Motekat (Munich, 1962), pp. 424–39. As Polheim (pp. 87–9) shows, this attempt fails completely: 'Das Ergebnis freilich ist negativ ... die Theorie erweist sich nicht als Hilfe, sondern also Hindernis.'

[2] Malmede (p. 15) formulates this assumption more clearly than most: 'Gattungsforschung ist demgegenüber bemüht, einen Begriff zu definieren, der ein gemeinsames einer bestimmten Gruppe von Werken bezeichnet.'

taken the word to refer to a kind of thing, and a definition to nvolve searching for those characteristics in virtue of which a member of the class of these things is included within it. Modern philosophers, notably Wittgenstein,[1] have questioned the adequacy of the reference theory of meaning to account for all types of concepts found in language. It is now thought that words function in a variety of different ways, and that the reference theory can only deal with one of them. Unfortunately, the general theory of definition is never brought to bear on the problem of defining the Novelle; yet there are clearly two ingredients to this problem: on the one hand, empirical knowledge of Novellen, and on the other hand, a conceptual framework provided by the theory of definition. The latter has been completely ignored; to it I shall now turn.

Leaving aside for the moment the question of the adequacy of the reference theory of meaning to this problem, we can first of all note the variety of literary genre words. There are great differences between them, and differences in what they are expected to do. The word 'sonnet' concerns a fixed formal organisation of a poem, and is a precise term involving a precise number and structure of lines. Even sub-types are describable in a precise way. But it is indeterminate as to subject-matter. The term 'tragedy', on the other hand, is something of an opposite to this; it concerns a certain type of subject-matter, and the formal issue is a very loose one – only the general form of the drama is concerned, but not a particular size, shape or structure of drama. The novel is different again, concerning primarily not subject-matter or structure, but the establishment of a considerable length within the basic prose epic genre. Note that length here is neither treated with precision (as in the sonnet) nor ignored (as in tragedy); yet length is concerned, but still not in a very definite way. A completely different kind of genre term is the fable, established not by length, form or subject-matter, but only by an overt purpose. The

---

[1] Cf. for example, Ludwig Wittgenstein, *Philosophical Investigations/Philosophische Untersuchungen*, bilingual edition, trans. G. E. M. Anscombe (New York, 1958: earlier edition, 1953).

important lesson to be learnt from this small survey of genre concepts is that we must not expect them all to be concerned with the same kinds of properties; and if, for example, we were to try to find some defining characteristic of, e.g., structure, for each one of them, we should be facing an impossible task. A second, related lesson would also emerge from such an attempt: if, for example, we pursued the question of the structure of the tragedy, we might find that very many of them had five acts. But however great the preponderance in terms of numbers, this would still have nothing to do with definition. We should have found out a fact about many tragedies, but not a feature that is part of the definition; indeed, the very fact that we can investigate the structure of tragedies presupposes the already formed category, and thus the existence of a definition which has already determined the question of membership within the class. A definition has *prescriptive* force and is a matter of the rules of language; it is therefore an error to go searching purely *descriptively* for common properties of a group of things to try to discover a definition. This would be descriptive research into the already defined category (which certainly is useful) but not descriptive research into the definition itself. Empirical research into the definition could only be conducted by close observation of the decisions made by speakers of the language when they are concerned to use this word rather than that, and especially of the points at which they stop using one in favour of any other. In other words, factual research into the characteristics of members of a category must not be confused with the kind of conceptual enquiry involved in definition.

A third logical principle must be mentioned before we return specifically to the definition of the Novelle. It is that the conceptual systems of languages originate more in the attitudes and needs of their speakers than in the properties of the phenomena around them which these conceptual systems are used to organise. Put more simply, concepts are more to do with what speakers of a language want from the things around them than they are to do with the nature of the things themselves. In practice, the relation between these two aspects of concepts is highly variable. Take the word 'weed' for example; weeds seem to be physical enough, as any toiling gardener knows, and we have the strong impression that the word 'refers' to things about the plants which we call weeds. But in fact, the only reasonable definition of 'weeds' would be something like: 'plants that we do not wish to culti-vate'. The fact of their being plants must enter into the definition, but there is no other fact of botanical structure relevant to it; size, odour, leaf pattern and botanical classification are all irrelevant.[1] In the case of this concept, the attitudes of the speakers of English, and their demands of their environment, have played a much larger part than actual botanical facts.

One more example from the same sphere will show a rather different relationship between these two elements of a definition, and one closer to the case of the word 'Novelle'. We commonly distinguish between trees and bushes, and are never in any doubt that trees 'exist'. Yet the distinction can seem hard to define. We think first of shape; the relation of trunk to crown is different in trees and bushes. But in fact this does not work: a 'bushy' shape which is well in excess of about ten feet in height is called a tree, while a woody plant with distinct stem but well under ten feet is called a bush. This seems to make height the overriding criterion, and shape irrelevant. Again, this would be incorrect; shape is indeed relevant, for within a certain size range, shape is the important factor. From something like eight to fifteen feet, shape determines the word we use. And so neither shape nor size can be called the defining characteristic, in the sense that a bush does not have to be smaller than a tree, nor a different shape to a tree; what matters is the relation of these two factors. But a factor which increases the problem of physical criteria is that the way man trains them has an effect on how they are classified too. One can make certain woody plants into tree or bush by cutting off or encouraging the branches low on the stem. When the last factor is taken into account, the case becomes clearer; the basis of the category 'tree' as opposed to 'bush' is again to a large extent one of use, and it is impossible to ignore the fact that this way of

[1] I have borrowed this example from P. H. Nowell-Smith, *Ethics* (Penguin, 1954), p. 72.

organising the botanical world has had in it a large element of man's need to use certain plants for timber, and others for hedging. And so the definition of these categories has to be partly in terms of physical characteristics (stem and shape relationships) and partly in terms of needs and attitudes superimposed on these things by man which have only a tangential relation to botanical properties; trees are plants that in virtue of some things about them can be used in a certain kind of way. Our use of language is so unreflective, our organisation of the environment into categories which we can use so deep-seated, that we commonly ignore the fact that a very large element in the definition of words is to do with our own convenience and with what we find useful distinctions for certain practical purposes. And thus we look for definitions in terms of precise physical criteria for the things we are talking about, not in terms of the dominant purpose of the category, even though this may be much more important in a given case; yet this attitude (which is the basis of the 'reference' theory of meaning) will make a great puzzle out of the definition of the very common categories which concern an amalgam of things having very little in common (weeds) or which concern a loosely interlocking set of criteria (trees),[1] in which no one is necessary or sufficient.

To summarise: in setting up a definition we must take care (a) to recognise the variability of genre concepts and not push the definition of this one into areas which it does not concern, even though apparently similar words concern those areas; (b) not to confuse the results of factual enquiry into a category of things with the definition of that category;[2] (c) to recognise that defini-

[1] Ironically, Wittgenstein's discovery that some concepts are not linked by common features but instead by 'family resemblances', i.e., a network of traits in which a certain number of the traits are necessary but *no one need be present*, might have offered Novelle theorists an easy way out of their difficulties in the standard theory of the Novelle. In fact, however, the standard Novelle theory cannot be a case of 'family resemblances' since its required features are too general and/or too vague in their applicability to distinguish one prose work from another, and thus not even a concentration of them in Novellen could reasonably be shown.

[2] Kunz, by contrast, argues (*Die deutsche Novelle zwischen Klassik und Romantik*, p. 9) that 'die rechte Weise nur in einem streng induktiven Verfahren bestehen kann. Was die Gattung "Novelle" konstituiert, ist primär nicht aus der einen oder anderen Gattungs-

tion must be as concerned with the dominant purpose of the category as with the question of defining physical characteristics. It can be seen quite readily that the traditional theory of the Novelle is logically faulty in all these respects.

To take the second of these points first, the traditional theory concerns itself with facts about the Novelle as if they could become part of a definition, and so tries to describe common features of Novellen in the attempt to find a definition. This is to confuse the results of research into the category with the constraints upon membership of the category; the relevant research would be not into the description of what the category contains, but into the prescriptive power of the word to determine what is and is not included. If we examine the usage of critics over the years, we find only one aspect of texts which has consistently caused hesitation as to whether the word 'Novelle' should be used: the aspect of length. Almost every historian of the Novelle includes Ludwig's *Zwischen Himmel und Erde*[1] and comments on its length with evident embarrassment; and it is this kind of hesitation which provides evidence for the meaning of the word. Because they have sought evidence for a definition in the wrong way, traditional Novelle theorists have also sinned in the first of the three ways I have outlined: they have ignored the variety of possible areas of concern of a genre concept, and have pushed the definition into areas which it does not concern. When one thinks about the Novelle in relation to other genre concepts it is obvious that it concerns length within the prose epic, and by no means obvious that it concerns anything else. I am not begging the question here by a simple denial of what others have asserted, namely that the definition is concerned with questions other than length; my point is a more substantive one, that definition is a

theorie abzuleiten', and that one must examine 'in detaillierten Untersuchungen die einzelnen Dichtungen'. This is tempting, but logically incorrect.
[1] Ludwig actually called his book an 'Erzählung', thus bringing it within the scope of Novelle historians. Himmel calls Ludwig's work a 'Romannovelle' (p. 198); Klein calls it a 'Grenzfall zwischen Roman und Novelle' (p. 202); Bennett (p. 146), though still wanting it to be called a 'Novelle', nonetheless feels compelled to comment on its length and the consequent temptation to call it a 'Roman'.

NARRATION IN THE GERMAN NOVELLE

matter of the immediate and even emotional responses of speakers of a language as to whether a word is appropriate or not in a given situation, to whether its prescriptive power is being properly applied, and to whether they have any *immediate* impression that its norms are being violated. To say that the Novelle must have a turning point, for example, is to push the definition of the Novelle (like that of 'sonnet') into the area of structure, with which it is not concerned, and the test of this is that no one has ever said instinctively, 'stop, you must not use the word like that', and *then* located their response in the absence of a 'Wendepunkt'. The only people who have ever said that a 'Wendepunkt' was necessary were advancing a theory derived from description and observation (albeit, as I have argued, very poorly formulated description) of the contents of what all concerned were quite happy to call Novellen. But it is just this question of being happy, or unhappy, at the use of the word that is the point from which evidence must be derived. In like manner, we have seen the definition of 'Novelle' pushed into the area of subject-matter, as if it were a word like 'tragedy', by a theory such as Lockemann's, that the Novelle concerns the clash of order and chaos, or by the standard theory, that it is concerned with striking events, or with situations rather than character.[1]

Now these first two kinds of error are easy to make once the third is made. To say that the closest relative of the Novelle as a concept is the novel – that is, that it concerns length above all – seems meagre as a definition, and whenever a sceptic[2] has come

---

[1] Cf. Lockemann, p. 14 ff. I should regard the attempt to define the subject-matter of the Novelle by contrasting it with the 'Märchen' also as an illegitimate extension of the field of the definition. To contrast 'Novelle' and 'Marchen' in order to tell us something about the Novelle is like contrasting 'Poetry' and 'Sonnet' to tell us something about poetry. In both cases there is not a binary opposition (where each concept defines the other by contrast) but a highly circumscribed and specific form of the first constituting the second. In practical terms, Novellen do quite commonly concern themselves with supernatural or unreal situations.

[2] B. von Arx reported, in his *Novellistisches Dasein. Spielraum einer Gattung in der Goethezeit* (Zurich, 1953), the definition of the Novelle resulting from a seminar given by Emil Staiger: 'eine Erzählung mittlerer Länge'. But von Arx was only partly a sceptic, and still wanted to say that the world of the Novelle was different from that of the novel, in an argument that has failed to convince other scholars. (Cf. Polheim, pp.

back to this all too obvious fact he has seemed not to offer us enough. But the point is that this is one of those categories where the use to which it is put is its most important feature. The word 'Novelle' is much used in criticism of German literature, and to say that it is only a question of a medium length story seems not to match that fact in importance. It can be seen to do so only when we consider the use of the category, and what need it answers in the community which uses it. In Germany in the nineteenth century there were few important writers of novels, but very many talented writers who wrote neither novels nor short stories but something of intermediate length. The thing which distinguishes German fiction in the nineteenth century from that of other countries is precisely this. An important need arose for a way of grouping together those literary productions which were most characteristic of that age in that community. The word 'Novelle' thus answered an important need, and that need in a sense created it.[1] To be sure it is a loose concept, with very blurred edges; in that sense its reference is not very clear. But its main purpose is clear, and that is to enable people to talk about a very characteristic development in German literature. I am of course aware that the word originates etymologically in the Italian 'Novella'; but that is not its real source as a German concept. A pre-existing word was taken up and it filled the vacuum that events had created; but it was the *character of the vacuum* that dictated what meaning the concept would have, not the original meaning of the word in the former context from which it was borrowed. And so Goethe's much quoted definition[2] has

21–2). Polheim himself shows some sympathy with the question of length, before deciding to take artistic quality as his main Novelle criterion (pp. 9–10; p. 106). But neither von Arx nor Polheim base their conclusions on the kind of logical analysis which I believe to be essential. Length as an adequate criterion is still widely rejected, e.g., by von Wiese, *Die deutsche Novelle*, I, 13; Silz, p. 6; Klein, p. 8.

[1] The classic form of the error of taking etymological origin as the 'real' meaning is in Adolf von Grolman's essay, 'Die strenge "Novellen"form und die Problematik ihrer Zertrümmerung', in *Novelle*, ed. Kunz, pp. 154–66, based on *Zeitschrift für Deutschkunde*, XLIII (1929), 609–27.

[2] Cited in *Novelle*, ed. Kunz, p. 34. Goethe's actual words (conversation with Eckermann, January 1827) are interesting for my purposes: ' . . . denn was ist eine Novelle anders als eine sich ereignete unerhörte Begebenheit. Dies ist der eigentliche Begriff, und so

little to do with the question of definition in our sense, for he is talking mainly of that former context, not of the situation that was to develop.

We thus reach the position that the concept is important, though its theoretical content is slight. To go back to my example of trees and bushes: these terms are very important to us, but as something to take as the basis of serious botanical research they are practically useless. Imagine what would happen, for example, if we tried to carry on botanical research by brooding on the meaning of these terms, convinced that if only we looked at trees and bushes long enough we should gain some real insight into the distinction in botanical terms. This is exactly what the traditional Novelle theorists have done, and it explains the impasse to which they were bound to come. A primitive and loose term which functions mainly to answer a simple need cannot be made the basis of research into the actual things it deals with; this is to take a term whose point was to make a convenient gathering together of texts with a loose relation to each other and pretend that it was a precise instrument which distinguishes phenomena very precisely according to their actual qualities. Naturally, critics who have tried to proceed in this way have achieved nothing. And so, the end result of this enquiry has been to show that the standard theory originates in a wholly mistaken attitude to definition, through which the real importance of the term is ignored and an importance is sought for it which it can never have.

There is another general framework within which the texts discussed in this volume are often considered, with very similar results because of very similar logical errors. The framework is that of the concept of Realism; and indeed when in German literary criticism a critic refers to nineteenth century Realism he is taken to be talking largely of the Novelle.[1] Much the same kind of arguments then arise; e.g., what really *is* Realism? The question

vieles, was in Deutschland unter dem Titel Novelle geht, ist gar keine Novelle, sondern bloß Erzählung . . . ' I am not in disagreement with Goethe's remarks.

[1] Cf. Walter Silz's *Realism and Reality*, and Richard Brinkmann's *Wirklichkeit und Illusion. Studien über Gehalt und Grenzen des Begriffs Realismus für die erzählende Dichtung des neunzehnten Jahrhunderts*, 2nd ed. (Tübingen, 1966.)

has certainly provoked much discussion.[1] By now we have
become used to the fact that the concept is discussed in this way,
and its meaning sought as if it were a very subtle and obscure
thing; and yet this fact seems very strange once we focus on the
use of the term. In literary works, over the centuries, there have
on occasion prevailed certain set conventions: for example, those
of classical tragedy, of the fairytale, of rococo verse, of the other-
worldly fantasy of German Romanticism, and so on. All of these
different kinds of literary work involve conventions which very
clearly set them off from any kind of real life impression. In so
far as we use the term 'Realism', we seem to be using it negatively: it notes the absence of any of these set conventions, but
scarcely anything positive. The variety of artistic products not
involved in any of these 'unrealistic' conventions is simply
enormous. The term is, then, as far as its use is concerned, a
catch-all, a very loose word affording easy reference to a large
and amorphorous group of literary works. There has sometimes
been a temptation to think that it means something like 'transcription of the real world', but on a moment's thought that
suggestion must seem meaningless; first, because people can argue
for ever about whether certain things are more real than others
(e.g., stones, God, money, beauty, time, thoughts, and so on)
without doing more than arguing over quite different senses of
the word which need not exclude each other;[2] and second, because
the artist, even if under the impression that he is giving us reality
unaltered, has still had to choose a very small amount from the
huge number of impressions by which he has become acquainted
with the world (even if we conceded that his impressions were
the same as everybody else's, which is not the case), and his
selection, juxtaposition and emphasis will convey his meaning,
not his having given us reality.[3] Anyone can describe what is

[1] Cf. the collection of essays edited by Richard Brinkmann, *Begriffsbestimmung des
literarischen Realismus* (Darmstadt, 1969).
[2] Obviously there are different senses here of real as (a) what can be seen; (b) what is
important to us; (c) what is a justifiable abstraction; (d) what one is aware of, etc.
[3] An especially odd aspect of the discussion of nineteenth century realism is that it often
touches on the classical 'imitation of nature' theory of art, which was so popular in the

going on around him, but an artist obviously has to do something else to gain attention for his work at all, and it is precisely that 'something else' that must be the value of his work.

An attempt to use the term 'Realism' in a precise way has been made through the assertion that it consists in a text having an objective narrator; presumably this must mean that in 'realistic' prose, the narrator presents his material in an objective way. Unhappily, the unworkability of this attempt is demonstrated only too clearly by the fact that there are two quite distinct senses of 'objective' current in critical literature, with the two excluding each other yet each claimed as the mark of 'Realism'. In one, it is 'objective' to have no narrator present, and to allow the characters to speak for themselves; in the other, the omniscient narrator is the mark of objectivity while the emergence of the perspective of characters through direct speech is 'subjective'.[1] Evidently, 'objective' is no better than 'Realism' itself as a word for use in a precise investigation.[2] Käte Friedemann argued sixty years ago, and very convincingly, that absence of comment on the part of the narrator was not sufficient to make a narrative 'objective', since the narrator still selected, included or excluded according to his concerns, which meant that no objectivity in any fundamental sense was achieved.[3] As for the rival sense of 'objective', it seems

eighteenth century. The drawbacks of this kind of 'realistic imitation of the world' theory appear to have been seen much more clearly in that earlier period; cf., for example E. M. Wilkinson, *J. E. Schlegel. A Pioneer in Aesthetics* (Oxford, 1945).

[1] Cf. W. J. Lillyman, *Otto Ludwig's Zwischen Himmel und Erde: A Study of its Artistic Structure* (The Hague/Paris, 1967), p. 15: 'There are two directly opposed uses of the terms "subjective" and "objective" in regard to narrative technique in the novel. Some critics...speak of a novel as "objective" when the omniscient narrator is present and as "subjective" when only the voices of the characters are heard... Other critics ...employ the terms with reverse significance, the essential of the "objective" novel being, according to Warren, "the voluntary absence from the novel of the omniscient novelist."'

[2] Brinkmann's use in *Wirklichkeit und Illusion* of the word 'objective' is criticised, for example, by two reviewers, G. Kaiser, in *Zeitschrift für deutsche Philologie*, LXXVII (1958), 161–76, and R. Heuer, in *Euphorion*, LIII (1959), 467–74. Cf. especially Kaiser, p. 174, and Heuer, p. 468. I have analysed the errors to which these terms lead in the context of Schiller's aesthetics in *Schiller's 'Kalliasbriefe' and the Study of His Aesthetic Theory* (The Hague/Paris, 1969), pp. 121–6.

[3] Käte Friedemann, *Die Rolle des Erzählers in der Epik* (Berlin, 1910), p. 6, diagnosed the error here very finely with her remark on Spielhagen's theory of the 'objective' narrator:

even less plausible: there seems to be no reason why we should call direct speech by characters in a book a 'subjective' element, any more than there was for us to call it 'objective'. To use this pair of terms meaningfully we must have in mind a clear contrast one to the other, objective to subjective. This is obviously why both kinds of use of 'objective' had opposed narrator and characters, even though they did this in opposite ways. But we must also have some other reason for setting up the contrast if it is not simply to be *another way of referring* to the narrator as opposed to the characters. This is where both views fall down, and the lack of content in the distinction subjective/objective in this context is shown clearly enough by the fact that it can be made as easily in either direction.

Let us examine the everyday use of the opposition 'subjective' and 'objective' in narrative reporting. In ordinary usage, the distinction is taken to refer to the presence or absence of evaluation, either directly through explicit evaluations, or indirectly through words which are 'loaded', that is, very much evaluatively charged. We can make this distinction because there is usually something to compare the reports to, namely the original event itself, and we can then judge how far the reporter's perspective has influenced the terms of the report. But this shows why the distinction is dangerous in literary criticism: there is *no* event to compare the narrator's account to; that account is the event in itself. All of what the narrator tells us is a composition,

'Was also Spielhagen verlangt, ist, um es noch einmal zu betonen, nicht geistige Objektivität, sondern – *dramatische Illusion*, die er mit dem Worte "Objektivität" bezeichnet.' Friedemann's whole argument against the view that the narrator should retire behind the events and not comment on them, thus allegedly achieving 'objectivity', is excellently done; by comparison Wayne Booth's recent discussion of the problem in *The Rhetoric of Fiction* (Chicago, 1961) is a laborious treatment which in substance goes very little, if at all, beyond Friedemann. Percy Lubbock, long before Booth in the English-speaking world, had also made this point elegantly and briefly, though still without Friedemann's logical finesse: 'Flaubert does not announce his opinion in so many words, and thence it has been argued that the opinions of a really artistic writer ought not to appear in his story at all. But of course with every touch that he lays upon his subject he must show what he thinks of it; his subject, indeed, the book which he finds in his selected fragment of life, is purely the representation of his view, his judgment, his opinion of it. The famous "impersonality" of Flaubert and his kind lies only in the greater tact with which they express their feelings – dramatizing them, embodying them in living form, instead of stating them directly.' (*The Craft of Fiction*, London, 1921, pp. 67–8.)

and the very scene itself is his creation as he reports it; we can scarcely use the word 'objective' in such a case. On the other hand, we may want to comment on his having given us this scene rather than that, or this aspect of the scene rather than that, a choice which cannot be called subjective or objective at all. We can of course say whether there is present any explicit evaluative language; but using the word 'subjective' to refer to this must seem to introduce the connotations of normal usage, which are impossible for works of literature. In any case, there is a simple alternative to such a term in this case: we can speak simply of the presence or absence of overtly evaluative language! Indeed, what reason could there be to abandon an accurate, informative description for a highly misleading one?

'Objective', then, cannot be made to save the word 'Realism' as a precise term. And so it seems clear that we have here very much the same kind of procedure as was employed in the case of the word 'Novelle'; a rather loose, catch-all term, more important for its use than for its precision of reference to a property shared by the group included by it, has been brooded upon with the conviction that it ought to yield some precise but as yet hidden meaning.[1] As before, research into the membership of the category has been thought to be a key to the definition of the category.[2] And again, as a result the definition of the category has

[1] D. G. Mowatt and I diagnosed a comparable error of logic in Staiger's poetics in 'Language, Metaphysics, and Staiger's Critical Categories', in *Seminar: A Journal of Germanic Studies*, 1 (1965), 122–5. E.g. '[Staiger] broods on the essential nature of the primitive categories inherited from popular usage... Ordinary language hands a researcher in any subject a set of terms reflecting the attitude which exists at a naive level in the language. As investigation proceeds and theory becomes more sophisticated there comes a point where these inherited terms are too undifferentiated to be of any use, and then there are two possibilities. The first is to force language, by re-definition and coinage, to carry the distinctions now considered necessary, and this is the fruitful path, for ordinary language cannot be allowed to prejudge what the analyst will find. The other is to keep the original terms, and marvel at their incommensurability...the whole idea of elaborating such a primitive set of distinctions was essentially unprogressive...' (pp. 124–5). The kind of logical error discussed here is very common in literary criticism; in many ways it is *the* basic error of standard theory of the Novelle, and of Realism.

[2] Brinkmann, in *Wirklichkeit und Illusion*, is an example here, since he tries to clarify the concept of Realism by analysis of three examples, so equating definition and research into the category.

been pushed into areas which it does not concern; a number of critics have even tried to speak of the specific 'Weltanschauung' of Realism, usually in terms of its optimistic tenor, and the empirical falsehood of this is very plain to see.[1] Worse still, Realism has been used as a standard with which to judge 'realistic' works, and the construction placed on Realism here is always one of direct, naive transcription of reality. Naturally, this standard damages any literary work if applied consistently.[2]

Throughout this discussion of Realism I have rejected attempts to characterise the narrator of realistic works in any specific way; there is, we shall find, so much variety of narrative type in what are loosely called 'realistic' stories that this restriction would entail a distortion of the texts. But in that critics concerned with Realism turned to narration as a key to it they were at last, however slowly, moving in the direction of a major issue in dealing with these texts: the relation of the narrator to his story.[3]

The emphasis given to the question of narration by the accepted definition of the Novelle was in the main a harmful one; for there, only one kind of narration was allowed for Novellen. When we look at the Novellen themselves, on the other hand, it soon becomes evident that they display the same variety of narrative stance as is found in fiction in general. It is doubtful whether the search for defining features of the Novelle has ever been of much assistance for the interpretation of the texts themselves; equally doubtful is whether it has furthered understanding of

---

[1] Cf. especially Bennett: 'The essence of Poetic Realism consists in its complete description of reality, the attribute "poetic" signifying that it is not concerned with a pessimistic dissection of life, but rather accords to it positive value...', and 'It is in essence optimistic...' (p. 125). Cf. also Martini: 'Der Erzähler des älteren Realismus ging, wie unsicher und fragwürdig auch diese Überzeugung bei Raabe und Fontane schon geworden war, vom Gefühl einer letzten inneren Harmonie des Daseins, einer letzten Gerechtigkeit des Welt-seins aus...' (Das Wagnis der Sprache, Stuttgart, 1954, p. 62).

[2] Cf. below, p. 174, for the comments of Stirk on the 'unrealistic' features of Bahnwärter Thiel, which, since the story has been categorised as realistic, must then be called flaws.

[3] Brinkmann, for example, is obviously moving in the direction of a concern with different types of narration and his discovery of three different types in the three stories he examines would be useful if well-defined. Unfortunately, Brinkmann is greatly hampered by his uncertainty as to the distinction between author and narrator, and by his framework of realism, which makes him deal with differing narrative styles in the unprofitable terms of objectivity and subjectivity.

individual texts to examine them in the light of concepts such as 'Realism'. But in the rest of this book I shall try to demonstrate that to examine individual Novellen with conscious and systematic attention to their narrative structures *does* further understanding of them. Indeed, I want to show that if there is any general theory or general set of concepts which makes a profitable framework of investigation for the interpretation of these texts, it is the theory of narration.

Narration in fiction is an issue in which interest has been growing in recent years, though less in Germany than elsewhere.[1] But in a remarkable beginning to this discussion Käte Friedemann pointed resolutely in the right direction. Arguing against Spielhagen's view that the narrator should disappear, not commenting but only showing the events themselves, Friedemann first showed that this was not sensibly to be termed a demand for objectivity but only for the kind of illusion to be found in drama; and then having begun in a negative way, she proceeded to some penetrating positive statements. Spielhagen was missing the whole point of the epic genre, she said, because 'das *Wesen* der epischen Form gerade in dem Sichgeltendmachen eines Erzählenden besteht'.[2] She went on to distinguish narrator and author: 'Es handelt sich nicht um den Schriftsteller Soundso, der in mehr oder

---

[1] Stanzl is no doubt substantially correct to claim that 'Es ist auffällig, daß sich vor allem englische und amerikanische Romantheoretiker und im deutschen Sprachraum Anglisten mit der Frage des Erzählerstandpunktes, des "point of view", beschäftigt haben...', in his *Typische Formen des Romans* (Göttingen, 1964), p. 73. Works such as those of Lubbock and Booth have no recent analogues in Germany, though some English and American Germanists have been concerned with narrative viewpoint. But Stanzl should mention also Wolfgang Kayser, admittedly a German Germanist strongly influenced by Anglo-Saxon theoretical trends (cf. his 'Wer erzählt den Roman?' in *Die Vortragsreise*, Berne/Munich, 1958, pp. 82–101); and above all Käte Friedemann, whose treatment of the status of the narrator still appears to me superior to that of Lubbock and Booth. Such more modern works as Käte Hamburger's *Die Logik der Dichtung* (Stuttgart, 1957) seem to me to compare unfavourably with Friedemann. It is fair to say that von Wiese, in his second volume of *Die deutsche Novelle*, raises the question of the narrator; but he is still hampered both by the conception of a style of narration which is characteristically Novellistic, and even by a lack of reliable distinction between narrator and author, as will emerge in many of the notes in my later chapters, where differences between my own interpretation of a particular story and that of von Wiese can be traced to this lack.

[2] Friedemann, p. 3.

weniger verblümter Form Indiskretionen gegen sich und andere begeht, denen nachzuspüren die literarhistorische Kritik noch immer nicht müde wird – sondern "der Erzähler" ist der Bewertende, der Fühlende, der Schauende.'[1] Friedemann realised that the existence of a narrator was not just a technical problem ('...daß es sich bei der Frage nach der Selbstdarstellung des Erzählers um mehr handlet, als um ein rein technisches Problem')[2] of getting the message across to the reader efficiently, a point not seen by Wayne Booth when he formulated his concern with narrative rhetoric in terms of the 'effort used to help the reader to grasp the work';[3] she knew already that it was the very meaning and existence of the work of literature, not merely its transmittal, that she was concerned with: 'Also nicht um einen außerhalb des Kunstwerks stehenden Schriftsteller handelt es sich, der seine Gestalten, denen er versäumt hätte, ein selbständiges Leben einzuhauchen, nachträglich zurechtrücken und erläutern müßte, sondern um den Erzähler, der selbst als Betrachtender zu einem organischen Bestandteil seines eigenen Kunstwerkes wird. Dieser aber, da er nicht einen Autmomaten, sondern einen lebendigen Menschen repräsentiert hat es auch nicht nötig, mit seinem Ich, d.h. also mit der Beurteilung der erzählten Begebenheiten, zurückzuhalten.'[4]

This account of the narrator and his importance can scarcely be bettered in even the recent critical literature; indeed most writers since Friedemann have ignored it completely. Others have attempted to abolish her distinction between narrator and

---

[1] Friedemann, p. 26. Compare Booth, making a similar point but with less telling formulation, to the last two quotations from Friedemann: 'The emotions and judgments of the implied author are, as I hope to show, the very stuff out of which great fiction is made' (p. 86).   [2] Friedemann, p. ix.

[3] W. Booth, *The Rhetoric of Fiction*, Preface. Some of the material in Booth's often interesting work transcends this limited and limiting theoretical concern, but the frequent repetition of the same viewpoint leave us in no doubt that his opening formulation was no accident. E.g., 'The third-person reflector is only one mode among many, suitable for some effects, but cumbersome and even harmful when other effects are desired' (p. 153), or '...the very concept of writing a story seems to have implicit within it the notion of finding techniques of expression that will make the work accessible in the highest possible degree' (p. 105). The last chapters of his book are devoted to a polemic against narrative stances which do not make the moral clear – a sad ending.   [4] Friedemann, p. 26.

author,[1] and even those who have agreed that some such distinction is necessary have commonly drawn it in a less useful way.[2] Friedemann's discussion is, however, incomplete in one respect: in insisting that the narrator is a distinct figure in his own right, she leaves open the question of what kind of figure he is. He is certainly not like any other character in the story; on the contrary, he is a highly conventional figure, to whom the convention of narration allows, on occasion and depending on the particular case, the ability to read other people's minds, to be present during conversations which could not have been overheard, to show extraordinary powers of memory, and so on.[3] The degree to which these conventional abilities are drawn upon in particular cases varies greatly, but without the existence of the convention in general no fiction is possible.[4]

[1] Notably Käte Hamburger in her *Die Logik der Dichtung*, p. 77: 'Die Rede von der "Rolle des Erzählers" ist denn ebensowenig sinnvoll wie es die von der Rolle des Dramatikers oder Malers wäre.' This is an unfortunate argument, since Friedemann's point was precisely that the presence of a narrator distinguished the epic from drama. A better comparison would be with the role of the 'Ich' of lyric poetry, but Hamburger's attitude to the distinction between author and lyric 'Ich' also misses the point: 'Zunächst haben wir, von unserer dichtungslogischen Sicht her, die Antwort zu geben, daß es ein ebenso unerlaubter Biographismus ist zu sagen, dieses Ich sei nicht Goethe, dieses Du nicht Friederike wie, daß dieses Ich Goethe und dieses Du Friederike sei' (p. 184). In spite of the appeal to logic here, the distinction is seen as empirical rather than logical. The 'Ich' may be identical with Goethe in a given case; but to say it is *not* Goethe is to make the logical point that even though the two may be identical, they are different in logical status; one relates to the rest of the poem, the other to the rest of what happens in Goethe's life. The same point holds for the distinction between author and narrator. Käte Hamburger's reply to the critics of her book on this point ('Noch Einmal: vom Erzählen', *Euphorion*, LIX, 1965, 46–71) asserts her view once more without coming to terms with contrary arguments, e.g., '"eine vom Autor geschaffene Gestalt" gibt es nicht und kann in keiner Weise aufgefunden werden. Es gibt nur den erzählenden Dichter und sein Erzählen' (p. 66).

[2] Cf. W. Wittkowski: 'Allerdings vermag ich selber keine strenge Grenze zwischen beiden zu ziehen' ('Skepsis, Noblesse, Ironie. Formen des Als-ob in Kleists *Erdbeben*', *Euphorion*, LXIII, 1969, 257). Without a clear conception of the distinction, it is doubtful whether talking about author and narrator can be very helpful.

[3] Wolfgang Kayser ('Wer erzählt den Roman?') is also concerned to show that the narrator of the novel, 'ob er sich die Maske eines persönlichen Erzählers vorhält oder ein Schemen bleibt' cannot be seen as analogous to the 'Erzähler des täglichen Lebens' (p. 98). But his substituting for this analogy another, 'die zum allwissenden und allgegenwärtigen Gott oder den Göttern', seems to me not entirely successful; narrators are only rarely omniscient, and practically never ubiquitous.

[4] The point is very commonly ignored, especially when the storyteller's memory of the precise details of a long passage of direct speech by one of the characters is concerned.

The distinction between narrator and author is, as I have discussed it so far, still a theoretical point; its justification in practical terms will, I hope, emerge from the interpretations of the stories I have chosen. Throughout these interpretative essays examples are noted of what happens if the distinction is not part of a particular critic's critical apparatus. A simple example is afforded by the case of stories in which the narrator is not omniscient. The author of a story must in a sense be omniscient about it; but the narrator he creates may be relatively unaware of the whole shape of the story, and of its values. In Keller's *Kleider machen Leute*, for example, the narrator hesitates over the motivation of Wenzel as he enters the Inn at the beginning of the story. The hesitation alerts the reader to the precariousness of the situation both factually and morally; the narrator is not quite sure how to judge his hero's behaviour as Wenzel gets deeper into deception, and is also uncertain as to whether he should put the whole thing down to chance or not. This is a very interesting use of the narrator, but for a critic who believes that he is the author, the results can only seem a baffling refusal to tell us what happened on the part of the only man who should know, namely Keller.[1] In von Wiese's essay on Kleist's *Erdbeben in Chili* the critic reaches an impasse because while the author must have a perspective reaching over the whole story, the narrator is tied to the scene he is narrating in his attitude and in the mood he creates. And so the narrator sounds unconcerned shortly before a terrible disaster occurs; and von Wiese, not being able to separate the knowledge of the author from that of the narrator, is naturally puzzled, and unable to appreciate the function of the narrator at this point of the story.[2]

The eight stories analysed in this volume are chosen because of the importance of their narration from the thematic point of view; that is, the narration is an essential part of the meaning of

---

This 'total recall' is as much part of the literary convention as the mind-reading narrator; to attack either one as improbable is equally mistaken. Cf. below, p. 119.

[1] Cf. this critical error discussed, in slightly different terms, in B. A. Rowley's volume *Keller: Kleider Machen Leute* (London, 1960), p. 15.

[2] See below, p. 69.

the story, and not a matter of technical value only, of helping the reader grasp what is there in the material without the narration itself.[1] If there are stories in which narration can be dealt with as Wayne Booth suggests, they must indeed be inferior; they do not exploit fully the resources of the fictional mode. I can best illustrate this point by taking an example of a story in which I believe that the narration *can* be in large measure described as a mere piece of technique. In Brentano's *Geschichte vom braven Kasperl und dem schönen Annerl*,[2] the narrator is a poet, who, while walking at night, meets an old woman; she in turn tells him a story of her godchild, Annerl, and her grandson, Kasperl, who were to have been married. At this beginning of the tale Annerl is, unknown to the first narrator, to be executed for infanticide in a few hours. Brentano makes the old woman hesitant about coming to the point of her story, yet just communicative enough to arouse suspicions of where her tale is leading. He juggles the narrative back and forward between the two, so that the first narrator becomes more and more involved, eventually finding himself on horseback racing to try to save Annerl, which he fails to do by a second. The shift in perspective from aloof narrator to involved character is, needless to say, striking. Brentano uses the two narrators to create suspense by contrasting the patient and

[1] R. Koskimies ('Die Theorie der Novelle', in *Novelle*, ed. Kunz) even though making narration the important criterion of the Novelle, still only regards it as a piece of technique designed to stop the audience yawning: 'Die Verschiebung des Gesichtswinkels, die also durch Abwechslung der Erzähler geschieht, läßt sich im Grunde wohl nicht aus einer überlegten Technik erklären, sondern von Anfang an haben die Schriftsteller es nur vermeiden wollen, ihre Leser (oder Zuhörer) zu langweilen...' (p. 410).

[2] The story has been much interpreted; cf. the survey of recent work by Polheim, pp. 90–8. It is by no means new to think of this story as a virtuoso performance technically, nor is it new to point out flaws in the tale, direct and simple errors at the lowest level of textual consistency. The direct relationship between these two points which I suggest, on the other hand, has not been asserted before. Polheim tends to think of critics who see flaws in the tale as simply not trying to understand it; this is in general a laudable instinct for a critic, but I cannot follow him in this rather blatant case. Indeed even Alewyn's essay ('Brentano's *Geschichte vom braven Kasperl und dem schönen Annerl*', in *Gestaltprobleme der Dichtung. Günther Müller zu seinem 65. Geburtstag am 15. Dezember 1955*, ed. R. Alewyn, et. al., Bonn, 1957), which Polheim thinks of as showing greater understanding of the text than any other, still points to some textual gaps; cf. e.g., his p. 149 and p. 173.

resigned old woman with the impatient and horrified younger man; the final night ride which just fails is a theatrical tour-de-force; and the treatment of the different attitudes of the two to the passing of time until the execution helps to create the basis for the desperate, but unavailing, final race against the clock. But it is difficult to say anything more positive than this about the narration, or indeed about the story. The narration is highly developed, but only used for excitement and local effect: it is not part of the thematic structure of the story. And this is because the thematic content of the story is exceedingly simple, not to say crude: the text bombards us with the interpretation it wants, that the story is about true and false honour,[1] and the word 'honour' occurs over and over again with increasing monotony. Having given us a story with this rather uninteresting thematic content, Brentano overlays it with artistic effects (notably the narrative scheme)[2] to keep our interest. Superficial artistic gloss is introduced to make up for lack of real content. Corroboration of this overall pattern is found in the symbolism; again, it is obvious, but irrelevant to the themes of the story. There are also fairly simple inconsistencies in, for example, the motif of the 'Schürze'.[3] But this is the

[1] Silz was surely right to speak of the 'unhappily moralistic' ending (*Realism and Reality*, p. 22) and Alewyn, too, concedes that the story had for Brentano a simple moral purpose: 'In ihrer erbaulichen Wirkung mag er einzig ihre Rechtfertigung gesehen haben' (p. 158), though he also argues, unconvincingly, that the concept of honour is not its central idea (p. 146).

[2] Alewyn argues that the narrative scheme is relevant, or rather that the old woman is thematically important, because of her concern with the grave. That seems to me insufficient, but even so, the more obvious and dramatic effects of the narration are obviously not thematic, nor is the thematic role of poet-narrator dealt with by this view. And the distinction between author and narrator is problematic in this essay: 'Das Vorteil dieser Einrichtung [the narrative structure] für den Dichter war ein mehrfacher. Er wurde der Verantwortung für seine Geschichte ledig. Er konnte den überlieferten Stoff um einiges ausbauen und anpassen, ohne aber genötigt zu sein, ein lückenloses Ganzes zu liefern oder über jede Einzelheit Rechenschaft abzulegen' (p. 155). In spite of Brentano's precautions, critics have not once blamed Anne Margareth for the story's shortcomings! Responsibility for its gaps as well as its details cannot, of course, be the narrator's, but only the author's.

[3] The most clear and unanswerable demonstration of textual inconsistency lies in the short essay by Alfred Walheim, 'Die Schürze der schönen Annerl', *Zeitschrift für Deutsch-kunde*, XXVII (1913), 791–3; Walheim shows a fundamental confusion between the 'Schürze' of the three year old Annerl, into which the teeth of the separated head of Jäger Jürge bit, and the old woman's 'Schürze' with which the head was covered up,

kind of thing that can easily happen if there is not thematic control over all aspects of the work; inconsistency can only occur easily in an area of the work that is thematically irrelevant to it, and where for this reason the inconsistency is not of fundamental importance. I have dwelt on the flaws in Brentano's story, but have done so only to delimit my concerns in the interpretations which form the main body of this book; the point I have wished to make is that I have excluded stories such as Brentano's which appear to use the possibilities of narrative framework intensely, and yet in an important sense do not use it at all.

In my choice of stories I have tried to include a wide variety of different kinds of narrative. In saying this, I do not mean to subscribe to any standard typology of narration; rather than adopt one of the simplified typologies of the narrator which have appeared in recent years,[1] I shall prefer to proceed simply by asking a series of questions[2] about the narrator. None of these questions results in a simple classification of a small number of distinct types (e.g., 'reliable' and 'unreliable', or first-person as opposed to third-person narrators), since they all involve matters of degree and of special individual situations. This point will become clearer in the course of the discussion which follows.

The first question which we can ask concerning the narrator of

with the wrong one returning at the end of the story, and many other improbabilities or impossibilities in the motif.

[1] Stanzl's work is very much to be welcomed as a serious move in the direction of the investigation of narration, but his typology of 'Erzählsituationen' seems to me too simple. Wayne Booth avoids the pitfalls of too rigid and simple a typology, but his discussion of the issues is still in general less than satisfactory. He needlessly attacks the distinction between first and third-person narrators as 'overworked', and even more needlessly attacks the first-person narrator convention: it 'is sometimes unduly limiting; if the "I" has inadequate access to information, the author may be led into improbabilities' (p. 150). This ignores the crucial point that the use of the first-person narrator consists precisely in the delimiting of the narrator and consequent creation of a distinct personality having a distinct interest in the story. Booth introduces into the discussion an 'implied author' whose status changes from time to time, but who is sometimes only a confusion of author and narrator. His other distinctions ('reliable' and 'unreliable' narrators, 'dramatised' and 'undramatised' narrators) never quite avoid the issue of the beliefs of the author; cf. p. 151 and p. 159.

[2] Wolfgang Kayser follows with much success this kind of cautious but fruitful path in his classic essay, 'Kleist als Erzähler', *German Life and Letters*, N.S., VIII (1954–5), 19–29.

the story is simply: To what extent does he emerge as a distinct character? The possibilities are numerous; he may be one character among others, an actor in the story but not an especially important one (e.g., Dr. Watson in the *Sherlock Holmes* stories), the central character of the book (e.g., *David Copperfield*), a story-teller having real physical existence within the story as a writer though not directly an actor in it (many of W. Somerset Maugham's stories, usually in the figure of the traveller), a story-teller having no physical existence in the story but still projected as a distinct figure through his explicit comments and thoughts, or, at the end-point of the spectrum, the distant unidentified narrator who makes no comment from the viewpoint of an observer, but who nevertheless can be endowed with a distinct outlook through the emphases he gives to what he reports. I shall use this series of possibilities as the main factor organising my discussion of the narrative structure of the eight stories. But other important questions about the narrator must be considered all the time: How much does he intervene? Why does he intervene? How much does he know? What kind of knowledge does he have of people (their appearances or their thoughts) or of the universe in which they live? Where is he – always in the company of one character, more than one, or no-one in particular? And most importantly: What are his concerns, and the emphases which predominate in his story? It must be remembered that any one of these questions may have to be answered in different ways at different points in any one story.

Among my eight authors, the one who most allows for the emergence of his narrators as distinct characters also tends to have the greatest mixture of types of narration within a single story: E. T. A. Hoffmann. *Rat Krespel* is told by one of the 'Serapions-brüder', and so by a kind of author-figure, a man involved in the telling of stories; but he is also one of the important characters in the story, as a young man interested in Krespel's daughter. Yet the central figure of the story also becomes involved in its narration, for part of the story is told as if from Krespel's own perspective, and it is the important part which (apparently) clears up its mysteries. This pattern of mixed narration is common in Hoffmann's work: *Das Fräulein von Scuderi* is narrated partly by the conventional anonymous story-teller, partly by Olivier, and partly by Cardillac as retold by Olivier. *Der Sandmann* begins with narration by letters between the characters – and so at one end of the spectrum as far as narration by distinct characters is concerned – and in the middle of the story switches to the other end, and to a highly self-conscious story-teller, who at first meditates on how to tell the story and from that point on remains in command of it. In *Die Elixiere des Teufels*, the narrators include Medardus, his 'Doppelgänger', the girl who obsesses him, and others.

This persistent characteristic is an important part of what Hoffmann writes about; he is concerned with the clash of different mental worlds, and thus narrates from several points of view. In *Rat Krespel*, Krespel's existence appears chaotic to the outsider, but by switching the narrative perspective Hoffmann can show its strictly consistent shape from an inside viewpoint; as a result we can see strongly contrasted the logic of Krespel's madness and its apparently random manifestation. In *Das Fräulein von Scuderi* something like the same thing occurs, except that there the conventional story-teller appears too, and pursues a doggedly rational path through the mystery of the events in Paris. And so the paradox emerges: from a reasonable point of view, these events are mystifying and terrifying, while from the point of view of the madman Cardillac they are very simple. From the contrast of these two emerges yet another perspective, in which the reader can see through the contradictions in Cardillac's account to the emergence of something that will at last explain what the real structure of the situation is.[1] The reader is actively involved in receiving and weighing different kinds of impression from different narrative sources; for Hoffmann's contrast between the rational outsider, the story-teller whose perspective produces nothing but bewilderment, and the aberrant central figure who though seeming

[1] Cf. my 'E. T. A. Hoffmann's *Das Fraülein von Scuderi*', *Modern Language Review*, LXIV (1969), 340–50, for an interpretation of the story in the light of its narrative structure.

complex is at bottom always too simple, having reduced his life to one obsessive idea, is a large part of his meaning. By this means, he turns our ideas on madness and loss of control upside down; in the initial narrative perspective, Krespel and Cardillac seem out of control, but by the end their failing emerges as the rigid control over them of one idea, and the greater health of those around them consists precisely in their ability to behave more randomly. *Der Sandmann* shows that there is still room for much variation within this preferred scheme of Hoffmann's; for here, after narration by the letters which show differing attitudes to Nathanael's concern with the figure of Sandman (all of which allows us to entertain the possibility that the Sandman exists only in Nathanael's mind) the conventional story-teller suddenly breaks in. From this point onwards everything, including the direct references to Coppola, has to be taken in a different and more serious way. Here Hoffmann exploits the contrast not just of two perspectives on the same event (as he did in *Rat Krespel*) but actually two ways of telling the story which make the events radically different kinds of events; in the first, they are primarily events of Nathaniel's consciousness but in the second they are 'real' events. Yet in all of these cases, the effect is to drive the reader out of any simple identification with the perspective of a narrator, since he must stand above all of them and weigh them against each other. Hoffmann demands constant action, interpretation, and then reinterpretation on the part of his readers.

Closest to Hoffmann's *Rat Krespel* in its allowing the narrator to emerge as a distinct character in the story is Grillparzer's *Der arme Spielmann*; and here too the narration is split between the main character of the story on the one hand, and a 'real life' story-teller on the other. But here, the emphasis is not so much on two views of the central character, as it was with Hoffmann, but instead on a direct contrast of the narrator and his subject, who turn out to be opposites, with this oppositeness the very theme of the story. The Spielmann is sincere but quite unable to bring this sincerity to any useful action, in his everyday life through his inefficiency, and in his art through his technical incompetence.

2-2

The narrator is the exact reverse; insincere and unfeeling but technically aware in an ostentatious and even pretentious way. The thematic structure of the story lies in the contrast of the values of the man telling the story and those of the man who is the subject of that story, and so the very act of story-telling is thematic, part of the meaning of *Der arme Spielmann*, in that it is an activity contrasted to that of the old man whom it ostensibly concerns.

Storm's *Der Schimmelreiter*, most of all these stories, shows the need for flexibility rather than rigid categorisation in talking of different kinds of narrators. For its narrators emerge in a sense as distinct personages having to do with the 'real life' situation they talk of, and yet in another sense they relate to the events as distant, self-conscious tellers of a story too. The contradiction is only apparent.

The story concerns the life of Hauke Haien, a great progressive figure in the history of the dyke regions of North Germany, and his struggle against the superstitions of the people which impede his work. But it is told to a traveller passing through the region several generations later by a schoolmaster who is unpopular among the people of the district. After bystanders tell the traveller that the old woman, Antje Vollmers, would tell it better, the schoolmaster agrees to try to make some concessions to the version she would give. This is a remarkable narrative 'frame', and achieves something technically quite brilliant: we have a *double* narrator, and the two narrators (the schoomaster and Antje Vollmers) correspond to the antagonists of the story (Hauke Haien and the old woman of the people, Trin Jans) in their attitudes to reason and superstition, progress and the old ways of the people. But while this is technically as involved as Brentano's narrative scheme in *Kasperl und Annerl*, unlike Brentano, Storm does this for thematic purposes; just as in *Der arme Spielmann*, we have here narration by distinct characters who have distinct thematic relevance themselves to the story, in Grillparzer's case as the opposite pole to the central figure of the story, but in Storm's case both as identical and opposite poles to the two main figures.

The emergence of distinct characters to tell a story has often been taken as a means of guaranteeing the 'truth' of it; a real identifiable person appears to tell us what he himself heard.[1] Nothing could be further from the point of narration by distinct characters, who, in fact, as Storm's story shows, do exactly the reverse; they limit the degree to which we can accept the story at face value by the fact that their own concerns, intelligence and stake in the story are delimited for us. In *Der arme Spielmann*, the telling of the story, far from being more 'credible' through a narrator telling us of his personal experience, becomes a process of coming to terms with a figure who is a polar opposite to the narrator; the 'truth' of his version of the Spielmann becomes a secondary matter. And in *Der Schimmelreiter*, Storm has given us a narrative in which the Schoolmaster will evidently side with Hauke, while the influence of Antje Vollmers on the narrative will be to give right to Trin Jans. What Hauke was really like is not the point; the narrative scheme stresses the fact that this is not a story of Hauke, but a local legend in which fact and fiction cannot be disentangled. The point of legends is the ideas they embody, not the distant and shadowy figures that are their historical source; and so the story is as much concerned with the attitudes of its co-narrators, their part in the creation of the legend, as it is with Hauke. Storm rounds off this process by making the traveller's account (itself remembered and committed to paper) something read, remembered, and retold fifty years later by another narrator, stressing once more that it is the existence of the story in the minds of those who tell it, and their reasons for their retaining and retelling it, that is important. Telling stories is a means of interpreting one's own life, and past. The frame narrators are struggling with each other over the dead body of Hauke, but their real struggle concerns themselves and their version of their own society. Storm's narrative scheme is the whole point of his story.

So much for narration by distinct characters; the other five

---

[1] Cf. below, pp. 156–7. The equation of 'frame' narration and objective narration is, of course, a legacy of the accepted theory of the Novelle.

stories I have chosen all dispense with them, in favour of conventional story-tellers. Yet here too, there is much variety of type and function, much more than is allowed for by the common designation of this kind of narrator as the 'omniscient narrator'. Omniscience in narrators is in fact exceedingly rare; they usually have distinct areas of knowledge, delimited in specific ways, for example delimited as to type (knowledge of facts, of minds, of values of the story), or as to extent (knowledge of the facts as experienced by one character or group of characters, or knowledge of the minds of only one or a group). Most important of all, it is very common for the conventional story-teller to have a distinct, limiting relationship with his story as far as his attitude to it is concerned. This means that the attitude of the narrator is offered to us as part of its thematic material, not as a key to it; something for us to think about and evaluate, not to accept as the attitude of the work as a whole.[1]

A common example of narratorial limitation is the restriction of the narrator to the environment of one character; the narrator knows facts occurring in the room or piece of ground in the field of vision of that character, and, so to speak, sits on his shoulder. He may or may not know everything within that field of vision. This is in fact one of the commonest conventions of a limited narrator. Hauptmann's *Bahnwärter Thiel*, and Kafka's *Das Urteil*, or *Die Verwandlung* are cases of this kind of restriction; in Kafka's stories, the narrator knows all that is happening in the mind of Georg and Gregor respectively, and all that they see. But, at least until the very end of both stories, he knows nothing else; in *Das Urteil*, the thoughts of Georg's father are as inscrutable to the narrator as to Georg himself, and the same is the case

---

[1] Booth, distinguishing 'reliable' and 'unreliable' narrators, defines a reliable one as one who '...speaks for or acts in accordance with the norms of the work' (p. 158). I am inclined to think that on this definition very few narrators are reliable, and that those who are so are usually the narrators of inferior works. For if we can accept that narrators' comments are a reliable guide to the norms of the work, and thus a reliable interpretation of it, it follows that the narrator is not himself thematically involved in the work, but separable from it. The eight stories I treat here are all the better for entailing unreliable narration, in this sense, which seems to me to make this reliable/unreliable distinction an uninteresting one.

with Gregor Samsa. Hauptmann's narrator occasionally shows a
little insight into Lene's thoughts and emotions, but otherwise is
always concerned with Thiel's mind, and field of vision. Telling
the story from the 'point of view' of the one character does not,
of course, mean any necessary sharing of attitude, though it may
do; essentially, this limitation is a physical one.

All these three cases involve the eventual death of the character
concerned, and in fact all three exploit the uncomfortable feeling
that we experience as the narrator no longer enjoys his previous
perch; part of the irreverence of the final tram-ride of Gregor
Samsa's family after his death lies in the narrator's joining them
there, so that their breaking away from his oppressive claustro-
phobic presence is paralleled by the narrator's doing the same
thing. The narrator violates his own established convention, just
as they do. The move in the last line of *Das Urteil* away from
Georg's limiting perspective is a smaller-scale version of the
same. In the Hauptmann and Kafka stories alike, this choice of a
narrator who is limited to the physical presence of his central
character correlates with a concern with the consciousness of that
character. Hauptmann's narrator is always turned towards Thiel's
reception of visual impressions from his surroundings, and their
build-up in his mind. His descriptions of the physical settings of
his story are grotesquely impressionistic, but they are always in
terms of the impression made on Thiel himself by the outside
world, for the weird shapes with which the narrator seems to
overlay the physical world are the shapes of Thiel's own mental
images; Thiel's sense of being constricted becomes the spider's
web in the narrator's description of Thiel's woodland post, and
his being barely in control of the forces inside him is the basis of
the repeated description of the overwhelming force of the train,
appearing as if from nowhere. As the narrator assaults his readers
with these grotesque impressionistic descriptions, he also gives
him a sense of the intolerable overloading of Thiel's mind with
impressions from the outside world that he cannot assimilate.
Throughout, too, the relentless and unavoidable quality of this
assault on Thiel finds expression in the narrator's absolute control

over the narrative; he appears as a sovereign figure, first including much detail, and then excluding any detail as he jumps to another part of the story, at will – a display of almost arbitrary exercise of power on his part.

Kafka's *Das Urteil*, too, is much concerned with Georg's consciousness; but whereas Hauptmann's narrator gives us projections of Thiel's consciousness in descriptions of the physical setting, Kafka's narrator takes us close to Georg's actual train of thought. For several pages we are drawn into Georg's mental world by this process, and become almost comfortable in the version of things which we experience with Georg; but Kafka has lured us into this position in order then to make us experience from within the frightening and grotesque appearance of a challenge to it. At first the father appears as a madman; only gradually does it become apparent that we were living with Georg in the deceptively comfortable world of his self-protective fantasy, and that it is this that has made the intrusion of sanity and reality a nightmare experience. The story is about what the narration produces: the shock caused by our being forced to face a brutal challenge to our own versions of what is happening around us, a version inevitably bound up with the need to protect ourselves from unwanted knowledge. The narrator takes us into the unreality of Georg's world to the point that it appears a norm we can be comfortable with, and then the intrusion of sanity appears monstrous. *Das Urteil* is at one level about the conflict of father and son, but in a much more important sense it is about the shock of the intrusion of light into a well-rounded and well-protected view of one's life which has lost contact with what is really happening in it; and that more important aspect of the story is the creation of its narrative structure.

The narrators of Kleist and Keller have some important things in common. To begin with – and unlike those of Hauptmann and Kafka – they are not tied to one character, but have more freedom of movement. In *Das Erdbeben in Chili*, the narrator can follow Jeronimo, Josephe, or Don Fernando; and this variability of position is there too in *Michael Kolhaas* and *Der Zweikampf*.

Keller's narrator follows various characters in *Die drei gerechten Kammacher*, as he does in *Romeo und Julia auf dem Dorfe* and *Kleider machen Leute*. In all these cases, then, the narrator has increased the scope of his knowledge and comment. But this does not mean that he is more knowledgeable in general; for with both Keller and Kleist this gain has been accompanied by a loss. In both, the narrator can make comments on the thoughts of any character, and yet on occasion he declines to do so, Kleist's narrator by describing the external signs of a reaction (e.g., a flush of anger) and leaving the matter there, Keller's going even further to acknowledge that he does not know why someone acted as they did. And Keller's case points to the really important limitation of the narrator in both Keller and Kleist: the narrator is uncertain of the values of his story, picking always a morally ambiguous situation to talk about and then noticeably attempting to grapple with it, taking different attitudes at different points in the story. In *Kleider machen Leute*, for example, Wenzel's situation is morally ambiguous; he is involved in a deception of others, but it is in large measure their own self-deception that produces the situation too. The important question arises: What does the narrator think of Wenzel? The answer is different at different points of the story, and the narrator's shifts of viewpoint keep us actively involved as readers in the basic issue of the story, the attitude to be taken to such a man. In *Die drei gerechten Kammacher* the narrator begins by thinking of the comb-makers as subhuman in their limitation of their horizons; but at the end he looks on them as only too human in their suffering. The thematic problem he poses is that of the difference between the comb-makers' narrow pursuit of a very limited goal, and Züs' random, apparently aimless and pointless behaviour, but much of the development of this theme lies in his own performance as narrator, oscillating as he does between direct and purposeful narration, and lengthy digressions which go into much seemingly irrelevant (and goalless) detail. By the end of the story his attitude to the morally and humanly ambiguous phenomenon of the comb-makers has undergone a complete reversal; and much of the point of the story lies in the narrator's gradual working towards this change of evaluation.

Keller is not usually thought of as being similar to Kleist, and yet it is instructive to see their sharing not just some features of narration, but actually a whole complex of behaviour on the part of the narrator: the physically freely moving narrator who is uncertain of the values inherent in what he sees, and continually attempts to come to terms with and interpret a situation difficult to evaluate. Yet there are important differences too; and not just that between Kleist's dominant tone being more forceful and tense, with Keller's narrator being more easy-going and relaxed. For the most important difference is that, while Keller's narrator is concerned above all with the evaluation of his characters, Kleist's is much more worried about the structure of the world in which they live, and only secondarily concerned with whether their actions are appropriate to that structure.

In *Das Erdbeben in Chili*, the narrator is very much 'der Bewertende, der Fühlende, der Schauende', to use Käte Friedemann's phrase once more. He has before him the ambiguous situation of the earthquake, because of which many good things and many bad things happen. He begins in a crisp, direct and factual tone, but as he proceeds his language shows first an attitude to the events, and then how this attitude evolves into another as new events come along which need to be integrated into what he previously thought. His concern is with the meaning of the whole situation which develops before him, and his striking metaphors are reflections of his looking at it now this, now that way, charting his intellectual and emotional progress through the story. The kinds of details which he records, suddenly and in the middle of a very broad narrative sweep, show the aspects of these events that he is most impressed by, and thus once more what his attitudes are to the sequence of events. *Das Erdbeben in Chili* is, in fact, about nothing less than the attempt to grasp and take some sensible attitude to what happens in the story, and for this reason its narrator must be considered its central character. *Der Zweikampf*, while still being within Kleist's basic pattern of a narrator concerned with the basis of the world he describes, varies it significantly. Its narrator tells a story in the stereotyped style of a medieval romance: there is a knight who fights for the honour of his lady, an evil villain who has insulted her, a duel between the two, an eventual wedding and everyone lives happily ever after. But the narrator's framework is superimposed on material that is much more like the real world; the knight is neither a brilliant tactician nor a heroic fighter, the villain is a man of considerable charm and resource, the lady appears often heartless and selfish, and the outcome of the duel, by a roundabout means, helps to retain a usurper on the throne. The narrator's serene stereotype of a just world in which clear evaluations are possible crumbles as he doggedly sticks to it in the face of events which make it laughable. In *Das Erdbeben in Chili*, the narrator attempts to move with the events, while in *Der Zweikampf* he stays still and they move away from him; but in both cases the narrator's vain attempts to evaluate the structure of the world of his story are essential thematic material. The narrators of the Keller and Kleist stories are closest to what would traditionally be termed 'omniscient' narrators; yet how misleading and even destructive such a term would be in these cases, for it is precisely the limitations of the narrators that give these stories their meaning.

Tieck's *Der blonde Eckbert* is a Märchen, but I have included it because its narration is an example of a very fixed convention which adds another dimension to the spectrum of possible narrative schemes. In the convention of the fairy-story are found remarkable complexes of features: language is much simplified, both as to vocabulary and syntax; explicitly ideological material is avoided (no direct philosophising); the time setting is somewhat archaic, but also very indistinct; many standard motifs appear – the old woman, the child, the cottage, the woods; certain inconsistencies, improbabilities and even supernatural features are allowed – the dead man who reappears, the character who changes into another, the bird who can sing a song in human language and lay golden eggs. A very important feature of this convention concerns motivation; characters are allowed to perform actions for no reason, and this is acceptable fairy-story style, causing no feeling on the reader's part that the story is deficient. The convention of the fairy-story is usually announced by a beginning with a standard formula: 'Once upon a time...', and the reader adjusts his responses accordingly. What can such a convention be used for and why should it have arisen? Tieck's own use of it will shed some light on the question. In *Der blonde Eckbert* the reduction of linguistic and situational complexity to the simple fairy-tale situation allows him to include a very tight system of motifs which dominate the story, and which concern the constant expansion and contraction of Eckbert's world. Implausible and impossible events (unbelievable coincidences by the standards of 'realistic' fiction) help to make this tight network of motifs, while the simplicity and absence of detail of the Märchen set it off even more sharply. In this respect (the development without any realistic hindrances or restrictions of a well developed system of motifs as the binding structure of the events) the Märchen is like the dream, and perhaps the convention owes its existence to the recounting of dreams. Another factor coming into play is that the dividing line between fantasy and reality vanishes; as in a dream, it does not seem necessary to distinguish clearly between imaginings and fact. A realistic story could only be *about* a paranoid and his delusions; but *Der blonde Eckbert is* a paranoid fantasy in which the world gradually closes in on its victim, and his attempts to break out only hasten its constriction of him. It is a paranoid *experience*, and finishes with the outside world becoming the blur that is inevitable as the fears of its paranoid central figure make everything around him a frightening, indistinct thing which is uniformly directed against him; he can no longer distinguish one thing from another, or himself from it.

As I have said, this discussion is not concerned with any kind of exhaustive 'typology of narration'; there is an infinite variety of narrative situations, and as we discuss more and more stories, new facts of and factors in narrative stance must appear. In this discussion, I have been concerned with some rather basic points of narrative technique and how they become part of the thematic structure of these eight stories; the interpretations are intended to extend the comparative framework of this discussion to pursue the meaning of the stories further.

2. KLEIST: 'DAS ERDBEBEN IN CHILI'

Das Erdbeben in Chili[1] has attracted more critical attention than any other of Kleist's stories, with the exception of the much

[1] The edition used for references to the text in this chapter is: H. Sembdner, ed., *Heinrich von Kleist: Sämtliche Werke und Briefe*, 3rd. rev. ed., II (Munich, 1964), 144–59. This chapter is a much revised and adapted version of my paper 'Kleist's *Das Erdbeben in Chili*', read before the English Goethe Society in May 1963, and published in the *Publications of the English Goethe Society*, XXXIII (1963), 10–55. A number of studies devoted specifically to this story have appeared: J. C. Blankenagel, 'Heinrich von Kleist: *Das Erdbeben in Chili*', *Germanic Review*, VIII (1933), 30–9; K. O. Conrady, 'Kleists *Erdbeben in Chili*. Ein Interpretationsversuch', *Germanisch-Romanische Monatsschrift*, N.F., IV (1954), 185–95; J. Klein, 'Kleists *Erdbeben in Chili*', *Der Deutschunterricht*, VIII (1956), 5–11; W. Silz, '*Das Erdbeben in Chili*', *Monatshefte*, LIII (1961), 210–38, reprinted as a chapter of his *Heinrich von Kleist: Studies in his Works and Literary Character* (Philadelphia, 1961), pp. 13–27; B. von Wiese, 'Heinrich von Kleist: *Das Erdbeben in Chili*', *Jahrbuch der deutschen Schiller-Gesellschaft*, V (1961), 102–17, also a chapter in his *Die Deutsche Novelle von Goethe bis Kafka*, II, 53–70; R. E. Modern, 'Sobre *El Terremoto en Chile*, de Kleist', *Torre*, X (1962), XXXIX, 151–55; W. Gausewitz, 'Kleist's *Erdbeben*', *Monatshefte*, LV (1963), 188–94; J. Kunz, 'Die Gestaltung des tragischen Geschehens in Kleists *Erdbeben in Chili*', in *Gratulatio: Festschrift Christian Wegner* (Hamburg, 1963), pp. 145–70; E. San Juan, Jr., 'The Structure of Narrative Fiction', *Saint Louis Quarterly*, IV (1966), 485–502; M. Ossar, 'Kleist's *Das Erdbeben in Chili* and *Die Marquise von O.*', *Revue des Langues Vivantes*, XXXIV (1968), 151–69; A. O. Aldridge, 'The Background of Kleist's *Das Erdbeben in Chili*', *Arcadia*, IV (1969), 173–80; W. Wittkowski, 'Skepsis, Noblesse, Ironie: Formen des Als-ob in Kleists *Erdbeben*', *Euphorion*, LXIII (1969), 247–83; R. S. Lucas, 'Studies in Kleist, II: *Das Erdbeben in Chili*', *Deutsche Vierteljahrsschrift für Literaturwissenschaft und Geistesgeschichte*, XLIV (1970), 145–70. Studies of the *Erdbeben* which have appeared since mine was written have not necessitated any change in my interpretation. Gausewitz's essay is slight, Aldridge is largely concerned with the historical source, San Juan and Ossar largely ignore previous criticism, and Kunz advances much the same view as did Koch, i.e., that the tragedy results from the poor judgment of the lovers. Wittkowski alone comments on my interpretation (Lucas does not do so, inexplicably, since he announces a special concern with narration, p. 145); but Wittkowski so misstates and misconceives my position that its central points are not met. At the lowest level, he does not refer to my pagination correctly; on his p. 251, he cites a word from my p. 28 which cannot be found there and on his p. 261 a statement from my p. 30 which I cannot find there or anywhere else; on his p. 252 he refers to my p. 99, while my essay ends on p. 55. This misquotation persists in more important matters: on his p. 257 he says of me: 'Freilich verkennt er den Sinn und darum auch den Bau der Novelle, die er für inkonsistent erklärt (42).' But my p. 42 discusses the *narrator's* inconsistency, and its function within the story: I neither state nor imply that the story is inconsistent. This misconception is the key to most of the others, since it is my point concerning the narrator's developing understanding and changing stance

longer *Michael Kohlhaas*, and has even been considered by many critics to be a more accomplished work of art. Bonafous[1] thought that 'cette nouvelle, par sa composition, ses nuances, son énergie et sa concision nous parait la meilleure que Kleist ait écrit', Herzog[2] that it was Kleist's 'stärkste und elementarste Novelle', and Korff[3] that it was the thematic basis of all the other stories, 'denn in allen diesen Novellen bebt die Erde'. But it is an intriguing fact about *Das Erdbeben in Chili* that one critical opinion immediately seems to provoke another which contradicts it: Gundolf,[4] for example, thought the *Erdbeben* a meaningless story in which Kleist introduced one disaster after another solely to maintain the tension; but this judgment again is opposed by Bonafous, who said that it was constructed very strictly according to a philosophical idea.[5] There is in fact an astonishing lack of agreement among its critics on every aspect of *Das Erdbeben in Chili*: its tone and style, its value, its theme and meaning, and even on the judgment of its characters.

Opinion is evenly divided as to whether the story is optimistic or pessimistic: Herzog, Witkop, Wolff and Silz[6] take the pessi-

which is ignored persistently. Thus Wittkowski glosses my word 'non-committal' as 'Neutralität', (p. 256) and asserts that I deny the 'Parteinahme des Erzählers'; and he cites *one* of the two possible views of Jeronimo which I had diagnosed in the early part of the story as *my* view of him. Throughout, Wittkowski in this way takes out of context points that I had made about the possible constructions that can be put on an event in the story and which the narrator may seem to put on them temporarily, and makes them into definite assertions on my part. A typical example is his 'daher ist es abwegig, wenn Ellis ihn [den Vizekönig] als Repräsentanten der verdorbenen Gesellschaft betrachtet' (p. 262). My pp. 25 and 29 make clear that it is the *possibility* of this construction which the text raises and then *removes*. Similar arguments apply to his p. 265, regarding my use of Leibniz; p. 272, on my alleged condemnation of Don Fernando; p. 262, on the phrase 'sehe würdige junge Damen'; and on my alleged view that 'Am Ende richte man sich bewußt ein in der lebensnotwendigen Lebenslüge, als hätte alles auf Erden einen höheren Zweck', the last inaccurate as to framework *and* content. I do not, therefore, think that *my* view is discussed at all here.

[1] R. Bonafous, *Henri de Kleist* (Paris, 1894), p. 383.
[2] W. Herzog, *Heinrich von Kleist* (Munich, 1914), p. 350.
[3] H. A. Korff, *Geist der Goethezeit*, IV (Leipzig, 1953), p. 86.
[4] F. Gundolf, *Heinrich von Kleist* (Berlin, 1932), p. 165.   [5] Bonafous, p. 380.
[6] Herzog, p. 352, speaks of the story's 'pessimistische Erkenntnis' of the 'gebrechliche Einrichtung der Welt'; P. Witkop, *Heinrich von Kleist* (Leipzig, 1922), pp. 181–2, stresses the story's fatalism on the question of the inherent evil of human nature; H. M. Wolff, *Heinrich von Kleist* (Bern, 1954), pp. 42–6, stresses social corruption;

mistic view, but each stresses different aspects of the story which lead them to this conclusion, while Pongs, Blöcker, Brahm and Bonafous[1] believe it to be optimistic, though once more none gives the same reason. There have been many statements of the theme of the story: Wolff[2] thought that it was Rousseauism, the corruption of society as against the inherent goodness of nature; Blöcker,[3] that the world is 'ein Rätsel'; Bonafous,[4] that the story shows the goodness of God to man; Bennett,[5] that the incomprehensible and irresponsible forces of the universe break into the ordered life of man; Conrady[6] that 'das Widerspiel zwischen den Wirkungen der Naturkräfte und den Folgen der Menschengewalt... bleibt ein wesentliches Thema dieser Novelle'; Klein,[7] that man can begin again by an act of 'geistige Neuschöpfung'; Staiger,[8] that it is about the conflict between 'Geist' and 'Gefühl'; and there are many others. Even the question as to who is the hero or central figure of the story is disputed. The candidates for the position are the two lovers, Don Fernando and the child Philipp. Faced with this series of disagreements about the story, it is not surprising that some commentators have thought the story obscure; but even here there is still dispute, for others insist on its lack of ambiguity.[9]

Now I have not introduced this welter of contradictory opinions in order to show that it gets us nowhere, and that a fresh start is needed; on the contrary, all this shows one very important fact about the story, that it provokes a great variety of

---

Silz, *Heinrich von Kleist*, pp. 23–4, stresses the fortuitousness of both life and death in the face of the earthquake.

[1] H. Pongs, *Das Bild in der Dichtung*, II (Marburg, 1939), pp. 152f. and 292f., sees the child as a symbol of divine redemption through the power of love; G. Blöcker, *Heinrich von Kleist oder das absolute Ich* (Berlin, 1960), p. 137, sees the earthquake as an influence which makes man stronger; O. Brahm, *Heinrich von Kleist* (Berlin, 1884), p. 172, thinks that Kleist shows 'wie unter dem Eindruck des Zusammensturzes alles Bestehenden eine neue, bessere Ordnung der Dinge sich vorbereiten will'; Bonafous, pp. 380–1, believes that it shows divine benevolence.

[2] Wolff, p. 42.　　　　　[3] Blöcker, p. 137.　　　　　[4] Bonafous, p. 380.

[5] Bennett, *A History of the German Novelle*, p. 45.　　　　　[6] Conrady, p. 186.

[7] Klein, p. 11.

[8] In *Heinrich von Kleist: vier Reden zu seinem Gedächtnis*, ed. W. Müller-Seidel (Berlin, 1962), p. 55.

[9] Herzog, p. 332, and Klein, p. 10.

different interpretations and ideas. Any new interpretation of the story must certainly come to terms with this fact, and explain why it should be so; and indeed on closer inspection it can be seen that many of these conflicting ideas are relevant to the story, and that it is precisely as *conflicting* ideas that they are relevant, though not as the competing complete explanations offered by the critics. They are rather thematic material which Kleist includes in his story, carefully structured and controlled by his overall design. In the *Erdbeben* there is constantly a struggle to interpret the events on the part of the narrator, and of the characters of the story; and so previous interpretations achieve a special interest for a story whose very theme is interpretation. This is because the point of the story lies not in the meaning of the events themselves, but in the attempts made by the narrator and the characters to give them meaning.

The setting of the story itself gives a clue to Kleist's thematic concerns, for earthquakes traditionally have been occasions on which men have been moved to think and even to quarrel about the structure and the precariousness of their existence. The most famous earthquake of modern times, the Lisbon earthquake of 1755,[1] had a profound influence on European thought; it was the occasion of a considerable sharpening of the dispute between differing theologies and theories of the universe. The most notable clash was that between the popular optimism of Leibniz' theory of the pre-established harmony (i.e. that this was the best of all possible worlds), a special case of the rational and the optimistic thinking of the eighteenth century, and the pessimistic strain of thought represented by Voltaire's poem on the Lisbon earthquake and his *Candide*. No other natural event provoked such intense philosophical and theological activity: this disaster made it pressing to think about how the universe worked, and whether everything that happened in it was ultimately an act of

---

[1] For a good account of the currents of thought, the 'earthquake theology', surrounding the Lisbon earthquake, cf. T. D. Kendrick, *The Lisbon Earthquake* (London, 1956). A factor which would have made a contemporary audience think of the Lisbon earthquake in connection with Kleist's story would have been the common feature: destruction of capital cities of Catholic countries whose languages were closely related.

God. Kleist's choice of the earthquake in Chile as his subject in
1810 was bound then to evoke memories of the Lisbon earthquake and to have overtones of the debate which followed it; but
even for the twentieth century reader, this choice of subject
matter still in itself raises the question of what attitude we can
take to suffering on such a scale, or to a disaster which is so uncon-
trollable and unpredictable, and before which human beings are
so defenceless. Throughout his story, Kleist alludes to and plays
on various kinds of attitudes to the earthquake; as the narrator
describes the events of the story, his formulation suggests a
series of such attitudes, and thus the ways in which he is inclined
to construe what he sees. The role of the narrator in creating the
meaning of the story is therefore crucial; and it is a role the point
of which can only be understood through close attention to the
sequence of his changing relationship to the events of the story.

The narrator begins on firm ground with the indisputable facts
of the situation: the place and year of the earthquake. But when
he comes to the description of how the love affair between
Josephe and Jeronimo began, he cannot avoid interpreting the
situation. He remains at first fairly distant from the emotional
tenor of the relationship, describing it cautiously as a 'zärtliches
Einverständnis' (144). Yet when he relates how Jeronimo
managed to see Josephe even after her father had placed her in a
convent, he says that this happened 'durch einen glücklichen
Zufall'. It is not clear here whether the narrator is reading
Jeronimo's reactions, or giving his own, so that he is not yet
committed to sympathising with the lovers;[1] but the formulation

---

[1] The classic statement on the evaluative language of Kleist's narrator, to which all
subsequent criticism must always be indebted, is by Wolfgang Kayser, in his 'Kleist
als Erzähler', (*Die Vortragsreise*, pp. 169–83); 'Die Wertungen, die sescheinbar Subjektivität enthüllenden Sprachgebärden, führen uns in Kleists Erzählungen auf keinen
sicheren Standpunkt außerhalb der Geschichte, und keineswegs zu einer festen
Beurteilung durch den Erzähler, die sein ganzes Erzählen trüge. Sie sind oft aus der
Perspektive einer Gestalt und immer unter dem Eindruck der jeweiligen Situation
gesprochen' (p. 172), and 'Der Erzähler steht ganz im Banne des Geschehenen, das er
erzählt and das Wirklichkeit ist. Er steht im Banne: er besitzt keine Überlegenheit über
die Figuren, wie wir es von Fielding und Wieland her kennen. Er überschaut nicht
einmal das Ganze des Geschehens...und seine Wertungen – an sich Symptome seiner
inneren Teilnahme... – gelten fast immer der jeweiligen Situation' (p. 176). One could

is bound to arouse in us the suspicion that fortune may be on the
side of the lovers, and that we can side with them too. The story
at this point looks like a conventional romance, with young love
opposed by the world; and with this would go the usual value
judgments, for the lovers, and against those who oppose them.
The narrator is non-committal when he says that the 'junge
Sünderin' (the pregnant Josephe) was thrown into prison, for this
is little more than a conventional phrase.[1] Neither we nor he need
feel yet that she is a sinner, or that she is not. But the description
of the meeting in the garden, on the other hand, was oriented
towards a picture of Jeronimo as seducer; *he* had 'in einer
verschwiegenen Nacht den Klostergarten zum Schauplatze seines
vollen Glückes gemacht'.[2] This is not the usual kind of language

add that in the case of the *Erdbeben* the narrator often seems to take refuge in reporting
the attitude of a character when in doubt as to what his own should be. These brilliant
and subtle observations have unfortunately been misunderstood and misinterpreted on
many occasions. Wittkowski, for example, not distinguishing narrator and author, takes
Kayser to be asserting that: 'Durchweg werte Kleist nur momentan und überblicke nicht
das Ganze' (p. 249), and so feels that Kayser 'für die Sinnlosigkeit der Ereignisse
plädiert' which he then answers by insisting that 'Der Schluss ist indessen deutlich in
den Bau des Ganzen einbezogen...' That there is a 'Bau des Ganzen', of which Kleist
(but not the narrator) is master, is not of course at issue in Kayser's view. Von Wiese
(*Die deutsche Novelle*, II) takes Kayser to be denying that the narrator is concerned with
the 'Wirklichkeit des Geschehens' (p. 57), since he evaluates 'vom jeweiligen Standort
der Gestalten aus' (p. 54). Lucas echoes von Wiese in this misquotation of Kayser's
'*oft* aus der perspektive einer Gestalt und fast immer unter dem Eindruck der *jeweiligen
Situation*' (my italics) and as an attempted corrective asserts that 'the narrator does not
always abstain from all comment, submerging his identity in the mentality of the
characters' (p. 149). But it is clear that Kayser thinks that the narrator is *concerned* with
the meaning of what happens (the 'Wirklichkeit des Geschehens') – but that he does
not know it. Kayser neither states nor implies that the narrator abstains from comment
or that he submerges his identity in that of the characters; Kayser's point is that his
comment is largely addressed to the present situation. Nor does he view the narrator
as 'largely detached' (Lucas, p. 145); Kayer's 'sein Bemühen um Sachlichkeit', taken
in the context of his argument (cf. the passages I cite above), does not justify this
summary remark. Evidently, an equation of author and narrator is a factor in this kind
of misunderstanding of Kayser's work: 'Vielmehr geht es ihm [Kleist] auch als Erzähler
um die Wirklichkeit des Geschehens...' (Von Wiese, p. 57).

[1] W. Müller-Seidel, *Versehen und Erkennen. Eine Studie über Heinrich von Kleist* (Cologne/
Graz, 1961), p. 65, makes the point that the impersonal 'man' is used to introduce
evaluations from which the narrator remains aloof, e.g., 'man brachte die junge
Sünderin'.

[2] The concentration on the episode as an experience of Jeronimo, his 'Glück', and words
like 'Schauplatz' all make this seem like an event which he has engineered for his own
satisfaction (on the model of a seducer and an innocent girl), rather than a relationship

we should expect in a description of young love thwarted by wicked authorities. Already, then, there are two distinct images of the relationship emerging: young and innocent love thwarted on the one hand, and this is the dominant image, but on the other hand seduction through exploitation of the privileged position of teacher and subsequent defilement of the sacred ground in which the nunnery stands. The fact that it is on the 'Fronleichnamsfest' that Josephe 'in Mutterwehen auf den Stufen der Kathedrale niedersank' tends to strengthen the latter image; the injury to the church is the greater for this. In some doubt as to how he should view this matter of the guilt or innocence of the lovers, the narrator nevertheless is more certain when he describes the feelings of the women of the city. A clear evaluation is implied as the narrator describes their *disappointment* that the decision of the Viceroy has replaced death by fire for Josephe with a mere beheading. And they are described with obvious irony[1] as the 'fromme Töchter der Stadt', when those whose houses command a view of the place of execution invite their neighbours to come to see it. It is as if the narrator were pleased to be able, at last, to give a clear judgment after his uncertainty as to how to judge the conduct of Jeronimo and Josephe, and the Archbishop and the other authorities responsible for their condemnation.

The next sequence of events begins with Jeronimo in prison. He prays to the mother of God for help, but without results, and decides to hang himself with a rope which had been left to him by 'der Zufall' (145). This is not the first mention of the role of

with devotion on both sides. Most critics have missed this and other innuendoes which show the narrator's uncertainty about the guilt or innocence of the lovers, and assume that the narrator is unambiguously on their side; e.g., Blankenagel gives a list (pp. 34–5) of the means by which Kleist arouses sympathy for the lovers, and leaves the matter there. The list is a good one, but another list pointing in the other direction could be made. Wittkowski's view of this episode as a 'Triumph des Natürlichen' and '"Provokation" des Christentums' (p. 258) does not account for the fact that all emphasis is given to the masculine triumph.

[1] Wittkowski again misquotes this point in my argument: 'Andererseits klingt es nach dem Gesagten zu gewagt, wenn Ellis dem Erzähler zutraut, ironisch zu urteilen, sich hinter den Gedanken der Personen zu verstecken' (p. 257). My point is reversed here: it is that the narrator emerges to make an ironic judgment which he commits himself to.

chance[1] in the story, and we must by now begin to ponder its significance. Could it mean that Providence offers him a fortunate release from a hopeless position? But at this point the earthquake occurs, and alters our problem for interpretation. For Jeronimo at the time of the earthquake was trying to fix his rope to an iron hook let into one of the 'Wandpfeiler'. When the shock came he clutched at the pillar, which prevented him from falling over and possibly being crushed under falling masonry.[2] This seems to invite the following interpretation of the chance by which Jeronimo got the rope: Providence, or Divine power, favours Jeronimo, so that he may be regarded either as not guilty, or as pardonable even if he is guilty. Then whether the earthquake itself is sent for the purpose of saving him or not, he has been sent a rope which will make sure that he is at the pillar when the earthquake comes, so that he will not be hurt by the earthquake, but instead saved by it. When formulated explicitly, this interpretation is implausible; but the point is that it is *not* so formulated, remaining instead as the implied conclusion towards which we feel almost instinctively directed as soon as we try to piece the events together.

The narrator's attitude to the earthquake is seen in the metaphor he uses to describe it: it happens 'als ob das Firmament einstürzte'. This is one of a number of similar striking metaphors in the story. But these metaphors do more than just add power to the description; they show the narrator's construction on the events at this particular moment, his attempts to understand his own story.[3]

[1] Throughout the story the very large number of references to chance as an explanation of an event in itself throws doubt on this kind of explanation. By his frequent use of the concept, the narrator clearly invites us to think again; this is another device through which the narrator tries to stick to his facts and avoid interpretation, but in so doing impresses us all the more with the need for some interpretation. Cf. Müller-Seidel, p. 86: 'Hinter dem vermeintlichen Zufall ahnen wir den Plan dessen, der ihn "schickt."' Silz (p. 20) points to the unlikeliness, even unreality, of these chances, but notes their enormous scope to produce great consequences.

[2] Silz (p. 14) notes the paradox of Jeronimo 'clinging for safety to the very pillar on which he was minded to die'.

[3] Both Silz (p. 20) and Müller-Seidel (pp. 138–40) stress the 'as-if' of the story. But Müller-Seidel gives too much weight to the middle section of the story here: 'Die Struktur Als-Ob bestimmt in *Erdbeben in Chili* den Mittelteil der Erzählung.' This is in fact true of the whole story. And while he correctly notes that 'Fast durchweg sind

For the moment it seems that the earthquake is a product of divine intervention, for the word 'Firmament' suggests cosmic significance. There follows, to strengthen this suggestion, a seemingly miraculous series of events; the prison starts to fall, but is met by the fall of the building opposite, so that an arch is formed. The prison collapsing by itself would have killed Jeronimo, but the arch allows him to crawl out through it and escape. As soon as he has got outside, no sooner and no later, the whole street collapses with a second tremor. After this he hurries along to get out of the city, for there is still death on all sides. But the narrator describes the scene as if some unseen hand were guiding Jeronimo through this maze of destruction, so that he finds the right path:

Hier stürzte noch ein Haus zusammen, und jagte ihn, die Trümmer weit umherschleudernd, in eine Nebenstraße; hier leckte die Flamme schon, in Dampfwolken blitzend, aus allen Giebeln, und trieb ihn schreckenvoll in eine andere; hier wälzte sich, aus seinem Gestade gehoben, der Mapochofluß auf ihn heran, und riß ihn brüllend in eine dritte. (146)

It is superfluous to say that nothing 'jagte' or 'trieb' Jeronimo, but this is the way he, and the narrator, see the events.

So far, then, there is one issue that has been present in the earthquake and the preceding events; whether the lovers are guilty or not, and hence how and why Jeronimo has been allowed to escape. The suggestion implicit in the way the narrator describes the situation is that the earthquake announces Jeronimo's innocence and frees him. But immediately another issue arises:

Hier lag ein Haufen Erschlagener, hier ächzte noch eine Stimme unter dem Schutte, hier schrieen Leute von brennenden Dächern herab, hier kämpften Menschen und Tiere mit den Wellen, hier war ein mutiger Retter bemüht, zu helfen; hier stand ein anderer, bleich wie der Tod, und streckte sprachlos zitternde Hände zum Himmel. (146)

religiöse Momente das eigentliche Charakteristikum dieser Sphäre des Als-Ob', Müller-Seidel then concludes from this that 'Im sprachlichen Ausdruck wird fassbar, wie Göttliches ins irdische Dasein hineinwirkt', making the narrator's provisional constructions into facts. Thus Müller-Seidel arrives at the view that God works for the good in the story, while man and his institutions are the source of the evil.

It may be all very well to think of the earthquake as representing divine intervention on Jeronimo's behalf, but how do all these other people fit into the picture? To free an innocent man at the expense of the lives of many others makes no sense. Certainly, Jeronimo cannot make sense of it. He oscillates between the good and the bad faces of the situation three times.[1] First, he is seized by a feeling of delight that he is still alive, but seeing the others around him 'er begriff nicht, was ihn und sie hierher geführt haben konnte' (146). Next he thanks God for his rescue (for to whom else can he attribute it?) but immediately remembers Josephe and changes his mind: 'fürchterlich schien ihm das Wesen, das über den Wolken waltet' (147). Thus the concept of God has disappeared, to be replaced by the vaguer concept of the Being, whoever he might be, and whether good or evil, who controls life. When he hears the erroneous report that Josephe is dead he goes further, and attributes the whole sequence of events to 'die zerstörende Gewalt der Natur'; this is as if to say that he was entirely mistaken to see any design or intelligence in the recent events, and certainly that he was mistaken to think of them as in his favour. His last turn to an optimistic interpretation of what has happened is hope, and he looks again for Josephe; but his hope dies as he cannot find her. When at last he does find her, the concept of divine intervention appears again: 'Mit welcher Seligkeit umarmten sie sich, die Unglücklichen, die ein Wunder des Himmels gerettet hatte!' (148). The favourable conclusion allows the return to the most optimistic of the attitudes which had passed through Jeronimo's mind, and even permits the feeling that only ignorance of the full story made any other attitude possible. Yet we must remember that this has only disposed of one fact that did not favour the idea of divine intervention, namely Josephe's having perished. There remains something still to explain: why the death of so many other people, all presumably as

---

[1] Lucas here seems remote from the tone and setting of the story (pp. 147–8): 'So many reversals may easily become comic; and yet, though one may smile at the naivety... each moment in itself has a natural justification that draws one's sympathy... It is unlikely to have occurred to anyone but Jeronimo to see the hand of God in what happened.'

innocent as the couple were? Josephe's story now follows, and seems almost to provide an answer to this, for in the telling of it a new attitude to the earthquake seems to emerge.

The narrator first tells us what happened to Josephe, and then that she now tells it all to Jeronimo. The procession to the place of her execution had been broken up by the earthquake; she had hurried to the nunnery to get her child, had found the building in flames, and seen the Abbess die before her eyes; she saw the cathedral in ruins, and the body of the Archbishop being dragged out of it; the Viceroy's palace was in flames, the court where she had been tried was demolished, and her father's house had completely disappeared. In the place of the house 'war ein See getreten, und kochte rötliche Dämpfe aus' (149). This seemed to Silz a Danteesque picture,[1] and its function is clearly to give the appearance of the paternal house having been consumed by hellfire; the demolition of the seats of all those agencies which had condemned the pair – church, state, family – seems like a series of exemplary punishments, pointing to the cruelty and corruption of all of them. And so it seems that the earthquake has not merely saved the lovers, but attacked a corrupt society, in which their fate was only an isolated example of that corruption. We can now reinterpret the first page of the story. The Archbishop prosecuted Josephe, and is now dead. The laws of the nunnery condemned her, and now it stands in flames. Her family obstructed her love, and they have been destroyed. The lovers were not guilty at all then, or so it seems; the nunnery was never sacred, and so they could not defile it. Add to this the glee of the women of the city at the forthcoming execution, and the image of the city begins to look like that of Sodom and Gomorrah; were these then the kind of people whom Josephe saw dead and dying? What is more, the child of the union is miraculously saved: Josephe rushes into the nunnery to collect it, and the building collapses as soon as she comes out, killing all inside. The narrator produces another of his very strong metaphors: Josephe escapes 'als ob alle Engel des Himmels sie umschirmten'. At this point, then, the narrator's

[1] Silz, p. 15.

formulations seem to explain the earthquake as the destruction of Sodom and Gomorrah through the wrath of God; this is a broader view than the former one which concerned only the safety of the couple, and it seems to allow a secure judgment of the situation.

But there are still one or two puzzling facts that do not allow us to be entirely comfortable in this attitude. The Abbess had attempted to intercede for Josephe when she was being tried; and when she was condemned this same Abbess promised to look after Josephe's child. When Josephe gets to the nunnery, the Abbess is at the door crying for help so that the child should be saved, instead of getting clear of the building and to safety. She ought not to deserve to die. The obvious conclusion to which we jump is that she dies as the symbolic head of a corrupt institution; this would be more or less consistent with the view which has been developing in the narrator's descriptions. Nevertheless, the narrator is clearly distressed by her death: while the body of the Archbishop is 'zerschmettert', a word which implies no sympathy for him, the Abbess is described as being 'auf eine schmähliche Art erschlagen' (148).[1] And if such an attitude is taken to the Abbess, the Viceroy becomes an embarrassment, for if anyone should suffer an exemplary symbolic death, it is he who should do so; he is the symbolic head of the whole society. Nevertheless, in the list of people seen dead by Josephe, his name is conspicuously absent. Yet once before, only ignorance (of Josephe's having escaped) stood in the way of a harmonious conclusion; and for the moment, the narrator's stance seems satisfactory enough, in spite of its problems. Moreover, Josephe notes as she leaves the town that many have survived the earthquake; it is still possible that the truly innocent may have escaped, and this impression becomes even stronger when the scene outside the city is described, for it is 'als ob es das Tal von Eden wäre' (140). The tone of the story tends to make us believe that evil has been left behind in the city, and only innocence preserved.

---

[1] Von Wiese (p. 60) sees this sign pointing in what seems at the time to be the wrong direction, but not its function of helping to break down one concept of the story and produce another.

The first section[1] of the story ends with an idyllic passage showing the happiness of the lovers after their troubles seem to be as good as over. A new and perfect existence appears to be beginning; but the description of the idyll makes us uneasy:

Indessen war die schönste Nacht herabgestiegen, voll wundermilden Duftes, so silberglänzend und still, wie nur ein Dichter davon träumen mag. Überall, längs der Talquelle, hatten sich, im Schimmer des Mondscheins, Menschen niedergelassen, und bereiteten sich sanfte Lager von Moos und Laub, um von einem so qualvollen Tage auszuruhen. Und weil die Armen immer noch jammerten; dieser, daß er sein Haus, jener, daß er Weib und Kind, und der dritte, daß er alles verloren habe: so schlichen Jeronimo und Josephe in ein dichteres Gebüsch, um durch das heimliche Gejauchz ihrer Seelen niemand zu betrüben. Sie fanden einen prachtvollen Granatapfelbaum, der seine Zweige, voll duftender Früchte, weit ausbreitete; und die Nachtigall flötete im Wipfel ihr wollüstiges Lied. (149–50)

Kayser noted that this was the one piece of its kind in the whole of Kleist's stories, and that it had the effect of a 'glatter Stilbruch'.[2] The general function of the 'Stilbruch' is fairly obvious: it separates this scene from the rest of the story, emphasising its idyllic nature. But in so doing it makes us uneasy; the language seems too far out of keeping with the rest of the narrative, and the idyllic quality thus appears strained. The whole scene appears consequently unreal, too good to be true. In a way, the narrator is very consistently pursuing the view of the situation which he seems to have adopted – an optimistic one; but this very consistency exposes its weaknesses.

There are many other ways in which Kleist makes the calm of the middle section of his story an uneasy one. Consider, for example, the fact that the lovers try to get away from the laments

[1] I refer here to the three sections into which Kleist divided his story in the *Erzählungen* of 1810. Sembdner (p. 902) regrettably reintroduces the much larger number of paragraphs used in the first printed version of the September 1807 *Morgenblatt für gebildete Stände*, on the grounds that only lack of space caused the reduction to three. The three sections do, however, have structural importance.

[2] Kayser, p. 175. Von Wiese (p. 63) and, following him, Lucas (p. 160) both take Kayser's remark to be an adverse criticism of the *Erdbeben*, and to ignore a possible function for the change of style. Again, Kayser's point is misunderstood. Conrady (p. 189) rightly describes this passage as 'märchenhaft', though his metaphysical treatment of this is not convincing. The point here is that fairy stories are unreal.

of those who have lost possessions and family in the disaster, 'um durch das heimliche Gejauchz ihrer Seelen niemand zu betrüben'; and the further report that 'sie dachten, wie viel Elend über die Welt kommen mußte, damit sie glücklich würden' (150). Both passages emphasise the great discrepancy between the good fortune of the couple, and the misery of everyone else; but worse still, this discrepancy seems not to worry the lovers, whose sense of well-being so overshadows their compassion that they can even think in terms of this widespread suffering existing in order that they should be happy. Even their moving out of sight of 'die Armen' in order not to disturb them is strange; to be sure, some consideration is shown for these poor people, and yet in telling us this, the narrator makes it clear that there is no question of the suffering surrounding them having any effect on the happiness of Jeronimo and Josephe.[1]

There is, however, still no progress made beyond the generally favourable attitude to the earthquake which has been reached by the narrator; yet against the background of this for the moment static viewpoint, the sense of unease continues to build up. The entry of Don Fernando and his family into the story is a tense moment, for here the past seems to catch up with Josephe. For a moment, it is not clear what his role is to be; the 'Verwirrung' experienced by Josephe may well be felt too by the reader, for here is a new character in the story when it seemed to have run through a complete cycle of events already. Josephe is confused because she recognises him as someone she knows. But Don Fernando does not understand this:

...doch da er, indem er ihre Verwirrung falsch deutete, fortfuhr: 'es ist nur auf wenige Augenblicke, Donna Josephe, und dieses Kind hat, seit jener Stunde, die uns alle unglücklich gemacht hat, nichts genossen'...(150)

Now we are left to interpret this scene for ourselves, and it is not

---

[1] Wittkowski (p. 251) misses the text's implied reservation about the couple's mood being unchanged by the misery which they see, and therefore thinks of even this self-centredness as displaying their nobility: 'Die Liebenden schleichen nicht beiseite, *obwohl* die Armen jammern, sondern *weil* sie jammern, weil sie diese nicht mit ihrem Glück "betrüben" wollen. Sie nehmen mitleidsvoll Rücksicht, und zwar mit feinem Taktgefühl.' Lucas also (p. 152) underestimates the text's doubts about Jeronimo and Josephe.

the only one of its kind, where the narrator says what he sees, but will not comment on it. We naturally assume that Don Fernando thinks Josephe's hesitation is due to her uncertainty as to whether she will be able to feed both children, but that Josephe is in fact worried because Don Fernando knows she is under sentence of death. But we must interpret this for ourselves. The episode stresses the theme of the whole story, and its inclusion is not mere perverseness on Kleist's part. Yet it is important that Don Fernando interprets wrongly here. For we might wonder whether the interpretation of the events prevailing in the narrator's formulations is wrong too. This episode is therefore a kind of microcosm of the whole story. We are also reminded at this point by Don Fernando that the earthquake has made everyone 'unglücklich', which emphasises once more the self-centredness of Jeronimo and Josephe. One last disturbing point, as far as the 'wrath of God' concept of the story goes, is the introduction of Don Fernando's two sisters as people whom Josephe knew to be 'sehr würdige junge Damen'. This sounds very reminiscent of the 'fromme Töchter der Stadt'. Could it be that worthy people, in the sense in which the term would have been employed in Santiago before the earthquake, have been saved? The feeling that they may constitute a danger subsides slowly. To be sure, 'Donna Elisabeth ruhte zuweilen mit träumerischem Blicke auf Josephe' (151), but we are also told in the same sentence that she had been invited to see the execution by a friend, but had refused. She seems after all not to be a threat to the safety of Jeronimo and Josephe, or – more importantly – to the interpretation of the events which the narrator has made the basis of his descriptions. Yet now, having produced this series of mildly disturbing observations, the narrator at last introduces further reports which make nonsense of the view of the story which had until recently seemed to prevail. The reports are introduced, characteristically, in mid-sentence, and as seeming relevant only to a very minor consideration: Donna Elisabeth's dreamy gazing at Josephe is diverted by 'der Bericht, der über irgend ein neues Unglück erstattet ward'. But we are then told:

...wie der Vizekönig in den schrecklichsten Augenblicken hätte müßen Galgen aufrichten lassen, um der Dieberei Einhalt zu tun; und wie ein Unschuldiger, der sich von hinten durch ein brennendes Haus gerettet, von dem Besitzer aus Übereilung ergriffen, und sogleich auch aufgeknüpft worden wäre. (151–2)

This puts the whole situation in a new light. Before this, the reports of the earthquake had tended to suggest that the guilty had been punished, the corruption of the city destroyed, and the innocent saved. Yet now it seems that the earthquake has provided new and better opportunities for thieves to flourish; an innocent man has been unjustly executed; and the symbolic head of the state is indeed alive, exercising the authority of the state just as he did before the disaster. The idyll of the Garden of Eden seems shattered, and with it the model of the earthquake as the destruction of a Sodom and Gomorrah. To make matters worse, Josephe is still untouched by this account:

Josephe dünkte sich unter den Seligen. Ein Gefühl, das sie nicht unterdrücken konnte, nannte den verflossnen Tag, so viel Elend er auch über die Welt gebracht hatte, eine Wohltat, wie der Himmel noch keine über sie verhängt hatte. (152)[1]

This is an alarming piece of self-centredness on her part; in full consciousness of the sufferings of the rest of the world, she still calls 'den verflossnen Tag' (*all* of it) 'eine Wohltat'; this is a reference not merely to her own salvation, but to the whole complex of events through which she was saved. Now it is important to note that any optimistic attitude to the earthquake depends heavily on the lovers' having been worth saving; this devaluation of Josephe is thus something of a blow to such an attitude.

The distinction between author and narrator is very important here; while the author in his selection of material is alienating our sympathy from Josephe, the narrator seems not to want to

---

[1] Lucas (p. 152) misconstrues this passage: 'Josephe feels that the disproportion of suffering is an argument against the happiness that is now hers, and has to overcome this feeling before she can gratefully acknowledge the blessings of the day.' The text puts the 'overcoming' of feelings very differently. Wittkowski (p. 251) calls this kind of 'Dankbarkeit', 'ein nobles Zuviel', again missing the fact that this 'too much' is much less conspicuous than a 'too little'; mention of 'nobility' seems out of place here.

abandon her. The narrator has one last attempt to produce a favourable interpretation of the story; favourable to Josephe, and to a belief that the world is rationally designed. He excuses her lack of concern with her fellow men by saying:

Und in der Tat schien, mitten in diesen gräßlichen Augenblicken, in welchen alle irdischen Güter der Menschen zu Grunde gingen, und die ganze Natur verschüttet zu werden drohte, der menschliche Geist selbst, wie eine schöne Blume, aufzugehn. Auf den Feldern, so weit das Auge reichte, sah man Menschen von allen Ständen durcheinander liegen, Fürsten und Bettler, Matronen und Bäuerinnen, Staatsbeamte und Tagelöhner, Klosterherren und Klosterfrauen: einander bemitleiden, sich wechselseitig Hülfe reichen, von dem, was sie zur Erhaltung ihres Lebens gerettet haben mochten, freudig mitteilen, als ob das allgemeine Unglück alles, was ihm entronnen war, zu einer Familie gemacht hätte. (152)

This passage no longer formulates in terms of miracles, or direct action by God to correct the human situation, but it refers in broader terms to the beneficial effects of the earthquake; men rediscover their common humanity, and can now bridge what had before seemed important differences of class and status. The brotherhood of man is re-established. The trivial conversations of society have been replaced by 'Beispiele von ungeheuern Taten', of people who had shown 'Römergröße', in self-sacrifice and courage. The important things in life have been rediscovered. All this results in the summing up: '...daß sich, wie sie meinte, gar nicht angeben ließ, ob die Summe des allgemeinen Wohlseins nicht von der einen Seite um ebensoviel gewachsen war, als sie von der anderen abgenommen hatte' (152–3). After so much confidence in the past, the formulation is now very cautious indeed, preceded as it is by 'daß sich, wie sie meinte, gar nicht angeben ließ'.[1] Nonetheless, there emerges here a recognisably different attitude to the events so far. A moderately optimistic attitude is now maintained by weighing the good and bad effects of the earthquake, and taking the sum of the whole; this new way

---

[1] The narrator's formulations gradually become more cautious where any general interpretation of the story is concerned. This present phrase seems guarded enough, but it becomes doubly so at the end with 'es war ihm fast, als müßt er sich freuen'. Thus Kleist shows the narrator learning to be more and more careful.

of seeing things can take up all the indubitable evil that has been caused by the earthquake – the deaths of the innocent and the encouragement to thieves, for example – and set against these negatives the impressive reawakening of the better side of human nature. And thus the earthquake can seem to be part of a world that is still on the whole rational and benevolent, instead of cruel and chaotic. This is reminiscent of Leibniz's theory of the pre-established harmony, popularised as the view that this is the best of all possible worlds; for there, too, the problem of evil is dealt with by putting it in the scale and weighing it against the good in the world, as well as by making of it the force designed to promote the good and so help the world on its slow road to perfection. Kleist's text at this point allows very much the same impression of slow progress towards a better state in which evil is a necessary mechanism. This in turn allows us some confidence in the continuation of the moral progress of the community and in the future safety of Jeronimo and Josephe. Yet another optimistic note in the central section of the story is the Rousseauistic notion that man in nature is innately good and innocent, while only his institutions corrupt him; this is what seems to be being shown.

The last section of the story now begins, the whole of what has happened having been reoriented to fit this new attitude. The news is heard that there is to be a solemn mass 'in der Dominikaner-kirche, der einzigen, welche das Erdbeben verschont hatte' (153). The inference from this is clear enough, indeed the narrator has drawn it for us in his formulation. The church is not just the only one left standing. It has actually been 'verschont'. The narrator fits the bare event into his adopted framework, and attributes purpose to the fact that this church and no other was left standing. When, therefore, there is the suggestion that Don Fernando's party should take part in this mass, it seems natural that they should do so. This church seems to have been singled out as the only religious institution worthy of remaining as a place of worship; it surely cannot be, as the others were, a place of bigotry. We are not surprised that the party, including Jeronimo and

Josephe, decide to attend the church. Critics[1] often point out that the lovers act unwisely, but this is only true in the sense that they do something which eventually turns out badly; for at this moment they seem to be justified in doing what they do, and the narrator shares their conviction.

Yet as before, the narrator, having once made up his mind, begins to have doubts. He gives a large amount of space to the description of Donna Elisabeth's anxiety before the party sets off – approximately one twelfth of the story, an unusual length of time for Kleist to dwell on such a trivial incident. Usually Kleist's narrator describes action rather than reactions. On this occasion, there are no further reports of the earthquake to make us rethink our view of it; only the present atmosphere seems uneasy. Donna Elisabeth's misgivings are expressed three times: first when she reminds the company of the dangers of going back to the church, second when she gets ready to go 'mit heftig arbeitender Brust' and says that she has 'eine unglückliche Ahnung' (154), and third, after she has decided to stay, her calling Don Fernando and whispering to him something which neither Josephe nor the reader is allowed to hear. All of this recalls a number of previous incidents in the story; for example, Jeronimo's three times turning from hope to despair, and the exchange between Don Fernando and Josephe in which the reader had to interpret for himself what the real content of the conversation was. Both previous incidents occurred as the narrator's interpretation of his story was about to change, a factor which must be borne in mind here too.

This all weighs on the narrator, and accordingly his description of the entry into the church is full of foreboding: 'die Pfeiler warfen, bei der einbrechenden Dämmerung, geheimnisvolle Schatten' (155). We may well remember here the ambiguity of

---

[1] Cf. especially F. Koch, *Heinrich von Kleist*, Stuttgart, 1958. Koch thinks that their 'naive Deutung der Welt und Menschen' (p. 84) is what leads to their downfall, and that they foolishly think that 'der Kosmos sei in Einklang mit ihrem Schicksal' (p. 77). Lucas again seems very distant from the setting and social conventions of the story in criticising Josephe's error of judgment; cf. also his comment that the declared purpose of the mass being to avoid further disaster is 'a gem of Kleist's humour, that speaks neither for the common-sense nor the religious insight of those organizing it' (p. 156).

the 'Pfeiler' in Jeronimo's prison cell.[1] But the narrator puts his doubt aside firmly: 'Niemals schlug aus einem christlichen Dom eine solche Flamme der Inbrunst gen Himmel, wie heute aus dem Dominikanerdom zu St. Jago; und keine menschliche Brust gab wärmere Glut dazu her, als Jeronimos und Josephens!' (155). The genuineness of that religious fervour strikes a safer note, but immediately the sermon begins which sets in motion the final sequence of events which ends in the disaster. The real catastrophe is not just the death of Jeronimo and Josephe, together with Donna Constanze and little Juan, the son of Don Fernando; this is its smallest part. The larger issue is that there remains no account of the coherence of all that has happened which will make sense.

The most shocking thing about the disaster is that it is set in motion by nothing more than the priest's letting his tongue run away with him: 'Hierauf kam er, im Fluße priesterlicher Beredsamkeit, auf das Sittenverderbnis der Stadt' (155). The phrase 'im Fluße priesterlicher Beredsamkeit', is among the most important in the whole story. For after all of the narrator's attempts to see some kind of shape in what has happened, it is eventually nothing more important than this on which the outcome turns. How much more trivial could the trigger event have been? How can reason deal with it? The only explanation now left is that the whole story has been a series of coincidences, sometimes looking as if they had a purpose, but in reality blind chance. Kleist, by letting everything turn on a preacher's loquacity, makes the disillusion as extreme as it could possibly be.

To make matters worse, there is a final sequence of events which several times raises our hopes for the escape of the party, and then dashes them again in the next line.[2] After the preacher

---

[1] This sinister picture also points forward to the death of the child Juan, who is dashed against one of these same 'Pfeiler'. This is one more relation that the reader is invited to ponder. A similar example of irony is Josephe's wish to lay her face 'in den Staub' before her creator; this is what she will do, but in a different way to that which she had imagined.

[2] Cf. Blankenagel (p. 33) for a very good account of this sequence, stressing the complete unpredictability of the next event at any point. Silz (p. 22) points to the nightmarish quality of this final sequence, with the voices that come from nowhere, Don Fernando's

has condemned Jeronimo and Josephe in his sermon, Don Fernando takes command of the situation and tells Donna Constanze to pretend to faint, so that they can all leave. But immediately the situation deteriorates again as a voice cries out that 'hier sind diese gottlosen Menschen' (156), and Josephe is seized. Don Fernando is at Josephe's side, and holds up any action by claiming, rightly, that he is not Jeronimo, allowing thereby the implication that the woman at his side is not Josephe. A lucky chance has put them out of danger, perhaps. But the next reversal is the appearance of Meister Pedrillo, a cobbler who knows Josephe because he has worked for her. He now asks who is the father of the child she is carrying; by chance (!) it is not her own child that she is carrying, and the confusion following her announcing this with conviction seems again to offer chances of escape. Yet no one is present who knows Don Fernando, the son of the Commandant of the town, which is strange; and this allows the small child's sudden and fortuitous reaching towards his father to be interpreted as confirmation that Don Fernando is Jeronimo. Don Fernando is seized, whereupon Jeronimo cries that he is the man they all want. But now, a 'Marine-Offizier von bedeutendem Rang' appears, who knows Don Fernando, and addresses him as such. All these turns of fortune seem to have eventually resulted in the escape of the party, for they are now able to get out of the church unharmed. If the reader were not by now fearful of making any more predictions, he might think that they could not possibly survive all this only to be killed outside the church; but that is just what happens. Jeronimo is struck down by a man who says that he is Jeronimo's own father; characteristically, it is never shown whether he really is or not. There now follow in quick succession the deaths of Donna Constanze, Josephe and Don Fernando's child. The reader is almost dizzy after this succession of changes of fortune; they are so many, so entirely fortuitous, and so serious in their eventual consequences, that it seems no sense can be made of this bewildering sequence.

weird loss of identity, and the strange figure of Meister Pedrillo. How the latter becomes so involved is one of the unanswered questions of the story.

Once again the question of interpretation appears in the series of misinterpretations made by the bystanders concerning the identities of the members of Don Fernando's party: a series of misleading images, such as Josephe's walking with Don Fernando and carrying his child, instead of walking with Jeronimo and carrying her own, leads to these misinterpretations. Could it be that we have been similarly misled all the way through the story by images that are equally deceptive? It is as natural for the crowd to reach its conclusions as it seemed for the narrator to suggest his, but both were equally wrong. There now seems to be no design in this confused and contradictory series of happenings where innocent and guilty suffer alike and miraculous escape is followed by brutal murder. Finally the naval officer appears again, to say that he regrets 'daß seine Untätigkeit bei diesem Unglück, obschon durch mehrere Umstände gerechtfertigt, ihn reue' (158). By now Don Fernando is too tired to ask why this was so; to even ask for the 'Umstände' would be to maintain a faith in the rationality of events which neither he nor the reader still has.

But Kleist will not let us rest here; for the story closes with an account of the way in which Don Fernando adopts Philipp, the child of Jeronimo and Josephe. At the beginning of this epilogue, there is yet one more chance event. Don Fernando wishes to conceal from his wife until she is well the death of their son, and he is also worried about what she will say of his conduct: '...doch kurze Zeit nachher, durch einen Besuch zufällig von allem, was geschehen war, benachrichtigt, weinte diese treffliche Dame im Stillen ihren mütterlichen Schmerz aus, und fiel ihm mit dem Rest einer erglänzenden Träne eines Morgens um den Hals und küßte ihn' (159). Here is a chance working propitiously again. The story ends with the words: 'und wenn Don Fernando Philippen mit Juan verglich, und wie er beide erworben hatte, so war es ihm fast, als müßt er sich freuen'. Kleist does not even leave us the belief that we can believe nothing, for the story seems to end on a note that at least raises the possibility of optimism again. The ending with the words 'es war ihm fast, als müßt er sich freuen' is, compared to the other occurrences of 'als ob', very cautious indeed.[1] And it is still not clear whether Don Fernando almost feels as if he ought to be glad simply because he can do nothing about the position, or because there really is something to be glad about, taking events as a whole. Perhaps it is just that to remain alive we must structure the events of our lives, and thus act as if they had an overall design; as we look back, for example, we are often aware of the fact that an earlier disaster had the effect of pushing us in a direction which had some satisfactory results, and it even seems that the disaster was a necessary part of the fundamental shape of our lives.

It is, however, the fact that the story ends with a child whose life is still to come that makes it so open, and gives the greatest impression of questions to be answered, events still unseen which will also need interpretation. What will the child become? Will he be worth his survival, whether or not this was accidental? Will he really bring happiness to Don Fernando? Hindsight brings with it the familiar illusion that everything has conspired to secure the child's existence, and to keep him alive. He owes his existence to the coincidences through which Jeronimo and Josephe met and were able to continue meeting. The earthquake allowed Josephe to take him from the nunnery only a moment before this building collapsed, and he had been cared for by the Abbess, which was inherently unlikely. He had been saved in the final scene by a number of accidents, beginning with the fact that Juan cried when given to Donna Elisabeth and so was taken to the church, and ending with Meister Pedrillo's killing the wrong child, and not making sure that he had the right one by killing both. And the effect of all this has been to give the child as foster-parents the admirable Don Fernando and Donna Elvire. What is his destiny to be? The question is posed but not answered. At last it is clear

[1] Wittkowski makes the sentence a flat assertion: '...trotz der schrecklichen Erfahrungen meldet sich die Freude' (p. 249). He justifies this simplification (p. 266) with a strange and unconvincing argument: '...wieder macht solch kritisch-redliche Reserve das Ergebnis, statt es zu beeinträchtigen, nur um so glaubwürdiger. Andererseits geht es hier nicht um Verneinung, sondern um Möglichkeit von Gewißheit.' Lucas too (p. 164) avoids the complexity of the text: 'there is at the very least a reason for joy'.

that every new event will raise new questions, however many of the questions already existing it may answer. We shall never be in any better position than we are in now, because to interpret the present we must know the future, which we never do. In a sense the story could now begin all over again, and this is why it comes to an end.

I have so far tried to show the importance in the *Erdbeben in Chili* of the developing and changing attitude of the narrator as the sequence of events unfolds; but I want now to turn to the many contradictory opinions which the story has provoked to show how its critical reception sheds further light on its interpretative problems. We are indeed led to interpret the story in a number of ways, each inconsistent with the other; but we should not, as did the interpreters to whom I have referred, stick to any one of them, but instead see that all of them are provisional, and seem to be appropriate for a particular stage of the story. To seize on any one to the exclusion of the others is to make that mistake which is the very theme and point of the *Erdbeben*. The narrator and characters make the error, but the critic must not. That critics have done so nevertheless is in large measure due to the failure to understand the function of the narrator, and to distinguish him from the author.

Throughout, the narrator struggles to understand the story, forming one view of it after another, and visibly abandoning each in turn. He is worried by it, and evidently emotionally involved in it. He does not know the ending of the story while he is telling it,[1] and since he is not omniscient he clutches at what looks like a

---

[1] Von Wiese assumes that the narrator knows beforehand what is to come: 'der Erzähler selbst scheint den Liebenden die Stunde des Glücks zu gönnen, zumal er ja genau vorausweiß, wie teuer sie bezahlt werden muß' (p. 56). This is due to his equating the narrator's perspective with that of Kleist: 'Wenn es zunächst in der Tat so aussah, als stände Kleist selbst ganz im Banne des Erzählten und seiner Furchtbarkeit, so wird immer deutlicher, daß der Erzähler sehr wohl eine Überschau über das Ganze hat. Das zeigt sich in der höchst kunstvollen und doch durchaus übersichtlichen Komposition, die den Erzähler leitet und seinem Erzählen das Gesetz vorschreibt' (pp. 61–2). For a similar mistake, cf. Wittkowski, p. 249. See also his 'Allerdings vermag ich selber keine strenge Grenze zwischen beiden zu ziehen' (p. 257), his bracketing 'Erzähler' and 'Dichter' (p. 258 and p. 271), his odd concept of the author looking over the narrator's shoulder and playing his cards (p. 257 and p. 263), and his even odder concept

reasonable inference and so makes mistakes; but he becomes more cautious as a result of these mistakes. Since, then, he is constantly trying out new concepts of the events, nothing he says at any one moment is conclusive. We are more used to the convention of the narrator's being authoritative in his judgments, and exceptions to this convention are usually indicated clearly by his having an identity as a character in the story, which will limit him in obvious ways. In such cases we are always aware of his perspective as a distortion. What is characteristic of this story is that there is considerable limitation, but that it is not indicated by such external means. The reader takes seriously any hint about the ending of the story (such as the report of the 'Dominikaner-kirche' having been spared by the earthquake), because he tends to assume that he can trust the narrator's judgment; but he is wrong, for Kleist's narrator is trying to read the signs just as much as the reader himself.

As to the widely differing critical attitudes to the style of the story, there is no need to choose between the alternatives of a gripping realistic narrative and a symbolic or moralising story. The narrator all the time tries to reconcile the two himself. He tries to be strictly objective and factual, and yet finds himself dwelling on certain aspects of the story more than others. He never makes an explicit moral statement[1] either for or against the lovers, but it is clear that he is always trying to disentangle the values of his story and to interpret it as he goes along. In this tension between the narrator's desire to see coherence in the story and his wish merely to relate what actually happened, letting this speak for itself, lies its most characteristic quality. Sometimes one pole predominates, sometimes the other; we have only to contrast, for example, the opening sentence of the story, on the one hand, with the narrator's strong metaphors on the other. Von Wiese is thinking of one and ignoring the other when he refers

of the narrator being 'teils allwissend' (p. 257), as a result of which Wittkowski selectively treats the narrator's comments as the author's authoritative evaluations whenever it suits his interpretation to do so.

[1] Cf. Herzog, p. 353: 'Aber er setzt an das Ende keine moralische Nutzanwendung, sondern er gibt in den Vorgängen, die er schildert, das Symbol seiner Anschauung.'

to the 'unbeirrbar sachlichen Stil, durch den sich der Erzähler jede Einmischung und erst recht jede Deutung und Reflexion über das Erzählte verbietet'.[1] None of Kleist's other stories, he maintains 'entzieht sich so radikal einer möglichen Sinngebung. Sie fordern von sich aus stärker zur Deutung auf'. Actually, the reverse is true: in the *Erdbeben*, interpretation is an ever-present problem.

Examples can be multiplied of contrary attitudes to the narrative; e.g., Silz stresses the omniscience of the narrator as against Conrady whose view is that: 'auch der Dichter selbst ist Fragender'.[2] Bennett,[3] on the other hand, discounts the existence of a storyteller at all; and this is what the narrator himself in a way tries, but fails, to achieve. It is this striving for anonymity that makes the narrator of the greatest importance in the story. His giving the impression of being a photographic instrument is conveyed, as Kayser[4] pointed out, by his relating irrelevant detail; and yet even his dwelling on apparently unimportant detail still shows his concerns.

Most of the disputes which I mentioned arise because the function of the narrator's inconsistency is not seen, and his momentary impressions are taken to be authoritative. Gundolf's view of the story that it is meaningless does seem appropriate to a certain point in it, as does Brahm's that it has a symbolic meaning; but both ignore the context afforded by the rest of the story. The meaninglessness of the story is something which we experience, but only as a disappointment after a search for meaning; and thus the tension which the 'getürmte Unglücksfälle' bring is the tension between alternative meanings, not tension instead of meaning.

Various commentators have chosen as *the* idea of the story one that has a temporary existence at a given point in it; to take only

---

[1] Von Wiese, p. 54. Cf. also R. Ayrault, *Heinrich von Kleist* (Paris, 1934), p. 548, who states that there is no 'immixion' in the factual narrative. Klein on the other hand comes to the opposite conclusion (p. 5); he notes that the many contradictions contained in the story immediately invite a thorough interpretation of it.

[2] Conrady, p. 194.   [3] Bennett, p. 45.

[4] Kayser, pp. 179–80. Cf. Silz, p. 15: 'As in Jeronimo's case the "camera" moves along with her.' Lucas also concentrates on one aspect of the text to the exclusion of its opposite with his 'Hardly a sentence interrupts the onward progress' (p. 168).

one example, Braig[1] is impressed by the Rousseauism of the middle section, and then practically ignores the last section of the story. Other critics have seen the surviving child as the most important figure of the story. Von Wiese, following Pongs and Conrady, thinks the child a 'Symbol für die ganze Erzählung und für die Beziehung des Menschen zum Absoluten... Es steht in seiner Unschuld stellvertretend für jeden dem Menschen neu geschenkten Anfang'.[2] Klein agrees that the child symbolises a new beginning. But this is altogether too unambiguous a view for a story which has treated attitudes and expectations so roughly, and the last sentence will scarcely support such confidence; it contains no less than four cautionary elements ('es war ihm', 'fast', 'als ob', and 'müssen'), which limit the simple 'er freute sich'. The real point of the role of the child Philipp can be found neither in the assertion that he represents the beginning of a new life, nor in the opposing assertion that he represents the blindness of fate,[3] but rather in the fact that both possibilities are equally tempting.[4]

It would seem natural that Jeronimo and Josephe[5] are most often taken to be the central figures of the story. For a long time the story seems in fact to be the story of their relationship, and its survival in a hostile world. On the other hand, the text, as we

[1] F. Braig, *Heinrich von Kleist* (Munich, 1925), p. 441: 'Kleist schwimmt hier in Rousseauischer Gefühlsseligkeit.'

[2] Von Wiese, p. 69. Conrady says the child is the 'geheime Mitte der Novelle, um die herum sie gebaut ist' (p. 194); and Pongs (p. 153) states: 'In der lebendigen Unschuld, die im Kinde immer wieder neu ins Leben tritt, löscht sich Schuld und Irrtum der Menschen aus.' Cf. also Klein, p. 10: 'Eindeutig war das Motiv des Kindes als Motiv des Neubeginns', and Braig, who thinks the child the 'Verheißung eines schöneren Lebens'.

[3] Silz, p. 24: 'The surviving child is not a symbol of the triumph of love over death and evil; it is an example of the fortuitousness of existence in an incomprehensible world.'

[4] Conrady (p. 192) sees the hand of God in the survival of Philipp, but 'sinnlose Verwirrung' in the death of Juan. The question then arises: why was God able to act in one case but not in the other?

[5] Most critics think that the couple have the approval of the narrator, missing his uncertainties. Klein (p. 10), however, noted that the 'Liebesfrevel' was 'durchaus nicht rechtfertigt'. Silz singled out Josephe as the most important figure: 'the others are seen in the main with reference to her' (p. 14). It is certainly true that aspects of the text support this view; e.g., the Abbess finds her 'untadelhaft'. But others do not. And even if the description of Josephe bathing the child is seen as an image of Virgin and Child (p. 26), it is still a momentary impression of the narrator, not a final judgment. The dominant characteristics of that description seem to me, however, only those of the whole middle section: i.e., purity and primitive innocence.

have seen, does at times show uncertainty as to the value of this relationship, and even as to the value of Josephe as a person; and it does continue after their deaths.

It is the suggestion that Don Fernando is the central figure of the story that is the most interesting one, because it raises an issue which adds to the interpretation of the story. Don Fernando contributes a new idea to the series of possible attitudes to the design of the world and to the behaviour appropriate to that design: the stoic ideal. In his behaviour is implicit the feeling that the structure of the world is unknowable, and that its blessings and disasters are equally unpredictable; the stoic learns to bear the latter with fortitude, and to accept the former without forming any unreal commitment to them. Yet it is in one's own power to preserve something that has a unique value and does not depend on the unpredictability of fate: dignity and self-respect. Don Fernando is indeed an impressive embodiment of the stoic ideal, and it is significant that he comes to the fore at the very point in the story when all other possible attitudes to the world have been destroyed by the sequence of events. When no other value remains, and when nothing else seems enduring or reliable, his character gives to the scene the only stability it has, and the only thing which can still be relied upon. He defends himself and the children with courage and skill, always behaves with impeccable tact, courtesy and even chivalry, and accepts what fate offers without complaint; on the death of his child he is silent, only raising his eyes, 'voll namenlosen Schmerzes' to heaven. Several meaningful contrasts are established between Don Fernando and the couple, Jeronimo and Josephe. Compare to Don Fernando's calm acceptance of disaster, for example, Jeronimo's instability and despair as he escapes from the earthquake, unable to control his thoughts or attitudes; compare, too, Josephe's enthusiasm and over-optimism, which interprets the world as being in harmony with her wishes, to Don Fernando's cautious search for the positive side of what remains in the story's last line.[1] The couple

---

[1] Wittkowski, by contrast, treats Don Fernando, Jeronimo, and Josephe as comparable in character (cf., e.g., his pp. 264 and 272).

seem completely overshadowed by this powerful, impressive figure. The narrator finds him so impressive that during the struggle outside the church he calls Fernando 'dieser göttliche Held' and this in turn has impressed many critics: for at no point does the story seem to give so unambiguous a judgment in favour of one of the characters.[1] Blöcker draws from this what he thinks to be the moral of the whole story: '...nur wer bereit ist weiterzuleben mit dem, was das alles verzehrende Schicksal übrigliess, und noch das Fremde als das Seine anzuerkennen, ja dessen Wert vermehrt zu sehen um das Gewicht des eigenen Leides – nur der besteht die schwere Prüfung des Lebens'.[2] Yet again, the point must be remembered that no one comment of the narrator is authoritative in this story; and a closer look at the text shows how Kleist has undermined the stoic answer to its world too. Near the end of the text, we are told that Don Fernando was uneasy about seeing his wife and finding out 'wie sie sein Verhalten bei dieser Begebenheit beurteilen würde' (159). The worry turns out to be groundless in the sense that 'diese treffliche Dame' does not criticise him, and we may even wonder why it was mentioned at all. The answer must surely be found in the earlier passage in which Donna Elisabeth whispered to Don Fernando as the party set off to go to the Church:

Donna Elisabeth näherte sich ihm hierauf, obschon, wie es schien, mit Widerwillen, und raunte ihm, doch so, dass Josephe es nicht hören konnte, einige Worte ins Ohr. Nun? fragte Don Fernando: und das Unglück, das daraus entstehen kann? Donna Elisabeth fuhr fort, ihm mit verstörtem Gesicht ins Ohr zu zischeln. Don Fernando stieg eine Röte des Unwillens ins Gesicht; er antwortete: es wäre gut! Donna Elvire möchte sich beruhigen; und er führte seine Dame weiter. (154–5)

---

[1] Cf. *Heinrich von Kleist, Three Stories*, ed. H. B. Garland (Manchester, 1959), p. 177: 'For a brief moment at this crisis Kleist's approval of Don Fernando is suddenly illuminated, as if by a lightning flash.' Also Servaes, *Heinrich von Kleist* (Leipzig/ Berlin/ Vienna, 1902), p. 74: 'Hier springt dem Dichter wider Willen das Herz auf die Zunge.' It is worth noting here that Kleist honours Don Fernando with quotation marks for his direct speech. Most editions unfortunately treat this as a mistake, and level off one way or the other. Cf. Sembdner, p. 903: 'Kleist setzt jeweils nur die Worte seines Helden Fernando in Anführungsstriche.'

[2] Blöcker, pp. 134–5.

The clues to the meaning of this enigmatic passage are in the two mentions of Josephe: Elisabeth says something that Josephe is not to hear, and Fernando's response is to lead Josephe forward with something of a flourish, with the narrator interpreting some aspect of this reaction with the words 'seine Dame'. Evidently, these words reassert the dignity of Josephe, where what had been said was felt by Fernando to call it in question; and so what was said was surely to do with Don Fernando's going into the town with Josephe at his side. His asking what harm can come of this is, of course, answered by the later events of the story. Don Fernando is here confronted with exactly those dangers in the situation which later prove disastrous. And the important thing is that he does not weigh them at all; he simply refuses to think in any way that will dishonour Josephe, even by implication. Many critics have said that he makes an error of judgment here, but it is important to see that this is not the case: he makes no judgment at all.[1] He relies on the stoic ideal: disaster can come at any time and is not predictable, but dignity and chivalry can be preserved. In this veiled way – a suggestion from a whispered exchange, and a brief allusion on the last page – the story makes that same complex of behaviour which is so impressive at the end also lead directly to the final disaster. Don Fernando was put in a position where the future disaster confronted him, and he was the one man who might have averted it; but that very ethic which we later admire prevents him from doing so. Small wonder, then, that he becomes aware that his behaviour can be questioned.[2] And thus the story's last possible answer to the question how the world should be faced is itself called into question.

[1] Cf. Lucas: 'Don Fernando, though less far-seeing, even to the extent of irritation at her warnings...' (p. 161). The irritation is, however, not to do with his judgment, but with the challenge to his code of behaviour. Cf. also Wittkowski: 'Fernando und das Paar machen also sicher einen Erkenntnisfehler' (p. 264). Wittkowski's misquotation of me (p. 272) would make me guilty of the same error.

[2] Wittkowski bases his interpretation on Don Fernando's ethic. He attempts to meet my argument by excusing Don Fernando's error: 'Aber er entsprang ritterlich-noblen Motiven' (p. 264). But that was precisely what I had suggested, i.e., that the value given to 'noble' behaviour in the story is to be judged in the light of this clear connection between acting from noble motives and acting inappropriately.

Kleist's *Erdbeben* is, then, one of those works which, like Voltaire's poem, though in a very different way, reflect on the structure of the world, and the possibility of the existence of providence. Throughout the story the characters and the narrator struggle to understand the earthquake in these terms; the reader too is led to find an explanation of what is happening, and the excitement of the story lies to a large extent in his constantly having his explanations overturned, sometimes quite gradually and almost unobtrusively, sometimes with a violent shock. At the end we have almost given up trying to see coherence when a new possibility emerges, and so we are left sceptical, but still wondering whether the world is patterned, or chaotic.[1] Finally, we are sceptical even of scepticism as a reaction to the world. In a way the *Erdbeben* is like a detective story on a cosmic scale. There are always facing us the questions 'who did it?' and 'what was his motive?' There are many suspects, and many false trails. The act being investigated is not an ordinary crime, but the whole shaping of human existence; so that the identity of the culprit involves not only the characters in the story, but all of those who read it too.[2]

[1] Pongs aptly terms the story a 'Netz von Hinweisen' (p. 153).
[2] On the question of God in the story, it is impossible to disagree with Silz that 'on this larger issue Kleist does not commit himself' (p. 25–6). Many critics attribute good in the story to God, and evil to man and his institutions. But this too is a concept which the text entertains and then abandons quite early; above all, the reference to the continued existence of the 'Dominikanerkirche' hampers this unduly selective attitude to God and His actions.

3. TIECK: 'DER BLONDE ECKBERT'

The simplicity of the narration in Tieck's *Der blonde Eckbert*,[1] and its 'smoothly-flowing surface',[2] make it seem an easy story. Nonetheless, it has proved very difficult to talk about. It is not just that the story presents difficulties of interpretation, or that interpreters have found much to disagree about; the problem is how to find a way of talking about the story at all. Its characters, for example, are stereotype figures: the little girl, the old woman, the knight; can we talk about them as we talk about ordinary people? It is natural to begin to consider their motivation, what makes them do what they do. But how can we talk about motivation in any ordinary way in a story in which a little girl meets an old woman in the woods and without any explanation on either side follows and goes to live with her? And there are countless other examples of the characters in the story doing things without any reason. Again, if we are to attempt to talk about the sequence

---

[1] References are to *Ludwig Tieck's Schriften*, IV (Berlin, 1828), 144–69. There are separate interpretations by: Kenneth J. Northcott, 'A Note on the Levels of Reality in Tieck's *Der blonde Eckbert*', *German Life and Letters*, N.S., VI (1952–3), 292–4; V. C. Hubbs, 'Tieck, Eckbert, und das kollektive Unbewußte', *Publications of the Modern Language Association of America*, LXXI (1956), 686–93; R. Immerwahr, '*Der blonde Eckbert* as a Poetic Confession', *German Quarterly*, XXXIV (1961), 103–22; G. Haeuptner, 'Tiecks Märchen *Der blonde Eckbert*', in *Verstehen und Vertrauen: Otto Friedrich Bollnow zum 65. Geburtstag*, eds. J. Schwartländer, M. Landmann and W. Loch (Stuttgart, 1969), pp. 22–6; W. L. Hahn, 'Tiecks *Blonder Eckbert* als Gestaltung romantischer Theorie', *Proceedings of the Pacific Northwest Conference on Foreign Languages*, 1967, pp. 69–78; V. L. Rippere, 'Ludwig Tieck's *Der blonde Eckbert*: A psychological reading', *Publications of the Modern Language Association of America*, LXXXV (1970), 473–86; J. Gellinek, '*Der Blonde Eckbert*: A Tieckian Fall from Paradise', in *Festschrift für Heinrich Henel*, eds. J. L. Sammons and E. Schürer (Munich, 1970), 147–66; W. J. Lillyman, 'The Enigma of *Der blonde Eckbert*: The Significance of the End', *Seminar. A Journal of Germanic Studies*, VII (1971), 144–55. The last of these is indubitably the best of them; also useful is the account of the tale contained in the introduction and notes of the edition in the series 'Blackwell's German Texts' by Margaret Atkinson (*Tieck: Der blonde Eckbert; Brentano: Geschichte vom braven Kasperl und dem schönen Annerl*, Oxford, 1951), unfortunately seldom discussed by interpreters. Of all the numerous accounts of the story to be found in general works on Tieck, or on Tieck's prose writing, the most useful is that in P. G. Klussman's 'Die Zweideutigkeit des Wirklichen in Ludwig Tiecks Märchennovellen', *Zeitschrift für deutsche Philologie*, LXXXIII (1964), 426–52.

[2] Atkinson, p. xix.

of events in the story, we must bear in mind that these events include the reappearance of a character who has been killed, just as if nothing had happened. Ordinary notions of the logic of a sequence of events do not appear to be adequate to deal with this, and yet some kind of coherence must be assumed if it is to be worthwhile thinking about this tale at all.

I raise these questions because the fact which they point to, though obvious, must be well-considered: it is that the story uses a distinct convention of narration, that of the fairytale. It will be of no use to discuss *Der blonde Eckbert* as if it were not a *Märchen*. We are obliged to recognise and accept as part of the story the convention of the Märchen narrator, with all that this involves, and then to take care not to use the kind of critical or interpretative arguments that are inconsistent with that convention. The language of the *Märchen*, for example is always simple, without complex syntax or a large and sophisticated vocabulary. There are certain set phrases ('once upon a time') and certain types of sentence structure which predominate, especially at the opening of the narrative, where their function is to announce that the *Märchen* convention is being used. *Der blonde Eckbert* opens, as Klussmann[1] points out, in typical *Märchen* style with the familiar adverbial phrase specifying place, the introduction of the hero, and an immediate adjectival clause giving a fact about him. Since the *Märchen* reduces the possibilities of language, and standard formulations are common, it would obviously be inappropriate to find fault with any story using this convention for its use of cliché, or for its reduction of the expressive power of language. In characterisation, too, the *Märchen* has certain obligatory features; the stereotype characters of *Der blonde Eckbert* are in fact part of the *Märchen* convention, and no depth or individuality of characterisation can be expected of them. Less obviously, but no less importantly, a critical argument cannot assume or attribute

---

[1] Klussmann, p. 435: '...so könnte der Anfang eines echten Volksmärchens lauten. Die adverbiale Bestimmung des Ortes, die Imperfektform des Verbums "wohnen" im Sinne von "leben", die Nennung des Helden und der auf ihn bezogene attributive Relativsatz, dies alles folgt dem Satzbauplan zahlreicher Märchenanfänge.'

to any of the characters that kind of complexity of awareness found in realistic stories or in real life.

In a realistic narrative, we expect that events will follow each other, and people will act, in a consistent and reasonable manner; it is this observance of ordinary rules of motivation and normal sequences of events that gives the narrative a recognisable structure. But this is not the case with the *Märchen*, in which surface improbabilities and inconsistencies abound, as well as apparently unmotivated actions. Instead, our need for a recognisable structure is generally satisfied by certain recurring *Märchen* motifs: the journey, the knight, the old woman of the forest, the cottage in the middle of the forest, and so on. Consider, for example, the last few lines of Bertha's story; she has described her escape from the woods, followed by her setting up a household, and is in the middle of depicting her fears at that time when she brings her story to a sudden end in three lines:

--Schon lange kannt' ich einen jungen Ritter, der mir überaus gefiel, ich gab ihm meine Hand, – und hiermit, Herr Walther, ist meine Geschichte geendigt. (161–2)

The move to the present from the past, the introduction of Eckbert and then of marriage to him, the ending of Bertha's tale – all of this is abruptly thrown at us in a few words, but it is acceptable within the convention. To end a story with marriage to a young knight is so familiar in the *Märchen* that its being introduced with adequate motivation is not felt to be necessary; and it is noticeable that whenever an event (e.g., the journey) occurs in *Der blonde Eckbert* which departs from realistic standards of consistency and motivation, it is usually associated with a *Märchen* motif. There seems to be no need of reasons for doing what normally happens in a *Märchen*.

The resulting narrative is anything but easy to deal with from an interpretative point of view; we have to make abstractions from seemingly incomplete and incoherent material, and make inferences from uncertain points of orientation. It is small wonder that interpreters of *Der blonde Eckbert* have disagreed constantly, or that on occasion a critic should have said that in certain ways the story 'defies analysis'.[1] On one point, at least, there seems to be considerable agreement. Made in very different ways by different critics, it is broadly that there is some psychological justification for and meaning in the strange character of the story's events.[2] That this has been so obvious a point to make is surely because *Märchen* narrative shares many of its characteristic features with the dream,[3] and the dream has been a unique field of exploration for psychoanalysis. It is even possible that the *Märchen* convention derives in part from dreams, for there too we experience the same supernatural events and superficial incoherence. For a figure to change identity is a common dream motif; and the same abrupt changes of location, theme, time, or in fact anything else, acquire a normality through their unquestioning acceptance both by the people occurring in the dream and the dreamer himself. The same standard figures recur, and with them the same lack of detail and simplicity of outline; and the same compelling quality emerges from this simplicity in both dream and *Märchen*. When we look at the *Märchen* convention by itself, it may seem strange that an author should voluntarily work with an impoverished language, and with correspondingly simplified characters. The nearness of the convention to dreams gives at least part of the answer: the *Märchen* enables him to create the same kind of symbolic fantasy which occurs in dreams, and it is therefore in its own way a powerful instrument of expression.

Yet there are many difficulties in speaking of a psychological approach to this story. To begin with, any mention of dream analysis and psychology tends to raise the question of biographical interpretation; a pitfall[4] must be avoided by insisting on the

[1] Atkinson, p. xxv; but Atkinson's remark does less than justice to her own very interesting analysis.
[2] Cf. Atkinson, p. xiv: 'A shifting of viewpoint from the naive fairy-tale angle to the sophisticated psychological one reveals the self-same series of uncanny events in an entirely different light...'
[3] Cf., e.g., Immerwahr, p. 117: '...it has a unity and compulsion such as one might experience in a vivid dream'.
[4] E.g., Immerwahr, p. 116: 'To what extent is the tale a deliberate literary revision of a part of the author's biography...and to what extent is it an imaginative re-creation, a

distinction between diagnosing Tieck's neuroses via the story, and being concerned with the more general meaning of the story that is not restricted to Tieck but is the basis of its impact on its readers. Another problem is presented by the competing doctrinaire schools of psychoanalysis. It is all too easy for anyone to approach the story armed with a fully formed psychoanalytic theory (or an aspect of one), and take some parts of the text out of context in order to refer them to that theory;[1] the disjointed character of the *Märchen*'s plot events makes this all the easier in that the hold of the immediate context on any of the story's parts seems weaker than is the case with realistic stories. And in this way the apparent vacuum presented by the *Märchen*'s unmotivated actions is filled. Typical of such an interpretation is an alternation of references to parts of the text and expositions of the psychoanalytic theory of the particular authority chosen by the critic, the former often much briefer than the latter; the psychoanalytic jargon introduced in this way always seems to stand disconcertingly on its own, and never to achieve any closeness to the literary text. Even if such an interpretation is offered only as one way of looking at the text, it must still withstand comparison with that text.

The lesson to be learnt from such analyses of *Der blonde Eckbert* is that the development of a psychology more appropriate to the story will need a more comprehensive, and less selective view of the text; for example, both overtly stated motivation and those many passages of the text where a character does something

poetic distillate of inner experience which might be interpreted on the basis of the text alone...?' Except for the last dozen lines of the tale, it is the latter.' The tale is biographical evidence for biography, and poetry for criticism; one need not think of the two types of enquiry as competing with each other, and certainly not as relevant to different parts of the text.

[1] Cf. the interpretation of Hubbs, whose procedure is in essence, as Rippere has pointed out, the assignment 'to its figures and configurations of labels from Jung's mythology', which treats 'not the story itself but a skeletal reconstruction of it' resulting in a 'two-dimensional critical *jeu de substitutions*' (p. 473); she therefore rejects as 'simplistically reductive' his 'Der Hund, Strohmian, repräsentiert die Treue' (Hubbs, p. 690). Perhaps some of her own statements do not completely avoid the same danger, however: 'She [the old woman] would seem to represent...roughly, a superego figure' (p. 485), or, the dog 'comes to represent the child she will now never have' (p. 482).

without knowing why he does it must be given due weight.[1] And the analysis must relate to the configuration of the whole text and of its characters taken together, just as in analysis of a dream the psychology of any one figure in it is not the point, and only the complete psychology of the whole dream is important.

In an analysis of this whole complex, the starting-point may seem to be random, just as breaking into a circle can occur at any point. Yet it is also possible to find a likely entry by making what seems to be an important abstraction from the apparent jumble. In *Der blonde Eckbert* a pattern of events occurs with great frequency: there is an opposition of isolation, loneliness, restriction and narrowness on the one hand, and expansion, escape, freedom and openness on the other. There is movement between the two constantly: expansion is always followed by a process of restriction, which then again turns towards its opposite. This appears to me to be the most important abstraction which can be made from all that happens in the tale. The pattern occurs equally in physical settings and in the characters' personal experiences of their relationships or lack of them. Its first occurrence is in Eckbert's castle; it is not only a small castle, but has constrictive 'Ringmauern', and when it is introduced, the quality of its enclosing Eckbert is emphasised: '...auch sah man ihn nur selten außerhalb den Ringmauern seines kleinen Schloßes' (144). It seems a safe place, one in which Eckbert and his wife sit 'um das Feuer eines Kamines' (145), while outside, nature seems threatening: 'Die Nacht sah schwarz zu den Fenstern herein...'; and thus the castle, in one aspect, seems a protective retreat, an escape from the outside world. The contrary aspect of the theme comes in when Eckbert is trying to throw off his feelings of doom following his wife's death; he goes hunting in the open countryside, or takes a journey into the woods, and so seems to be escaping from his past existence in the castle, which had itself seemed a

---

[1] Characters in the tale frequently do things unaccountably, mostly with accompanying comment on that fact (e.g., 'ohne daß ich es wußte'); cf. 151, 154, 156, 162, 165, and 168. Characteristically, it is the major events of the story which are introduced in this way, e.g., Bertha's journey, Eckbert's killing Walther, and so on.

retreat. Bertha, too, grows up in a 'kleine Hütte' (148) escapes from it into the woods, but still comes to rest once more in another 'kleine Hütte' (152) just like her foster-parents' dwelling. The protective little cottage had become oppressive, and she escapes to a new one; and the pattern is repeated twice more as she escapes to the 'kleines Haus' (160), followed by the final 'kleines Schloß'. In the old woman's cottage is another symbol of restriction, a bird in a cage.

The personal situation of Eckbert and Bertha is much like their physical environment. Eckbert lives isolated and protected from people: 'Er lebte sehr ruhig für sich, und war niemals in den Fehden seiner Nachbarn verwickelt...' And as for friends: 'Nur selten wurde Eckbert von Gästen besucht...' (144). Bertha shows the same tendencies; at the beginning of the story we are told that 'Sein Weib liebte die Einsamkeit eben so sehr...' Bertha had also run away from her fosterparents to live in 'Waldeinsamkeit', a motif which recurs in the refrain of the bird.[1] The way in which this theme shows a constant swing between opposite poles is present here in Bertha's having first run away from her parents to an isolated existence, then from her loneliness to a marriage with Eckbert, which then itself falls into a lonely childless existence again. In fact, both characters show a pattern of seeking solitude and then attempting to break out of it as it is found unsatisfying; they are always trying to find another person to bring into their lives to expand their narrow little circle. There is, first, their marriage, by which they (but only apparently) break out of a solitary existence; second, their wanting (but failing) to have a child: '...nur klagten sie gewöhnlich darüber, daß der Himmel ihre Ehe mit keinen Kindern segnen wolle' (144); and third, Eckbert's search for friendship: 'Niemand kam so haüfig auf die Burg als Philipp Walther, ein Mann, dem sich Eckbert angeschlossen hatte, weil er an diesem ohngefähr dieselbe Art zu denken fand, der auch er am meisten zugethan war' (144).

---

[1] Gellinek's interpretation of 'Waldeinsamkeit' (p. 157) as a paradise of natural innocence misses the negative side of 'Einsamkeit' in the story, and the swings to and from isolation.

Eckbert sets much store by this friendship, and 'mit jedem Jahre entspann sich zwischen ihnen eine innigere Freundschaft' (145).

Both the main characters, then, gravitate towards lives which are physically and personally isolated, but try to escape from the restriction which comes with protection and safety, personally by searching for a spouse, friend, or child, physically by leaving the safe little home. But each time, the attempted escape or expansion fails, or it becomes an even greater restriction. The marriage turns out not to be an expansion, a taking in of something new, different, and therefore fructifying, but only a marriage by members of the same family, sterile and incestuous; it only makes them more like themselves and thus more isolated. The circle has not been increased, no reaching out from it to another person has taken place, and this is crystallised in the second failure, the failure to have a child. The failure to find friendship is another example of an illusory expansion in Eckbert's world. Here too, the pattern of the collapse of apparently separate people into related, even identical ones, occurs, with the reduction of the old woman, Walther, and Hugo to one person. It is this reduction which makes Eckbert exclaim: 'in welcher entsetzlichen Einsamkeit hab' ich dann mein Leben hingebracht!' (169). The response is in terms of the theme of expansion and contraction; a world of different people has collapsed into only one person with the result that Eckbert was isolated, after all; and we should note that this is what is given emphasis in his exclamation, not the fact of his friends turning into an enemy. Physical escapes collapse in the same way; the flight from one constricting environment always leads eventually to another. Bertha seems to spend her life in such escapes; she ends her life in the 'Ringmauern' of the castle in anxiety, following initial peacefulness; to this castle she had come from a 'kleines Haus', where also anxiety had followed her first feelings of relief; and she had come to the house from the old woman's little cottage, where she had at first been satisfied but later had developed feelings of anxiety: 'Es war mir enge und bedrängt zu Sinne' (158). But to this she had come as an escape from her fosterparents' little cottage where she was afraid of her fosterfather. The pattern of escape into a protected but restricted life, followed by the development of feelings that this state is insufficient and even unprotected, which then lead to a further escape: this is a recurring cycle which dominates the story. The significance of the cycle must now be investigated.

Eckbert's attempts to escape from his personal isolation tell us why it is that they are doomed to failure. Eckbert had formed a friendship with Walther, 'weil er an diesem ohngefähr dieselbe Art zu denken fand, der auch er am meisten zugethan war'. Eckbert wants not just a friend, but a friend exactly like himself. This is a very similar thing to his marrying his own half-sister; his wife is then exactly like himself too. Ideally, all his relationships would be incestuous, anyone different from himself being avoided. The text again stresses his wish for total identification when it discusses his desire for total communication with a friend:

Es giebt Stunden, in denen es den Menschen ängstigt, wenn er vor seinem Freunde ein Geheimniss haben soll, was er bis dahin oft mit vieler Sorgfalt verborgen hat, die Seele fühlt dann einen unwiderstehlichen Trieb, sich ganz mitzutheilen, dem Freunde auch das Innerste aufzuschließen, damit er um so mehr unser Freund werde. In diesen Augenblicken geben sich die zarten Seelen einander zu erkennen, und zuweilen geschieht es wohl auch, dass einer vor der Bekanntschaft des andern zurück schreckt. (145)

Bertha enters into this wish: 'Ihr müßt mich nicht für zudringlich halten, fing Bertha an, mein Mann sagt, dass ihr so edel denkt, dass es unrecht sei, euch etwas zu verhehlen' (146). Eckbert's later friendship with Hugo develops along the same obsessive lines, with the same exclusiveness and intensity; 'in allen Gesellschaften trafen sie sich, kurz, sie schienen unzertrennlich' (166). And once again, Eckbert feels the urge to make the friendship total:

Eckbert war immer nur auf kurze Augenblicke froh, denn er fühlte es deutlich, daß ihn Hugo nur aus einem Irrthume liebe; jener kannte ihn nicht, wußte seine Geschichte nicht, und er fühlte wieder denselben Drang, sich ihm ganz mitzutheilen, damit er versichert sein könne, ob jener auch wahrhaft sein Freund sei. Dann hielten ihn wieder Bedenklichkeiten und die Furcht, verabscheut zu werden, zurück. In manchen Stunden war er so sehr von seiner Nichtswürdigkeit überzeugt, dass er glaubte, kein Mensch, für den er nicht ein völliger Fremdling sei, könne ihn seiner Achtung würdigen. Aber dennoch konnte er sich nicht widerstehn; auf einem einsamen Spazierritte entdeckte er seinem Freunde seine ganze Geschichte und fragte ihn dann, ob er wohl einen Mörder lieben könne. Hugo war gerührt und suchte ihn zu trösten; Eckbert folgte ihm mit leichterm Herzen zur Stadt. (166)

Here is found the same urge for complete communication, but in terms which help to interpret its occurrence, both here and earlier; what is at issue here for Eckbert is to find out whether Hugo is really his friend. Eckbert evidently feels constantly threatened and insecure; his compulsion to confess is part of a general paranoia, a constant need for reassurance. And in fact, the basis of the whole pattern which we have observed so far is paranoia: the cycle of seeking security in an escape into isolation, which itself then becomes threatening and oppressive. This is the common factor in Bertha's constant running to a protective retreat, only to find it inadequate and run again, and Eckbert's self-defeating attempts to make friends to relieve his isolation and to find allies against the hostile world surrounding him. But the paradox of the paranoid's attempts to find new security is that they must result in new dangers and so increase the paranoia. For only *total* allegiance is adequate, and this inevitably develops a view of the world as being composed of two camps and two only, that which is hostile and that which is friendly. In *Der blonde Eckbert*, as in real life cases of paranoia, this division is always exceedingly clear and well-articulated, and no one is allowed to escape it; a newcomer to the situation is first greeted as a ray of hope and potential ally, and given a complete account of the paranoid's obsessive problems, which itself constitutes a demand for them to be shared. And so Eckbert exposes himself completely to Walther and Hugo. Having initially found some identity ('die selbe Art zu denken'), he pushes the relationship to total identity and total communication, and then, when they do not accept this complete identification with him, sees them become his enemies. Nothing less than their being a *complete* copy of him will do, and that never occurs;

therefore, they become a complete copy of the witch. Thus the identity of his friends with the witch is only the obverse side of his trying to make them identical with himself – it is the paranoid's reduction of the world to only two images, one his own, the other that which threatens him. The confession, then, is the paranoid's means of sorting out his world, of forcing everything into one of his images. Yet since no one is completely like himself, he is doomed to the terror of having exposed himself totally, and so made himself completely vulnerable, to one who has refused identification with him; Hugo and Walther are so feared and hated that Eckbert tries to kill them. Eckbert's attempts to win friends must win him enemies; his attempts to become less isolated and threatened are bound to have the reverse effect; his attempts to gain security must rob him of it completely. The impulse of a paranoid to confess everything to everyone is part of his obsession with his own problems, his demand for security, but so repels everyone that his paranoia comes to seem more justified; and this is exactly the function of Eckbert's confessions in the story.[1] The confessions are also part of the general paradox of the alternation of attempts to expand his world and its becoming increasingly narrow; his demand for complete friendship is what destroys his friendships.

The most general pattern of the story, then, is a pattern of paranoid behaviour; the alternation of expansion and contraction is the form of an obsessive quest for security. Security is found initially in physically and psychologically closed situations, which then become oppressive prisons from which escape is necessary; and the escape is followed immediately by a return to an even more closed and protected situation once the openness has been found intolerable. Each full circle sees a worsening of the situation and brings a speeding up of the next round; the pursuit of security produces situations which are even more insecure, and so necessi-

---

[1] Rippere (p. 475) also diagnoses here a 'compulsion to confess'. Gellinek attributes Eckbert's compulsion to confess to his guilt feelings, in support of her thesis that 'the central theme of the story is precisely that – to show how wrong punishes itself, namely through the workings of the human mind' (p. 153). But Eckbert exhibits the compulsion to confess *before* assuming any guilt that he has to confess to.

tate more and more desperate measures to alleviate insecurity, thus increasing it even faster. And as anxiety increases, grasp of reality becomes weaker; to this development in Eckbert I shall return.

Der blonde Eckbert is best regarded as a paranoid fantasy; it contains a fully developed 'conspiracy' against its central figure. It is not just that several apparently unrelated figures were secretly united against him, for there are two further points which make the conspiracy even more threatening. The first is that it is precisely his closest friends who are involved – a horrifying projection of paranoid fear and suspicion. The second is that this is not just an alliance: involved is one ever-present person, another projection of the paranoid's reduction of the reality of the world to two people: himself and his enemy. At the same time, all of nature seems involved in the conspiracy: the realm of the old woman and of Walther is nature, for while the old woman lives in the woods, Walther collects herbs, and his name (Wald-herr) also suggests his origin in the woods. Natural phenomena, in the shape of the weather, also seem to threaten Eckbert and Bertha.[1] And yet another aspect of the theme of paranoia lies in Eckbert's struggles to escape merely getting him deeper into trouble and bringing him finally to the place of his punishment.[2]

Eckbert's marriage is one of his attempts to escape from his lonely condition, and to reach someone outside himself, yet Bertha turns out to be not another different person, but instead his half sister. Incest is in itself a striking idea, but its significance

---

[1] Cf. Atkinson, xiii.

[2] My interpretation is not inconsistent with Klussman's observation that: 'Weder die wirkliche Existenz Berthas noch die Wirklichkeit der Hexe können vom Ende der Novelle her also bloße Erscheinungen des Verfolgungswahns gedeutet werden. Das Wissen der Hexe um Eckberts und Berthas Geschick ist fiktive Realität...' (p. 441). These facts are indeed fictive reality within the narrative convention of the *Märchen*. But within such a convention it is hardly relevant to ask whether the figures of the story are imaginings of Eckbert – only in a realistic novel would such a question be feasible. The story is a fantasy about paranoia, not a realistic story about a paranoid character. Thus I would view as insufficient, unless further analysed, Atkinson's statement that 'the supernatural element allows of two contrasting interpretations. It may be regarded on the one hand as a power external to man and independent of him, or, on the other hand, as a product of the irrational activity of man's own mind' (p. xi).

here must be determined by its context in the story.[1] That significance lies partly in the marriage being one of Eckbert's attempts
to break out of his isolation which collapse, because Bertha does
not bring the fruitful contact with a different person that he needs.
But it is also in part another example of his compulsive pattern of
choosing people to alleviate his loneliness who must be copies of
himself. At the end of the story Eckbert's dim awareness of his
relationship to Bertha, and therefore the compulsive aspect of his
choice of a partner nearly identical with himself, is conveyed by
his exclamation: 'Warum hab' ich diesen schrecklichen Gedanken
immer geahndet?' (169). But even their names had suggested it:
Bertha and Eckbert have a common syllable.[2] Incest here, therefore, refers mainly to the incestuous quality of the paranoid's
world, its feeding on itself, inbreeding, and refusing any life-giving
fructification from outside. This is the point, too, of the childless
liaison: it is part of the sterility of the 'Einsamkeit'. And it is
another aspect of the reduction of the world to two camps; on the
one side, Hugo and Walther turn out to be the witch, while on the
other, Bertha turns out to be (almost) Eckbert.

Bertha's experiences before marriage add a further dimension
to the story, and complement those of Eckbert; while Eckbert is
more overt, active and even manic, she is passive – the female
child component of the complex of paranoid themes. She is the
unwanted child, illegitimate,[3] rejected by her real parents and
mistreated by her foster-parents. She is constantly threatened with
punishment, and runs away to find the ideal, kindly parent; but

[1] Taking incest out of context and referring it to Tieck's own relationship with his sister
is characteristic of the interpretation by Hubbs, for example, and of most biographically
oriented critics. Most others scarcely mention this important element of the story.
Incest is related to narcissism by Klussmann, p. 441; he is followed in this by Rippere,
p. 485.

[2] That Bertha is similar to Eckbert has been commonly acknowledged, but the function
of their being nevertheless *two* similar people not considered. To say that they are two
sides of a split personality (Immerwahr, p. 116) implies a difference of the two sides,
which would need to come together to make a whole and complement each other – not
the case here.

[3] Lillyman's interpretation is the first to stress the full importance of Bertha's illegitimate
birth; her being an unwanted foster-child is a fact which explains her relationship to
her (only presumed) parents better than, e.g., Rippere's postulation of inherent selfish-
ness and anti-social attitudes.

in the reversal typical of the story, the benign parent becomes the real enemy (just as the closest friend does for Eckbert) after Bertha has alienated her. As a figure she thus adds to the story the theme of guilt and inevitable punishment, and the overt projection of what is only implicit in Eckbert, that the paranoid brings punishment upon himself. It is Bertha who also contributes to the thematic structure of the story that concomitant of all paranoid fears, the fantasy of a life with no problems, the world of riches and ideal marriage.[1] In the same vein is the fantasy of childish innocence, an unproblematic life shattered by her growing up, which inevitably brings sin, and invokes the forces which threaten her. The degree of the intertwining of the characters of Eckbert and Bertha is evidenced by the fact that we naturally accept Eckbert's becoming heir to his sister/wife's sins, and finally going to the old woman's cottage to pay for them.

The beginning of the end for Eckbert comes with his feeling that he must integrate Walther totally in his life, thus initiating an ever-quickening cycle of attempts to escape from his insecure lonely state which will progressively intensify it. The mention of the dog's name by Walther is sinister, while Walther's coolness after hearing Bertha's story gives more cause for alarm. Eckbert's need to kill the man to whom he has made himself vulnerable leaves him with no friend, and his wife dies as a result of telling the story which Eckbert has urged her to tell. His attempts to include Walther in his private world have made it contract, and the search for another person has made him even more solitary: 'Eckbert lebte nun eine lange Zeit in der größten Einsamkeit' (165). Loneliness produces the need for another friend, but the friendship with Hugo quickly goes through the cycle of friendship, trust, total communication, and then suspicion; 'Es schien aber seine Verdammniss zu sein, gerade in der Stunde des Vertrauens Argwohn zu schöpfen, denn kaum waren sie in den

---

[1] Rippere (p. 482) and Lillyman (p. 146) argue against the view that Bertha's fantasies are those of a poetic imagination; this view was put forward by Immerwahr, and more recently by Belgardt, in 'Poetic Imagination and External Reality in Tieck', in *Essays in German Literature in honor of G. J. Hallamore* (Toronto, 1968).

Saal getreten, als ihm beim Schein der vielen Lichter die Mienen seines Freundes nicht gefielen' (166–7). As Eckbert looks at Hugo, he seems to see Walther: 'Indem er noch immer hinstarrte, sah er plötzlich Walthers Gesicht, alle seine Mienen, die ganze, ihm so wohl bekannte Gestalt, er sah noch immer hin und ward überzeugt, daß niemand als *Walther* mit dem Alten spreche' (167). As the cycle of paranoia quickens, Eckbert's grasp on reality weakens: 'Oft dachte er, daß er wahnsinning sei, und sich nur selber durch seine Einbildung alles erschaffe' (167). And so for the last time, a journey to escape his fears takes place; but the projection of those fears accompanies him, and is expressed in his meeting an old peasant:

Endlich traf er auf einen alten Bauern, der ihn einen Pfad, einem Wasserfall vorüber, zeigte: er wollte ihm zur Danksagung einige Münzen geben, der Bauer aber schlug sie aus. – Was gilt's, sagte Eckbert zu sich selber, ich könnte mir wieder einbilden, daß dies Niemand anders als Walther sei? – Und indem sah er sich noch einmal um, und es war Niemand anders als Walther. (168)

Eckbert arrives at the centre of the wood, where he finds the old woman and hears the song of the dead bird and the barking of the dead dog. Here occur the last two developments of the paranoid fantasy: the completion of the pattern of his persecution, and the total loss of contact with reality. The helplessness of Eckbert is stressed by the inevitability of his fate, as the theme of 'Erbsünde' appears: it is his father's sin that started the process.[1] Yet the contrary motif appears too: his fate was *both* the ultimate result of things beyond his control, *and* exacerbated by his own action, and that of Bertha, in their offending the old woman.

Throughout the story an air of unreality and of indistinctness has prevailed, and a large part in the creation of this effect was played by the reporting of sounds[2] and avoidance of visual descriptions of situations; we often seem to lose sight of what is going on. Over and over again the impressions reported by

---

[1] For a full account of the impact of the chronologically first event of the tale on all that happens afterwards, see Lillyman's cogent account.

[2] Cf. Atkinson, p. 53.

Bertha, for example, were of the sounds, rather than the sight, of the woods, the bird, the dog, while she said that the old woman's face was moving constantly so that she could not tell what it really looked like. And now, at the end of the story, Eckbert's experiences are almost totally aural, no visual experience being reported at all. He arrives at the end of his journey:

Er stieg träumend einen Hügel hinan; es war, als wenn er ein nahes munteres Bellen vernahm, Birken säuselten dazwischen, und er hörte mit wunderlichen Tönen ein Lied singen:

> Waldeinsamkeit
> Mich wieder freut,
> Mir geschieht kein Leid,
> Hier wohnt kein Neid,
> Von neuem mich freut
> Waldeinsamkeit.

Jetzt war es um das Bewußtsein, um die Sinne Eckberts geschehn; er konnte sich nicht aus dem Rätsel herausfinden, ob er jezt träume oder ehemals von einem Weibe Bertha geträumt habe. (168)

It is these sounds that produce the confusion in his mind; the physical world has no clear orientation points for him any more. Tieck's use of these sounds in the final words of the story to suggest the final slipping away of all contact with the outside world from Eckbert is remarkable: 'Eckbert lag wahnsinnig und verscheidend auf dem Boden; dumpf und verworren hörte er die Alte sprechen, den Hund bellen, und den Vogel sein Lied wiederholen' (169).

This is above all a consistent ending to the story. All of the monotony of paranoia is here in the tedious repetition of the same sounds; and there is a final loss of any ability to take in the shapes of the outside world, or the distinctions present there, as even Eckbert's final impressions, the three sounds, begin to blur and to grow remote. The ultimate state of loneliness and being cut-off from everything has at last come. Relating to anything outside oneself involves seeing its distinctive quality and responding to the distinctions which exist in reality; this blurring of everything, the loss of all distinctions between one thing and another, in short,

the complete loss of any contact with reality, is the logical outcome of the process beginning with Eckbert's seeking in his
friends only what was in himself, and ignoring their real existence
as themselves.

Tieck's exploitation of the narrative convention of the *Märchen*
affords an interesting illumination of the possibilities of that
convention; and conversely, the meaning of his story is illuminated by the manner of its use of those possibilities. In a realistic
convention, any element of fantasy would have to be clearly
marked as the imaginings of one of the characters of the story;
but in the convention of the *Märchen* narrator, a complete paranoid fantasy is possible in which the conspiracy against Eckbert
does exist, and his friend really can be his enemy in disguise. We
can, in fact, scarcely talk of the unreality of any one part of the
text within its context in the story; it makes no sense to ask, for
example, whether the peasant really was Walther, even though
Eckbert's compulsively seeing Walther everywhere is explicit in
the text. The point is that illusion and reality are in a different
relationship to each other in the *Märchen*; only the whole story
can be an illusion, as though it were a nightmarish dream embody-
ing a fantasy of paranoia. In such a fantasy 'objective' evidence
of the existence of the global danger (such as the mention of the
name 'Strohmian' by Walther), cannot be contrasted with unreal
imaginings; for the distinction between imaginings and what is
real exists as little in the *Märchen* as it does in the dream. Because
Der blonde Eckbert is a *Märchen*, imaginings take on a life of their
own, and the paranoid fear of Eckbert that the world is closing
in on him can – with terrifying effect – come true.

4. HOFFMANN: 'RAT KRESPEL'

Rat Krespel,[1] like many of Hoffmann's stories, includes narrative by several figures, all of them actors in the story itself. Most of the narration is by Theodor, but there are important contributions by the Professor, as well as Krespel's own account of his life as retold by Theodor. The result is that we have a number of different perspectives on the puzzling events and figures of the story. For, even by Hoffmann's standards, *Rat Krespel* is a bizarre tale. Its central character behaves in a very strange way throughout; his weird tone of voice and manner, his dress, the apparent nonsense he talks on many occasions, the unusual way in which he has his house built, his dismembering of old violins – these are only some of the ways in which his behaviour is strikingly peculiar. It is easy to regard him as an eccentric figure and leave it at that, and yet the story suggests on many occasions that his actions may all be coherent in their own way, if only their logic is understood. The end of the story provides Krespel's own explanation, retold by Theodor, but it only deals with his behaviour towards Antonie and her suitors; most of the really bizarre things about Krespel are not mentioned. But while all seems bizarre from the standpoint of Theodor's or Krespel's narration, the Professor's suggests a possible line of explanation, and it is precisely this difference in perspective which makes it so important to dis-

---

[1] References are to E. T. A. Hoffmann: *Die Serapionsbrüder* (Munich 1963), 31–51. The only separate interpretation of the story to have appeared so far is that by Benno von Wiese in his *Die deutsche Novelle von Goethe bis Kafka*, II (Düsseldorf, 1962), 87–103. Brief accounts of the story found in general books on Hoffmann all tend to view Krespel as he is viewed by Theodor (cf. H. W. Hewett-Thayer, *Hoffmann: Author of the Tales*, Princeton, 1949, pp. 207–13 for a fairly typical example) but there is one exception to be made to this generalisation: a view of Krespel which interprets further than Theodor does is found both in W. Müller-Seidel's 'Nachwort' to the edition cited (pp. 1018–20), and also in *Autobiographie und Dichtung. Eine Studie zum Werk E. T. A. Hoffmanns* (Stuttgart, 1966), by W. Segebrecht, Müller-Seidel's collaborator in the edition cited (p. 134 and pp. 169–70). I am indebted to my former student, John M. Phillips, for the stimulus provided by many discussions of the story with him.

tinguish the impressions gained from the different narratives in the story:

'Es gibt Menschen,' sprach er, 'denen die Natur oder ein besonderes Verhängnis die Decke wegzog, unter der wir andern unser tolles Wesen unbemerkter treiben. Sie gleichen dunngehäuteten Insekten, die im regen sichtbaren Muskelspiel mißgestaltet erscheinen, ungeachtet sich alles bald wieder in die gehörige Form fügt. Was bei uns Gedanke bleibt, wird dem Krespel alles zur Tat.' (43)

In the Professor's insect image, Krespel's behaviour is just as normal and functional as that of the insect's muscle; all that makes both grotesque is their visibility, by lack of a thicker skin in the insect's case, and of dissembling or observance of social norms in Krespel's.

Krespel's house presents an essentially similar image: everything about it appears crazy and grotesque, whether we think of Krespel's method of building it, its strange external appearance, or the unusual party he gives after its completion. And yet, once certain preconceptions are discarded, there is obviously much sense in what Krespel does. It may be unusual, but it is by no means unreasonable to celebrate the completion of a house with those who built it. Moreover, though Krespel has built a house which is externally strange, it is also one 'dessen innere Einrichtung aber eine ganz eigene Wohlbehaglichkeit erregte' (33). As such, it serves to remind us of the difference between an outside and an inside view of Krespel's world, between an outer perspective in which all seems disjointed, and an inner one in which everything falls into place. And if Krespel's method of building seems strange, it is certainly not haphazard: much stress is given to the care of his preparations, and the exactitude of his measurements (31–2). Something very precise is being done, even if its nature is not immediately ascertainable by builders or spectators. Likewise, his clothing may seem 'sonderbar', but he made it himself 'nach bestimmten eigenen Prinzipien' (31). The position of the story within the *Serapionsbrüder* collection makes the point again, as does the reference back to the preceding story of the

'Einsiedler Serapion' implicit in Krespel's way of life being termed 'anachoretisch' (35).[1] For the hermit, too, was from one point of view mad – but his own world was completely consistent and had a definite structure.

What, then, is the structure of Krespel's world? At the end of the story we are given Krespel's own view of his life, as narrated by Theodor. Theodor accepts it without qualification and critics of the story have followed him.[2] But Theodor is not an omniscient narrator who gives us the ultimate truth about the facts and values of the story; his action here is part of the story, the behaviour of one of its characters, and of a man much concerned with Krespel's daughter, just as Krespel's explanation is also part of the story in being the central figure's view of his own life; none of this precludes our thinking further about the adequacy of this explanation, or of its place in the story as *part of* (not necessarily a comprehensive account of) the structure of Krespel's world.

If the first thing to be said about Krespel's narrative is that it only deals with his treatment of Antonie, and not with his other enigmatic behaviour, the second thing to be said is that it leaves much relating to Antonie unexplained too. Why the secrecy about Antonie's physical condition, for example? For this made the situation with Theodor more, rather than less dangerous to Antonie. How did Antonie die? Apart from the strange report of Krespel's dream, we are not told. Not only is Krespel's account inadequate in these ways; it brings with it large new enigmas from his earlier life. To take only one of them: Krespel's pushing his pregnant wife out of the window, no less than his subsequent thoughts on this action, are extremely strange:

Der Rat blieb erstarrt zur Bildsäule vor ihr stehen, dann aber wie aus dem Traume erwacht, fasste er Signora mit Riesenstärke, warf sie durch das Fenster ihres eignen Lusthauses, und floh, ohne sich weiter um etwas zu bekümmern, nach Venedig – nach Deutschland zurück. Erst nach einiger Zeit wurde es ihm recht deutlich, was er getan; obschon er wußte, dass die

---

[1] Cf. pp. 18–19 of the edition cited.
[2] The list of those doing so would be a very long one, but it should be noted that it includes the only essay specifically devoted to the interpretation of the story, that by von Wiese.

Höhe des Fensters vom Boden kaum fünf Fuß betrug, und ihm die Notwendigkeit, Signora bei obbewandten Umständen durchs Fenster zu werfen, ganz einleuchtete, so fühlte er sich doch von peinlicher Unruhe gequält, um so mehr, da Signora ihm nicht undeutlich zu verstehen gegeben, dass sie guter Hoffnung sei. (45)

The use of 'Notwendigkeit' and of 'um so mehr' here seems that of a mind working with an odd logic, and the addition of the news of Angela's pregnancy at the very end of the sentence, as an afterthought, is also strange. This passage must strike the reader rather as a report of further puzzling behaviour by Krespel than an explanation of a puzzle.

We should not, of course, expect Krespel's account of himself to be the whole story, or even that part of the story which he tells to be in the right perspective; nor would it be in general surprising if another character-narrator in the story – Theodor – were to fail to rise above his own limited viewpoint. As it happens, the story gives us several incidents in which Theodor's lack of perceptiveness about Krespel is demonstrated; this strengthens the possibility that his conclusions may be inadequate and limits the extent to which we as readers are bound by Theodor's attitudes to Krespel's explanation at the end of the story.

One of these occasions consists in a radical discrepancy between the Professor's account of an event, and the account given by Krespel of the same event in his explanation to Theodor. Here we have two conflicting narrators. The Professor describes it as follows:

Den andern Abend nach seiner Rückkehr waren Krespels Fenster ungewöhnlich erleuchtet, schon dies machte die Nachbarn aufmerksam, bald vernahm man aber die ganz wunderherrliche Stimme eines Frauenzimmers von einem Pianoforte begleitet. Dann wachten die Töne einer Violine auf, und stritten in regem feurigen Kampfe mit der Stimme... Nicht einer war, den der süßeste Zauber nicht umfing, und nur leise Seufzer gingen in der tiefen Stille auf, wenn die Sängerin schwieg. Es mochte schon Mitternacht sein, als man den Rat sehr heftig reden hörte, eine andere männliche Stimme schien, nach dem Tone zu urteilen, ihm Vorwürfe zu machen, dazwischen klagte ein Mädchen in abgebrochenen Reden. Heftiger und heftiger schrie der Rat, bis er endlich in jenen gedehnten singenden Ton fiel, den Sie kennen. Ein lauter

Schrei des Mädchens unterbrach ihn, dann wurde es totenstille, bis plötzlich es die Treppe herabpolterte, und ein junger Mensch schluchzend hinausstürzte, der sich in eine nahe stehende Postchaise warf, und rasch davonfuhr. (36)

But Krespel's version is not the same:

B...mußte an den Flügel, Antonie sang, Krespel spielte lustig die Geige, bis sich jene roten Flecke auf Antoniens Wangen zeigten. Da befahl er einzuhalten; als nun aber B...Abschied nahm von Antonien, sank sie plötzlich mit einem lauten Schrei zusammen. 'Ich glaubte' (so erzählte mir Krespel), 'ich glaubte sie wäre, wie ich es vorausgesehen, nun wirklich tot und blieb, da ich einmal mich selbst auf die höchste Spitze gestellt hatte, sehr gelassen und mit mir einig.' (49)

Krespel's narrative has omitted what appears to have been a very angry scene in which all three were shouting at each other, he himself being more animated than the others. Antonie's cry and collapse in the Professor's version occurs as Krespel is screaming more and more, not as she is saying goodbye to B... Krespel in his own account is 'gelassen und mit mir einig' but not so according to the Professor. Krespel's story continues with a long denunciation of B... for *his* having caused Antonie's collapse – but in the Professor's account it is Krespel's shouting which is interrupted by Antonie's cry, and more importantly it is Krespel's vehement voice which appears to start the argument, while it is B... who reproaches Krespel, and Antonie also 'klagte'. The Professor has no reason to distort the incident, and in general shows himself favourably disposed to Krespel; Krespel, on the other hand, tells a version of the event which shows him in a rather better light than the Professor's, and which puts a wholly different emphasis on the whole scene. Doubt is thrown on Krespel's narrative by this fairly objective check, and on Theodor's simple acceptance of what Krespel says. And doubt is thrown more directly on Theodor's perceptiveness and judgment by a second incident.

On the occasion of Theodor's meeting Krespel for the first time, he reports that:

Es war von Musik die Rede, man rühmte einen neuen Komponisten, da lächelte Krespel, und sprach mit seiner leisen singenden Stimme: 'Wollt ich doch, daß der schwarzgefiederte Satan den verruchten Tonverdreher zehntausend Millionen Klafter tief in den Abgrund der Hölle schlüge!' – Dann fuhr er heftig und wild heraus: 'Sie ist ein Engel des Himmels, nichts als reiner Gott geweihter Klang und Ton! – Licht und Sternbild alles Gesanges!' – Und dabei standen ihm Tränen in den Augen. Man mußte sich erinnern, dass vor einer Stunde von einer berühmten Sängerin gesprochen worden. (34)

Theodor reports this as an example of Krespel's strange speech, of how he:

...schnell von einer Sache auf die andere [sprang], bald konnte er von einer Idee gar nicht loskommen, immer sie wieder ergreifend, geriet er in allerlei wunderliche Irrgänge... Sein Ton war bald rauh und heftig schreiend, bald leise gedehnt, singend, aber immer passte er nicht zu dem, was Krespel sprach. (33–4)

Yet in the incident cited by Theodor, it is easily possible to follow Krespel's train of thought, to see beyond the apparent jumps in his conversation, and to understand how his tone matches what he is talking about. The violent threat which Krespel here utters is one always reserved for Antonie's suitors (cf. 40 and 49). The composer B... was one of them, and so either it was B... himself who was being spoken of, or the idea of a young composer led Krespel to think of B... His mind then turns to Antonie: it was not her fault, she is pure, an angel.[1] Theodor assumes that Krespel has changed the subject, to take up the earlier conversation topic of another famous singer; but even though he failed to see all the other clues, Krespel's tears should have given him the answer, for just a few minutes later, he sees the mention of Antonie by the Professor having the same effect, with the same protestation of Antonie's goodness accompanying it:

'Antonie ist ein gutes Kind,' sprach der Professor. 'Ja wahrhaftig, das ist sie!' schrie der Rat, indem er sich schnell umwandte, und mit einem Griff Hut und Stock erfassend, schnell zur Türe hinaussprang. Im Spiegel erblickte ich, dass ihm helle Tränen in den Augen standen. (35)

---

[1] On p. 44, Krespel refers to his wife with the same word.

NARRATION IN THE GERMAN NOVELLE

Again we have the contrast between Krespel's appearance to others and his own world; while he may appear to wander and jump about, to change the subject rapidly, and to speak in a diffuse way, a close look reveals the opposite: his conversation concerns itself with very few themes, and these occur in a rigid, obsessive way.

The two incidents I have discussed so far both show Theodor unable to go beyond the surface of Krespel, as well as Krespel's own unreliability in his telling his own story. Moreover, the whole tone of Theodor's narrative makes it impossible to view him as an objective and reliable narrator; he is clearly much too involved. Even before he has met Antonie, for example, he shows a strange excitement: '"Wie ist es aber mit Antonien?" frug ich schnell und heftig.' (35). And he later admits 'Ihr wisst, daß ich auf solche fantastische Dinge ganz versessen bin...' (37), and thus shows an irrational fascination with Krespel and Antonie. It should not be surprising, then, that in the narrative frame of the *Serapionsbrüder*, Lothar shows his annoyance when Theodor concludes his story, and refuses to accept Theodor's view of Krespel, instead judging him to be 'spleenisch' and 'grauenhaft' (51).

But what all these incidents show is not only negative; it is not only that we cannot rely on Theodor, for example, but that we can rely on *ourselves*, as readers, to penetrate the surface strangeness of the story, and to perceive its coherence. The task facing readers of the story is to understand the 'Sprünge' and 'wunderliche Irrgänge' of all of its episodes as part of its overall design, just as that same kind of mental operation was necessary to understand what then turned out to be a relatively simple sequence in Krespel's conversation. And, as in that case, versions of an event given by its characters are important as facts about those characters rather than as acceptable interpretations, for neither Krespel nor Theodor can be regarded as reliable narrators.

Certainly, that there exists a coherence to all the puzzling episodes does not seem too unlikely at the outset. The motifs: windows, doors, singing and violence are easily seen to be interconnected, and to bring together such diverse things as Krespel's house building, his life with Angela, and the scenes which include Antonie's suitors. On investigating this interconnection, an important fact comes to light: Krespel's concluding narrative, though it may prove full of gaps and discrepancies (or rather because of them), provides the key[1] to the situation experienced directly by Theodor. It does so because the Angela story contains all the motifs surrounding Krespel and Antonie, but in a configuration which allows us to see how Krespel's later 'Sprünge' operate.

To begin at the beginning, Krespel's life with Angela was a very unhappy one for him, largely because of her singing. This attracted to her many admirers, and the situation was made even worse for Krespel by Angela's wishing to conceal her marriage, for the sake of her career and because she disliked his name, 'das übeltönende "Krespel"' (45). Krespel describes his unhappiness with Angela:

Mit der tollsten Ironie beschrieb Krespel die ganz eigene Art, wie Signora Angela, sobald sie seine Frau worden, ihn marterte und quälte. Aller Eigensinn, alles launische Wesen sämtlicher erster Sängerinnen sei, wie Krespel meinte, in Angelas kleine Figur hineingebannt worden. Wollte er sich einmal in Positur setzen, so schickte ihm Angela ein ganzes Heer von Abbates, Maestros, Akademikos über den Hals, die, unbekannt mit seinem eigentlichen Verhältnis, ihn als den unerträglichsten, unhöflichsten Liebhaber, der sich in die liebenswürdige Laune der Signora nicht zu schicken wisse, ausfilzten. (45)

Not only was he ridiculed by 'Abbates, Maestros, Akademikos', and tormented by her; he is already ascribing her faults to her being like any 'erste Sängerin'. And even this early, music and

---

[1] My reading of the relation of the Angela story to the rest of *Rat Krespel* therefore is at variance with that of Hewett-Thayer: 'It may be a question whether Hoffmann's story might not have been more effective without Krespel's narrative. In story after story he adds this type of "flashback" which establishes the roots of later happenings in the soil of past days. That Antonie is Krespel's daughter was a natural inference from the outset, and the introduction of Angela, her mother, adds little of value...' (p. 212). That Hewett-Thayer should say that the story of Angela adds little is understandable enough, however, from the point of view of the interpretation of the story which he himself (following Theodor) accepts. But that is an argument against the interpretation, not a reason to abandon a part of the text which has many thematic connections with the rest.

singing are not just a bone of contention, but almost an offensive weapon, an instrument of aggression. In marital squabbles, Angela uses the admirers she has won by her singing as a weapon against Krespel – and they are often musicians too; thus her singing becomes doubly threatening to Krespel. She even makes the *sound* of his name part of their unhappiness. Krespel, on the other hand, had used his violin-playing to win Angela, and in one of their arguments he strikes her with his bow (45) – accidentally, according to his narrative. All of this is in one way a perfectly understandable domestic situation; in this situation the essentials (jealousy, marital quarrels, conflict of career and marriage, etc.) are distinguishable from the accidentals (music, violins, composers, academics). The difference between this scene and the later developments can be seen, for example, in Krespel's later wearing his bow as a sword. A metaphorical weapon has become an actual weapon. Elements of the earlier situation have become rigidified, so that its accidentals seem to have been fixed upon by Krespel and preserved as anything but accidentals. In this light, Krespel's adoption of a 'singing' tone is not something which does not match what he is saying, once it is realised that it is an aggressive, threatening tone in Krespel's mental world. Earlier, singing was associated with a threat to Krespel's security; now, singing is simply equated with threatening. Each reference in the text to Krespel's singing tone occurs clearly in conjunction with what he construes as a threat to all that he wishes to defend. And his wearing the bow as a sword is part of the same pattern. Hence, too, the Professor's impression, when he overhears the musical evening, that the violin's notes 'stritten in regem feurigen Kampfe mit der Stimme' (36).[1]

[1] Müller-Seidel, noting Krespel's and Angela's use of art, says that 'Die Kunst, wo immer sie geübt wird, ist nicht von vornherein heilig... Es ist kein Zweifel, daß hier Kunst von jemand benutzt wurde, der damit etwas für sich selbst gewollt hat' (p. 1019). But his conclusion is that the story is about the sin of misusing art for a practical purpose, and that Antonie is an allegorical figure, who innocently bears an affliction born of the sin of her parents. This view of the story (common, as I have noted, to Müller-Seidel and to his collaborator Segebrecht) is the only one known to me which makes anything of the conspicuous fact that art is used in extraneous ways, but it puts that fact in the wrong perspective. What is stressed by the details of the text is not that this is a sin

Given this pattern of transferring much of the past to the present, and given the way in which certain aspects of the past are endowed with a very fixed but unusual significance derived from their past associations, Krespel's strangeness at the time of his living together with Antonie is not difficult to understand. With Antonie, Krespel tries to relive his life with Angela without the threat that his marriage contained: he tries to prevent Antonie from singing. Antonie becomes the complete substitute for Angela: 'Alle Liebenswürdigkeit, alle Anmut Angelas wurde Antonien zuteil, der aber die häßliche Kehrseite ganz fehlte' (47). Though she is his daughter, he has not seen her as a child, nor has he seen his wife since she was about Antonie's age! Thus his life with Angela has a large gap in it, but begins again with a woman of the same age and similar qualities. Krespel plays his violin for her, as he did for Angela, but where outsiders ridiculed him with Angela's help, Antonie is kept away from the outside world, especially composers, since a composer like B... 'nicht der Versuchung würde widerstehen können, Antonien singen zu hören, wenigstens von ihm selbst komponierte Arien' (48). Singing means admirers, and the destruction of Krespel's security once more; composers are an especial danger. The excellence of Antonie's voice (36) is both a measure of the threat, and of her identification with Angela: Krespel's friends describe them as 'zwei ganz sublime Sängerinnen' (47). But what allows Krespel's fantasy of living his earlier life without its outstanding flaw to continue undisturbed is the fact that Antonie is docile, where Angela was not, and only for that reason can she play the role of what Angela might have been.

So far, I have argued that Krespel's isolating Antonie, and refusing to allow her to sing, spring from his psychic problems, rather than from her physical disposition; and in so doing I have not yet mentioned Antonie's physical defect which is Krespel's justification for what he does. This illness might seem to be a

against the principle of art for art's sake, but that art provides the weapons for the domestic arguments between Krespel and Angela, and that from this situation develops Krespel's rigid association of art with threat and aggression.

difficulty for my interpretation of the story; but on the contrary, the view developed so far is the sole means of making comprehensible the strange reports of Antonie's illness and death. Theodor relates how Krespel told him of the first occasion on which Antonie's singing was heard by her father:

Krespel schwamm erst in Entzücken, dann wurde er nachdenklich – still – in sich gekehrt. Endlich sprang er auf, drückte Antonien an seine Brust, und bat sehr leise und dumpf: 'Nicht mehr singen, wenn du mich liebst – es drückt mir das Herz ab – die Angst – die Angst – Nicht mehr singen.' –

'Nein', sprach der Rat andern Tages zum Doktor R★★; 'als während des Gesanges ihre Röte sich zusammenzog in zwei dunkelrote Flecke auf den blaßen Wangen, da war es nicht mehr dumme Familienähnlichkeit, da war es das, was ich gefürchtet.' – Der Doktor, dessen Miene vom Anfang des Gesprächs von tiefer Bekümmernis zeigte, erwiderte: 'Mag es sein, daß es von zu früher Anstrengung im Singen herrührt, oder hat die Natur es verschuldet, genug Antonie leidet an einem organischen Fehler in der Brust, der eben ihrer Stimme die wundervolle Kraft und den seltsamen, ich möchte sagen über die Sphäre des menschlichen Gesanges hinaustönenden Klang gibt. Aber auch ihr früher Tod ist die Folge davon, denn singt sie fort, so gebe ich ihr höchstens sechs Monate Zeit.' (48)

There are many peculiarities here. The 'Familienähnlichkeit' which Krespel perceives, for example – what can he be talking about? For Angela died 'an den Folgen einer Erkältung im Theater', and after a long and successful career of singing, not just six months. How then can there be any family resemblance in this illness, and how can Krespel have feared it, or been able to diagnose it, since Angela did *not* suffer from it? The symptom is a very odd one – redness on the cheeks sounds more like a sign of health than a symptom of a weakness of the chest. The answer is surely very simple; there *is* a family resemblance between the two women, one which Krespel could have feared, and could have diagnosed: their superb singing. In the sense that Angela died of over-exposure to her public in draughty theatres, it is what caused her death. Once we see the passage in this way, everything else falls into place. Krespel's becoming 'in sich gekehrt' and 'nachdenklich' (rather than observant and outward-directed, which would be the case if his attention were on Antonie's physical symptoms), his exclaiming 'nicht mehr singen, wenn du mich liebst' (the conditional stressing Antonie's love for him rather than her life), the anonymous doctor's confirming Krespel's diagnosis apparently without examining Antonie (cf. 'Der Doktor, dessen Miene vom Anfang des Gesprächs...'), – all this becomes comprehensible if we assume that the physical defect is illusory,[1] and that the real problem is in Krespel's mind; it is in his need to produce an excuse to stop Antonie singing, and so to keep her free of any capacity to threaten and torment him. And the (imaginary?) doctor's incompetence is mitigated by his having put his finger on the real problem: the fact that the weakness and the beauty of the voice are causally connected. The pattern of the singing tone and the violin bow is repeated; a metaphorical weakness has become an actual physical weakness. Another detail indicates the same point: while in Krespel's account Antonie's collapse occurs immediately after she has finished singing, according to the Professor it occurs after a long argument. The emotional scene, rather than the singing, would seem the more likely cause. And even if we allow that Antonie's rapid recovery (49) might be consistent with a severe physical illness – though it seems unlikely – Krespel seems at that time not to behave like the worried father of a very sick daughter: 'Tags darauf erschien der Rat sehr heiter, und niemand hatte den Mut, ihn nach der Begebenheit der vorigen Nacht zu fragen' (36).

Again, Antonie's death is no stumbling-block for the view that

[1] It is precisely the avoidance of these discrepancies concerning Antonie's illness and its diagnosis, resulting as it does in a simple acceptance of Krespel's narrative, which is the failing of previous criticism of the story. This leads Hewett-Thayer to believe that the theme of the story is the rather trite 'Shall life itself be sacrificed to art...or shall art be sacrificed to mere existence?' (p. 212), and as a result he judges that Krespel acts wisely to keep Antonie from marrying B... (p. 211); similarly, von Wiese believes that this shows Krespel acting as a 'liebevoller Vater' (p. 98). Müller-Seidel rightly insists that the 'Vorgeschichte' must not be taken simply (p. 1018), and that it does not prove Krespel's innocence: 'Wird das alles erzählt, damit wir seiner Unschuld versichert sein sollen?' (p. 1019). But he does not follow his own advocacy of a more complex attitude to the 'Vorgeschichte' in the matter of the illness: 'Denn entweder entsagt sie der Kunst, dann entsagt sie, weil ihr die Kunst alles ist, auch dem Leben. Oder sie widmet sich dem Gesang, und dann ist erst recht der Tod die Folge' (pp. 1019–20). The text makes it clear that art is *not* everything for Antonie: 'Nur einmal ihn sehen, und dann sterben' (49) shows that she has other strong interests.

her physical weakness is an illusion; on the contrary, Antonie's death was very difficult to square with Krespel's account of her 'Fehler':

Kurz vor meiner Ankunft war es in einer Nacht dem Rat so, als höre er im Nebenzimmer auf seinem Pianoforte spielen, und bald unterschied er deutlich, daß B... nach gewöhnlicher Art präludiere. Er wollte aufstehen, aber wie eine schwere Last lag es auf ihm, wie mit eisernen Banden gefesselt vermochte er sich nicht zu regen und zu rühren. Nun fiel Antonie ein in leisen hingehauchten Tönen, die immer steigend und steigend zum schmetternden Fortissimo wurden, dann gestalteten sich die wunderbaren Laute zu dem tief ergreifenden Liede, welches B... einst ganz im frommen Stil der alten Meister für Antonie komponiert hatte. Krespel sagte, unbegreiflich sei der Zustand gewesen, in dem er sich befunden, denn eine entsetzliche Angst habe sich gepaart mit nie gefühlter Wonne. Plötzlich umgab ihn eine blendende Klarheit, und in derselben erblickte er B... und Antonie, die sich umschlungen hielten, und sich voll seligem Entzücken anschauten. Die Töne des Liedes und des begleitenden Pianofortes dauerten fort, ohne dass Antonie sichtbar sang oder B... das Fortepiano berührte. Der Rat fiel nun in eine Art dumpfer Ohnmacht, in der das Bild mit den Tönen versank. Als er erwachte, war ihm noch jene fürchterliche Angst aus dem Traume geblieben. Er sprang in Antoniens Zimmer. Sie lag mit geschlossenen Augen, mit holdselig lächelndem Blick, die Hände fromm gefaltet, auf dem Sofa, als schliefe sie, und träume von Himmelswonne und Freudigkeit. Sie war aber tot. (50–1)

Here, Antonie's singing occurs in Krespel's dream only: B... is not actually present, and there is no music.[1] But Antonie's

[1] Hewett-Thayer attempts to meet this point as follows: 'The inner force of her divine gift was only slumbering, and, since Hoffmann doubtless intended us to interpret Krespel's dream as more than a dream, as in part reality – at any rate, to allow this possibility, Antonie eventually chooses a transitory exercise of her artistic gifts, with death at the end of her song, rather than a continuation of life without art' (p. 213). There is actually no reason to assume such an intention, which simply changes the text; Hoffmann chose not to show Antonie's end that way. Von Wiese attempts to explain away this fact: 'Der Autor verzichtet auf eine solche plumpe Wiederholung... Krespel wird hier zu einer Art Medium, sein visionäres Hören, Sehen und dann immer noch übersinnliches Weiterhören erfährt genau das – so dürfen wir wohl interpretieren – was sich bei der schlafenden Antonie in ihrem Unterbewußtsein als höchstes Glück des Gesanges und der Liebe abspielt...' (p. 102). But this is most unconvincing, and his metaphysical elaboration of the point even less so; there is no evidence in the text for the view of Krespel as a visionary: 'Das Innerste der Antonie ist für den visionär schauenden Krespel vernehmbar und sichtbar geworden; damit hat es eine Gegenständlichkeit und Objektivität besonderer Art gewonnenen; es ist nicht nur unwirklich,

supposed defect will only kill her if she sings, and Krespel has kept her from singing; therefore, she cannot die of that. What, then, does she die of? Krespel's account of her life with him makes this easy enough to guess. Antonie is indeed prevented from dying the death of her mother: she is not exposed to the great outside world, the public, and the openness of theatres. But she suffers the opposite fate, as Krespel's treatment of her slowly stifles her.

Her life becomes progressively impoverished, as she is cut off from other people, from possible husbands, and from her own talent. Her pathetic condition emerges in the descriptions of her indulging her father's whims and follies (50), and again the descriptions put more weight on her caring for him than his caring for her. Towards the end, Krespel's reports of her conversation show almost a simple-mindedness, the natural result of his preventing her personal growth. In Krespel's dream B... occurs again; he knows that her love for B... was a threat to him, and that it is this kind of deprivation that kills her. For what can the happiness on Antonie's face be but the memory of B...?

Theodor had reported that Antonie was pale (38) 'aber wurde etwas Geistreiches und Heiteres gesagt, so flog in süßem Lächeln ein feuriges Inkarnat über die Wangen hin...' Yet he later accepts Krespel's account of the symptom of her illness, another proof of his lack of perception. For if we take the normal view that colour in the cheeks is a sign of health, and that Antonie's *paleness* is the danger signal, we can see that it is her being shut up with Krespel that threatens her; even a brief stimulus from the outside world makes her immediately look better.

That the dominant factor in the relationship between Krespel and Antonie is his possessiveness is obvious from the first, and goes on being so. The first mention of Antonie in the story occurs when the Professor's niece asks Krespel 'Was macht denn unsere Antonie, lieber Rat?' Krespel immediately seizes on one of her words: '"Unsere? Unsere liebe Antonie?" frug er mit gedehn-

sondern überwirklich. Das Geträumte übersteigt hier gleichsam die Realität und gewinnt dadurch eine eigene unheimliche Existenz...' (pp. 102–3).

tem, unangenehm singenden Tone' (34). Angela belonged to her public as much as to him; but Antonie is his alone, and he adopts the tone[1] which we recognise as his aggressive voice, to ward off this claim to co-possession. That the niece's words are innocent, and need not be regarded as such a claim, indicates that this idea is an obsession for Krespel. Krespel's possessiveness again is evident when he gives Antonie a choice, not between singing and living as we might expect, but in quite different terms:

> Er sagte Antonien alles, er stellte ihr die Wahl, ob sie dem Bräutigam folgen und seiner und der Welt Verlockung nachgeben, so aber früh untergehen, oder ob sie dem Vater noch in seinen alten Tagen nie gefühlte Ruhe und Freude bereiten, so aber noch jahrelang leben wolle. (48)

What is supposed to be largely a matter of Antonie's physical well-being contains a rather well-developed consideration involving her father's own happiness; and that consideration receives a stress which we might well feel to be inappropriate where the main issue should be life or death for Antonie. Similarly, we might expect concern for Antonie's life when she insists on seeing B... again, and not the following:

> Die Tochter, das einzige Wesen auf der weiten Welt, das nie gekannte Lust in ihm entzündet, das allein ihn mit dem Leben versöhnte, riss sich gewaltsam los von seinem Herzen, und er wollte, dass das Entsetzliche geschehe. (49)

Here the perspective seems quite wrong: Krespel seems now not to be concerned with saving her from B... in order to preserve her life, but in order to keep her for himself – and it even seems that he envisages her death as a punishment for her giving B..., and not her father, her heart. When on the other hand she later says 'Ich will nicht mehr singen, aber für dich leben' (50), we again feel that the important issue ('leben') receives less weight than the less important one ('für dich'), and that Krespel's possessive claim is paramount. Yet there is a more natural way to

---

[1] Other incidents which corroborate the view that the singing tone is a response on Krespel's part to a real or imagined threat to himself are, for example, the occasions when Theodor tries to bring the conversation between Krespel, Antonie, and himself to the subject of music (39), when he tries to get Antonie to sing (40) and when he asks Krespel to play his violin (38).

understand this sentence; if we forget about the supposed physical weakness, and remember Angela, it can be taken simply at face value. This is exactly what Krespel wanted Angela to say to him, and to do; to live for him, give up singing and her public, and devote herself to being Krespel's wife.

Not only are Krespel's dealings with people easier to understand in this way; his other bizarre behaviour also becomes more comprehensible. When Krespel supervised the building of his house, he made the builders first construct solid walls two storeys high, and only then instructed that windows should be cut into those walls; standing inside the house, he gave very precise measurements in what seemed to all the onlookers to be an arbitrary way. Krespel's life with Angela again provides the key. After a particularly stormy incident between them, Krespel had fled to a country house. Angela had followed him. After the scene that followed, Krespel pushed Angela out of the window and fled. He never again met his wife. Pushing her out of the window was obviously a symbolic gesture for him; it meant her expulsion from his life, and thus his flight and lack of concern for her condition become comprehensible. The action he took in regard to Angela was his last, and as such could not be allowed to have any consequences or sequel. That this was an involuntary act, resulting from something like an intolerable traumatic experience, is indicated by his slow realisation of what he has done: 'erst nach einiger Zeit wurde es ihm recht deutlich...' And now he thinks of the height of the window, in precise terms, a motif which recurs later. The depth of his being wounded by Angela is shown when, even in the face of reports that his decisive action has completely changed Angela, he dares not go back to her and expose himself to any possibility of the same thing happening again. Even after years of loving letters, he still experiences relief when Angela dies; it was as if 'ein störendes unheimliches Prinzip aus seinem Leben gewichen, und er könne nun erst recht frei atmen' (47). That he conceived of Antonie as the same kind of threat, and that even though he managed to control it, the same strain and feeling of imminent danger oppressed him, is shown when his reaction to Antonie's death is in similar terms: 'nun bin ich frei – frei – frei – Heisa frei!' (42). In spite of his love for Antonie, he has felt constantly threatened by her presence.

Krespel's house-building is recognisably a continuation of his earlier gesture of pushing Angela out of his life. Here too, the kind of development takes place which is visible in the case of his violin bow and singing voice. Throwing Angela out of the window was a symbolic gesture; years later the symbol has taken on an independent existence, and a motif having local significance in a particular situation has acquired for him a fixed general significance. Krespel's house is a kind of psychic defensive fortress. In its being built the emphasis is first of all on the shell which is sealed off from the outside world. From the inside, Krespel then has a certain number of windows cut into the walls, in arbitrary positions which stress his very personal and idio-syncratic choice of where and how he will allow anything to penetrate into his existence. The very precise measurements both remind us of the precise height of the window from which Angela was pushed, and indicate the strictness of the control which Krespel exercises in regulating his contact with the outside world. Only through one of these windows are the citizens of the town H– permitted to experience Antonie's voice. Meanwhile the motif of physical ejection from Krespel's house, recalling Angela, occurs whenever a person has become a threat to Krespel. Theodor is ejected early in the story (38) and realises that there is some deeper meaning to Krespel's gesture: 'Eigentlich wurde ich doch von ihm auf symbolische Weise zur Tür hinausgeworfen.' On other occasions, Krespel expels Theodor (40) gently threatening violence, and the composer B..., threatening him a great deal less gently (49). Thus Krespel protects his precarious world.

It remains to consider Krespel's most bizarre feature: his making, and destroying, violins. In this case, the connection with Antonie and Angela is made very obvious, though not the nature of that connection. Before Krespel met Angela, we are told, he did not build violins, and with one of these twisted pieces of logic which come to appear self-evident and natural, his not destroying violins is made a natural corollary: 'Selbst baute er damals noch keine, und unterliess daher auch das Zerlegen jener alten Geigen' (44).

Similarly, his violin-building ceases with Antonie's death: 'Nun bau ich keine Geigen mehr – keine Geigen mehr – heisa keine Geigen mehr' (42). Another obvious fact is the identification of Antonie with the single violin which Krespel preserves, an identification made by Antonie herself: 'Ach das bin ich ja – ich singe ja wieder' (50), and in other ways. There is a reference to Antonie as a 'Königin des Gesangs' shortly followed by one to the violin in question as a 'Königin' among others (37); and this violin was saved from destruction only at Antonie's request (50). Meanwhile the first destruction of a violin in the story was when Angela smashed Krespel's instrument during a quarrel – the immediate result of which was his own violent reaction and flight.

All of this shows that the two women must be the focal point of Krespel's strange treatment of violins. That Krespel himself does not understand all this is plain; when he decides not to destroy the Antonie-violin, for example, it is something he does without knowing 'welche unbekannte Macht ihn nötigte...' (50). Krespel's violins indeed display the most pathetic side of him. As I have noted above, early in his history the violin became an instrument of aggression and conquest, and beautiful music a danger. Later, Krespel buys violins of great quality to destroy them, ostensibly to find the secret of their tonal excellence; but this sounds curiously similar to his obsession with that aspect of Antonie which is responsible for her vocal quality, especially in view of the fact that both are silenced. And thus Krespel destroys one set of violins and builds large numbers of his own: as though to disarm potential enemies, and amass a huge armoury of his own! With Antonie dead, the battle is over; no further violins are bought or made, and the bow/sword is broken. It would be hard to describe all that is at work when Krespel plays his violin for Antonie; for her, it is an enactment of her wish to sing, and for him a reminiscence of his winning Angela, but there is also the joining of the two in one voice, a unity not possible with Angela, and finally the distinct sexual overtones to the whole scene[1] given by the physical identification of Antonie and the violin, an identification retrospectively strengthened in their joint burial.

After Theodor's narrative is over, Lothar is angry. Theodor had promised a story less concerned with madness than was Lothar's story of the hermit Serapion:

> Du warnst vor Blicken in die schauerliche Tiefe der Natur, du magst von derlei Dingen nicht reden, nicht reden hören, und fällst selbst mit einer Geschichte hinein, die in ihrer kecken Tollheit mir wenigstens das Herz zerschneidet. Was ist der sanfte glückliche Serapion gegen den spleenischen, und in seinem Spleen grauenhaften Krespel! Du wolltest einen sanften Übergang vom Wahnsinn durch den Spleen zur gesunden Vernunft bewirken und stellst Bilder auf, über die man, fasst man sie recht scharf ins Auge, alle gesunde Vernunft verlieren könnte. (51)

Thus Hoffmann raises the possibility that his 'Bilder' might be looked at sharply, and that their surface oddness might conceal a 'schauerliche Tiefe'. Krespel's behaviour may seem complex, diffuse, even random, but the reverse is actually the case; in his fixation he simplifies his life so that everything in it depends on one issue, which rigidly governs all that he does. Hoffmann's Rat Krespel is a vulnerable, sensitive man whose marriage increases his personal insecurity to an intolerable degree; fixing on certain things associated with rather than causing his suffering he spends the rest of his life fighting imaginary battles to avoid such experiences and to relive a happier version of his earlier life, but in so doing he stifles his only daughter. If the story has a strong appeal, it is not because of its bizarre surface quality, but because its theme of an obsession which is defensive in nature but destructive in effect is bound to strike a familiar chord in any reader.

[1] Again, von Wiese interprets this scene in metaphysical terms which cannot be related to the text rather than relating it to the rest of the story and to the development there of the motifs which it contains: 'Vielmehr deutet die Duplizität von Geige und Stimme, die dennoch identisch sind, hier auf die mysteriöse Sphäre des Heiligen und Schönen hin, die sich der Menschen und der Dinge nur bedient, um in zeichenhafter Weise im Irdischen sich anzukündigen, die zugleich aber auch eben hier immer wieder der Gefahr einer dämonischen Zerstörung ausgesetzt ist. Antoniens Stimme und der Klang der Geige sind nur scheinbar von den Voraussetzungen der Wirklichkeit aus zu begreifen. In Wahrheit gehört beides einem zwar noch sinnlichen Bereich an, der aber doch schon auf übersinnliche Erscheinungen hindeutet' (p. 101).

5. GRILLPARZER: 'DER ARME SPIELMANN'

Grillparzer's story *Der arme Spielmann*[1] has long been regarded as one of his best works,[2] and its popularity even seems to be increasing; since 1964 no less than ten interpretations of the story have appeared, a remarkable number in such a short period.[3] Most interpretations have been concerned almost exclusively with the figure of the Spielmann, so that an evaluation of the story has seemed to be much the same thing as an evaluation of the Spielmann, and the question as to how we should understand the story has seemed to be identical with the question of how we should

---

[1] References are to: *Grillparzers Sämtliche Werke in zwanzig Bänden*, ed. A. Sauer (Stuttgart, 1892), XIII, 225–66.

[2] Cf., for example, Papst's judgment that the story 'bears comparison with the best of his plays as one of his great masterpieces' (*Grillparzer: Der arme Spielmann and prose selections*, ed. E. E. Papst, London and Edinburgh, 1960, p. xviii).

[3] These recent interpretations are the following: J. P. Stern, 'Beyond the Common Indication: Grillparzer', in his *Reinterpretations* (London, 1964), pp. 42–77; J. De Cort, 'Zwei arme Spielleute: Vergleich einer Novelle von F. Grillparzer und von Th. Storm', *Revue des Langues Vivantes*, XXX (1964), 326–41; H. Politzer, 'Die Verwandlung des armen Spielmanns. Ein Grillparzer-Motiv bei Franz Kafka', *Jahrbuch der Grillparzer-Gesellschaft*, IV (1965), 55–64; O. P. Straubinger, '*Der arme Spielmann*', *Grillparzer Forum Forchtenstein* (1966), pp. 97–102; M. W. Swales, 'The Narrative Perspective in Grillparzer's *Der arme Spielmann*', *German Life and Letters*, N.S., XX (1967), 107–18; H. Politzer, *Franz Grillparzers 'Der arme Spielmann'* (Stuttgart, 1967); A. Gutmann, 'Grillparzers *Der arme Spielmann*: Erlebtes und Erdichtetes', *Journal of the International Arthur Schnitzler Research Association*, VI (1967), 14–44; W. Paulsen, 'Der gute Bürger Jakob. Zur Satire in Grillparzers *Armem Spielmann*', *Colloquia Germanica* (1968), pp. 272–298; G. Jungbluth, 'Franz Grillparzers Erzählung: *Der arme Spielmann*. Ein Beitrag zu ihrem Verstehen', *Orbis Litterarum*, XXIV (1969), 35–51; H. Krotkoff, 'Über den Rahmen in Franz Grillparzers Novelle *Der arme Spielmann*', *MLN*, LXXXV (1970), 345–66. Even before this a number of separate interpretations of the story had existed: E. Alker, 'Komposition und Stil von Grillparzers Novelle *Der arme* Spielmann', *Neophilologus*, XI (1925), 15–27; B. Seuffert, 'Grillparzers Spielmann', *Festschrift August Sauer zum 70. Geburtstag des Gelehrten am 12. Oktober 1925* (Stuttgart, 1925), pp. 291–311; W. Silz, 'Grillparzer: *Der arme Spielmann*', in his *Realism and Reality* (Chapel Hill, 1954), pp. 67–78; B. von Wiese, 'Franz Grillparzer: *Der arme Spielmann*', in his *Die deutsche Novelle von Goethe bis Kafka*, I, 134–53; R. Brinkmann, 'Franz Grillparzer: *Der arme Spielmann*. Der Einbruch der Subjektivität', in his *Wirklichkeit und Illusion* (Tübingen, 1957), pp. 87–145; and the introduction to E. E. Papst's edition of the story (cited above). There are, of course, numerous treatments of the story in general works on Grillparzer and on the Novelle.

view the Spielmann.[1] Very often there has been a strong biographical slant in this criticism, so that the Spielmann has been
identified in certain crucial respects as Grillparzer himself. '*Der
arme Spielmann* ist Grillparzers offenstes Geständnis', said Alker
in 1925,[2] a position adopted by many critics subsequently. The
biographical identification, whether true or false, is of little use
for criticism of the story; even granted that this were in some
sense a confession, so are most works of literature in the same
sense, and the critical question still remains to be considered:
what kind of human experience is considered in the story, and how
relevant is that experience to its readers? Even granted we knew
what the Spielmann meant to Grillparzer, our analysis of the story
as a work of literature must proceed from what he communicated
in it; it is more relevant to take the Spielmann as a challenge for
the reader than as a self-image by Grillparzer.

Since the attempts that have been made to consider the critical
questions of the story were concerned for the most part with the
personality of the Spielmann himself, very little attention was
given to its other important character, the narrator; indeed, he
was rarely recognised as that kind of figure at all. This was an
important omission, for almost a third of the text precedes the
Spielmann's story, and this section is largely devoted to the
narrator's talking about himself, his attitudes to the Spielmann,
to the 'Volksfest', and to other things. Klein's plot summary[3]

---

[1] This is, for the most part, the emphasis of the interpretation of von Wiese, and on his
p. 136 he gives a survey of previous critics who had a similar concern.

[2] Alker, p. 17. Cf. also E. K. Bennett, *A History of the German Novelle*, p. 155: 'It
would seem rather that Grillparzer had at last arrived at the truth about himself.' That
the story had many roots in Grillparzer's life and experiences is by now so well-
documented that it is surprising to see that many of the recent crop of interpretations
consider the point to need further assertion; e.g., Straubinger (p. 98), noting the
'widerstreitende Meinungen' concerning the story, suggests that biographical facts
need to be taken into account; Gutman's essay is entirely biographical; while Jungbluth
recommends a return to a biographical approach such as that of Alewyn, which he
finds neglected: 'Es ist eines der furchtbarsten und schonungslosesten Bekenntnisse
der Weltliteratur' (R. Alewyn, 'Grillparzer und die Restauration', *Publications of the
English Goethe Society*, N.S. XII, 1937, cited by Jungbluth, p. 38). Jungbluth also
makes the assumption that in the narrator 'man ohne Skrupel den Autor selbst erblicken
darf' (p. 41).

[3] J. Klein, *Geschichte der deutschen Novelle*, pp. 195–7. Klein himself calls his summary
of the story a 'Strukturskizze'.

avoids these expressions of his attitudes on the part of the narrator, while Bennett's account minimises the existence of the story's long introduction.[1] This neglect of the function of so obtrusive a narrator is again partly to be traced to the biographical identification of narrator and Spielmann as two sides of Grillparzer;[2] once more, this identification is irrelevant to (and deflects attention from) the critical question of the nature and function of the juxtaposition of the two figures in the story.

Only a few recent critics (for example, Brinkmann, Swales and Politzer) have examined the position taken in *Der arme Spielmann* by the narrator, yet the value of their studies lies more in individual perceptions about specific parts of the text than in the emergence of any comprehensive view of the function of the narrator. Brinkmann's painstaking discussion of narration in the story is mainly concerned with the literary historical category of realism, and as a result treats narration as a technical rather than thematic element in the text.[3] Equating author and narrator,[4] he investigates only the question of the objectivity or subjectivity of the narrator's transmission of the story to the reader, not the function of the narrator's highly specific character in its system of values.

Swales and Politzer are the only critics so far to have taken the first step towards an investigation of the narrator's intrusion into his story by according him full status as a character in it, with his

---

[1] Bennett, pp. 152–8. Cf. especially his statement that Grillparzer's aim is to 'present a complete picture of a given character...' (p. 158).

[2] This is, in fact, now the most persistent cliché of *Spielmann* criticism, but is regularly 'discovered' as if a new point. The first to make the point, according to Straubinger (p. 98), was Wedel-Parlow, in his Grillparzer biography of 1932. But Seuffert (p. 295) made it in 1925. In the interpretations of the last twenty years, the point appears first in Silz, p. 74, and is repeated in von Wiese, p. 149; Brinkmann, p. 141; De Cort, pp. 340–1; Stern, p. 77; Swales, p. 115; and Jungbluth, p. 42. Papst warned against the dangers of this kind of interpretation in 1960, p. xxi.

[3] Cf., for example, his conclusion on p. 131: 'Was der Spielmann ist, was sein Wesen ist und wie er in der Welt steht, das erfährt man – formal – nicht durch entschiedene, zuordnende "objektive" Aussagen, sonden nur aus den relativen Sichtweisen begrenzter "empirischer" Subjekte, die *da* sind, nur insofern sie dem Erzähler wirklich begegnen.'

[4] Brinkmann makes this clear in saying: 'Daß auch der Erzähler Grillparzer selbst ist, bedarf kaum der Erwähnung (so wenig selbstverständlich das auch a priori so sein müßte)' (p. 141).

own reactions (not necessarily ours or the story's taken as a whole) to the Spielmann. Swales concludes that the narrator is ambivalent about the Spielmann, part of him wishing to identify with the old man while he also feels the need to defend against this identification as against a weakness.[1] But the Spielmann's own direct narrative already makes the reader ambivalent about him in just the same way, for there too we feel drawn to and exasperated by him. Can the space and emphasis devoted by the text to the narrator's personality be considered justifiable if this contributes nothing that we do not already feel without him? A view which attributes so little function to so much text must remain unsatisfying. Politzer's account of the function of the narrator also has its problems; for when he abstracts the thematic point that the narrator, unlike the Spielmann, undergoes a 'Verwandlung' through genuine 'Begegnung' with another person at the end of the story in his encounter with Barbara, and thus that communication with another human being makes an impact on him,[2] we must surely agree with his reviewer[3] who points out that the text's ending contains no trace of all this. All the reader sees is the narrator's probing a sensitive spot in Barbara and looking without comment at the results, Barbara's tears, which he might easily have predicted. The function of the narrator must be derived not from non-existent material at the end of the story, but instead largely from the wealth of material in the first third of the text.

Though the Spielmann has often been said to be a problematic character, there are at least some important ways in which he is not. Much that is factual about him is not in any doubt; he tells his own story very openly, and there seems no reason to fear that he deliberately conceals anything from us. We do not feel that there are any secrets about him, or that we need further information and

---

[1] Swales says that this is a narrator who 'intellectually is determined to report from the perspective of the real world, but who emotionally assents to the ideal, if impossible world of the "höchste Stufen der Kunst"' (p. 116).

[2] Politzer, 1967, pp. 58–60.

[3] F. Maxwell-Bresler's review of Politzer, 1967, in *Modern Language Review*, LXIV (1969), 950–1. The point is actually not stated strongly enough; Maxwell-Bresler allows that this can only be 'Vermutung', not categorical statement. But *some* evidence is needed for the former, too; even 'Vermutung' has its limits.

reports on more of his experiences; nothing new seems to be required to complete our picture of him. There seems also to be little difficulty in summing up and conceptualising all that we know of his personality. I do not mean that there have not been misconceptions: when, for example, a critic asserts that the Spielmann's failures are compulsive, or another that he inhabits the ideal world of music, both seem to give insufficient weight to the fact that he is always shown to be genuinely simple-minded and incompetent;[1] this amply-demonstrated fact allows us neither to postulate a deep-seated efficiency behind it all, nor a world inside his head that can be thought of in terms of a communicable value like music. But these misconceptions are certainly very easy to clear up, and the available features of the text which show them to be misconceptions are extremely plentiful and obvious. Again, while one might take either a positive or negative view of the Spielmann, depending perhaps on one's taste,[2] there will be little disagreement as to the nature of the positive and negative sides of Jakob on which the whole judgment would be based; its ingredients are not obscure. His main characteristic is a lack of a certain kind of judgment and competence, a simple-mindedness visible both in his dealings with others, and in his abilities whether musical or otherwise. This makes him defenceless in his human contacts, and renders him of little practical value to anyone else, whether as musician or provider. But this defect has attendant advantages. Because he is without suspicion, he is also entirely without malice; because he cannot conceive of others being dishonest, he is himself entirely honest; and because he cannot recognise self-seekingness in others, he is entirely generous. Above all, because he is not in the least competitive, and because his ability to recognise the difference between good and bad

---

[1] Politzer, 1967, p. 40: 'Es gibt, scheint Grillparzer sagen zu wollen, kein Versagen in der Wirklichkeit, das nicht in einem Seelenwinkel des Versagenden zu Hause wäre'; and Swales, p. 115–16. Stern's (pp. 76–7) introduction of a Christian perspective also gives insufficient weight to the Spielmann's defective judgment. His attractiveness is a consequence of that defect, rather than a matter of faith.

[2] Only in this sense do I agree with Papst that 'either of two apparently conflicting assessments of the Spielmann seems to be equally tenable'. These assessments are reactions to, not accounts of, the Spielmann.

playing is so limited, he is entirely without pose or pretensions; his most noticeable feature is his complete sincerity in his music and in his relations with others. As far as his happiness is con-concerned, he is almost without ability to produce or preserve situations which will make for his security and happiness, but is possessed of a remarkable ability to be happy with what he has. It is by no means certain, therefore, that he does not have a happier life than his more gifted father and brothers. To them, achievement meant so much that they could not be happy without it. Paradoxically, then, although Jakob seems to be exceptionally vulnerable in the world, he is in one sense invulnerable too; and in that sense his competitive family are very fragile indeed. His father is so vulnerable to a decline in his influence that a stroke, and death, result. One brother makes too ambitious a wager, and dies; the other chooses exile to escape the consequences of a dishonest attempt to harm a competitor. The Spielmann, on the other hand, survives them all, and appears to experience great happiness in his playing. The question remains of the real human value of happiness which depends on the reduction of one's horizons to this extent. But that, once more, is a problem for the reader; and its uncertainty is not caused by any uncertainty as to the facts of the Spielmann's existence. It is not necessary to quarrel, as critics in the past have done, over whether he is or is not a saint; we can simply say that it is natural that he should seem so to the 'Gärtnerin' at the end (264) of the story, though we should usually reserve the use of such a word for one who displays the attractive features of the Spielmann *without* these features being produced by, and thus dependent on, his simple-mindedness.

So much for the characteristics of the Spielmann; but if as the central character he is perfectly comprehensible from his own story, then what can be the reason for the well-developed narrative framework? For it cannot change what we know of the Spielmann. I am, of course, assuming here that the Spielmann's story is indeed his own, in his own words. One critic, Brinkmann, does not share this assumption, believing that the Spielmann's story is coloured by its being retold by the narrator. The narrator's emphasis and bias would have crept into the direct speech of the Spielmann after all, and on such a view we should (though Brinkmann does not draw this conclusion) need the narrative framework in order to evaluate the Spielmann, since it would be a key to the kind of bias which had been at work in the retelling of the old man's story. But there is no need for this conclusion. Brinkmann argues from such factors as the feat of memory required for the narrator to remember the Spielmann's story word for word after two years,[1] but overlooks the fact that this is one of those literary conventions without which fiction would be impossible. Direct speech in a work of fiction could never be given its full value if we did not accept the convention of the long memory of story-tellers, just as theatre is impossible without the acceptance of such conventions as the curtain, soliloquies, and so on. And so our question remains: given that the Spielmann presents himself fully enough, why the long preamble to his story? If with Jungbluth we want to call this device of two 'Ich-Erzähler' a 'raffinierter Trick', we have condemned it as an ingenious piece of irrelevance;[2] and if, with biographical critics, we say that Grillparzer here presents aspects of himself, we have still not considered their relevance to the Spielmann. Least of all can one agree with Stern that 'the narrator's taciturnity about himself is one of its [the story's] minor triumphs', or that in the narrator's introduction there is established a laconic mode 'with a sparseness, an economy of means rarely achieved elsewhere in German narrative prose'.[3] These judgments seem most inappropriate to a text which is remarkable for precisely the reverse, a conspicuous presence of the narrator's personality, achieved by a

---

[1] Brinkmann, p. 126. Brinkmann's attempt to show stylistic features in the Spielmann's direct speech which are attributable to the narrator seems to me unconvincing.

[2] Jungbluth (p. 43) does not draw this consequence of his view since he uses it as a bridge to a biographical excursion; the irrelevance can be explained ('findet daraus seine Erklärung') in biographical material. But this view of the process of artistic creation – haphazard inclusion of anything that happens to concern Grillparzer at a given moment – is not at all generous to Grillparzer's artistic talents.

[3] Stern, pp. 63–4. It is not clear in any case why taciturnity should constitute a triumph; it is rather unusual for epic narrators to obtrude their presence.

particularly lengthy and digressive introduction to the story of the Spielmann.

If we are to take seriously this large part of the text as relevant to the whole, it would seem unavoidable to consider the contribution it makes in presenting the narrator as one of the two main characters of the story. He is not presented to us through the events of his life story as the Spielmann is, but nonetheless becomes a distinct character in his own right through the attitudes he strikes, the emphases of the descriptions he offers us, and on occasion through his direct comment on himself. From the very beginning of the story we must constantly evaluate what he says, and build up an impression of him. When, for example, he professes to a love for the common people, it is not enough to take this as a simple fact, to be accepted at face value and then passed over. The fact that the assertion is made so directly and explicitly is important, and we must consider both why the narrator raises the issue, and whether his actions are consistent with his claim.[1] Yet none of these questions is worth raising except in the context of the thematic structure of the whole story.

That there is something in these opening pages to which we instinctively react negatively seems clear; Alker, for example, found them a blemish on the story, badly and dilettantishly written.[2] Unlike many later critics, Alker allowed himself a direct response here, and yet his critical framework was inadequate to deal with it; what is unpleasant in these pages must be attributed not to the author's bad craftsmanship, but to the projection of an

---

[1] Almost all critics accept the narrator's professions of love for the people and his claims to have an 'anthropologischen Heißhunger', at face value, in spite of their obsessiveness: e.g., Straubinger, p. 100; von Wiese, pp. 137–8; H. Pongs, 'Möglichkeiten des Tragischen in der Novelle', *Jahrbuch der Kleist-Gesellschaft*, XIII–XIV (1932), p. 79; Brinkmann, p. 88, and so on. Swales is the only critic who consistently evaluates rather than accepts the narrator's pronouncements concerning himself, though Politzer (1967, p. 13) questions the narrator's claim that he is 'leidenschaftlich' about anything.

[2] E. Alker, p. 18: 'Doch die ersten drei Seiten können weder in stilistischer noch in kompositorischer Hinsicht als sehr glücklich gelten; sie machen einen jungdeutsch–dilettantischen Eindruck.'

unpleasant character on the part of the narrator; and the kind of unpleasantness turns out to be very relevant to the Spielmann.[1]

The narrator begins his story by describing the July 'Volksfest' in Vienna:

In Wien ist der Sonntag nach dem Vollmonde im Monat Juli jedes Jahres samt dem darauffolgenden Tage ein eigentliches Volksfest, wenn je ein Fest diesen Namen verdient hat. Das Volk besucht es und gibt es selbst; und wenn Vornehmere dabei erscheinen, so können sie es nur in ihrer Eigenschaft als Glieder des Volks. Da ist keine Möglichkeit der Absonderung; wenigstens vor einigen Jahren noch war keine. (225)

Two pages later the narrator follows this with the assertion that 'Ich versäume nicht leicht, diesem Feste beizuwohnen' (227). But this turns out not to be the case,[2] for he is very easily diverted from the festival by the sight of the Spielmann; and even when he loses the Spielmann he simply goes home instead of back to the festival. This is only one of the things said by the narrator which either immediately rings false, or turns out to be so in the light of later events. The rather self-conscious reference to the 'Volk', with the immediately following introduction of class-awareness in the word 'vornehm' distances the narrator from the people rather than shows his feeling for them; the choice of word in contrast to 'Volk' is one suggesting superiority and refinement, and the resulting impression is of condescension to the inferior 'Volk' by a man conscious of his own status as 'Vornehmer', the pose of an aristocrat whose appreciation of a certain quaintness of the common people depends on his being quite safe from the realities of their life. These suspicions, derived from the tone of the first sentence, are confirmed in what comes later. There is a great deal of 'Absonderung', no visible dropping of class barriers,

---

[1] Politzer (p. 9) finds the narrator here pedantic. But while his style can be criticised, it must be criticised from the other end of the spectrum; it is a rather mannered, self-conscious and pretentious style.

[2] Swales (p. 110) notes that his interest in the Spielmann seems 'to be somewhat inconsistent with the narrator's avowed purpose in attending the Volksfest'. Swales' interpretation of this discrepancy is mainly concerned with the relative importance for the narrator of Volksfest and Spielmann; I should think of it more as an indication of his insincere posturing.

and no levelling of human beings, in the description of what happens on the way to the festival:

Schon mischen sich einzelne Equipagen der Vornehmeren in den oft unterbrochenen Zug. Die Wagen fliegen nicht mehr. Bis endlich fünf bis sechs Stunden vor Nacht die einzelnen Pferde- und Kutschen-Atome sich zu einer kompakten Reihe verdichten, die, sich selber hemmend und durch Zufahrende aus allen Quergassen gehemmt, das alte Sprichwort: Besser schlecht gefahren, als zu Fuße gegangen, offenbar zu Schanden macht. Begafft, bedauert, bespottet, sitzen die geputzten Damen in den scheinbar stille stehenden Kutschen. (226)

The narrator's description is concerned more than anything else with social levels. The 'vornehme Damen' are as separate from the crowd as they could be, and description of the attitude to them of the people emphasises that distance. The people behave as the 'Vornehme' would expect them to, i.e. badly, thus allowing them a comfortable feeling of their own superiority.[1] The narrator goes on to reinforce this by a description of the 'schreiende Weiber- und Kinderbevölkerung des Plebejer-Fuhrwerks' (228). There are here many pairs of words of opposite emotional force. 'Plebejer' is as negative a word for the people as 'Vornehme' was positive; the 'Damen' of the latter correspond to the 'Weiber' of the former, and while one group sit proudly and quietly on display, the other is 'schreiend'. The narrator himself in his language is producing that very 'Absonderung' the lack of which he professes to find so valuable a feature of his favourite festival. The narrator may claim (225) that 'Der Unterschied der Stände ist verschwunden', but it never disappears from his own consciousness or from the scene as he describes it. He separates himself from the people, remains always distant from them, and develops an interest in the Spielmann only after having heard him utter a piece of Latin: 'Der Mann hatte also eine sorgfältigere

---

[1] It is unnecessary to introduce Grillparzer's possible fear of social revolution here, e.g., Brinkmann, p. 88, and Politzer, 1967, p. 10. The attitude of the narrator to the people is a motif in the story, only to be evaluated in relation to its other occurrences and to contrasting motifs. Only the complete results of this kind of analysis could be referred to Grillparzer's beliefs, or to anyone else's, not an isolated piece of text seen without the controlling factor of its position in the whole story.

Erziehung genoßen, sich Kenntnisse eigen gemacht, und nun ein Bettelmusikant!' (229). The apparent move down the social scale is what attracts the narrator's attention, not the Spielmann's more evident (and more interesting) strangeness as a violinist. The phrase 'sich Kenntnisse eigen gemacht' is an interesting key to the narrator's system of values, too; education and knowledge is a possession of the privileged class, of which he too is a member. Throughout the story, the narrator is never really impressed by anything which represents the culture of the Viennese people as a whole. On the other hand, he is very impressed by the mention of Jakob's father 'Der Einflußreiche, der Mächtige' (238). And when Jakob gives the narrator his address, the latter responds to the information that it is 'im ersten Stocke' with '"In der That", rief ich, "Im Stockwerke der Vornehmen?"' (232). By contrast, the narrator's references to the people are always perjorative; they are noisy and 'genußlechzend' (228), and he is pleased to be away from them: 'Die Stille des Ortes, im Abstich der lärmenden Volksmenge that mir wohl' (233). As one who claims to be a lover of the people, the narrator is simply an impostor, and his lack of sincerity is well shown in the exaggerated tenor of his claim to be one:

Als ein leidenschaftlicher Liebhaber der Menschen, vorzüglich des Volkes, so daß mir selbst als dramatischem Dichter der rückhaltlose Ausbruch eines überfüllten Schauspielhauses immer zehnmal interessanter, ja belehrender war, als das zusammengeklügelte Urteil eines an Leib und Seele verkrüppelten, von dem Blut ausgesogener Autoren spinnenartig aufgeschwollenen literarischen Matadors; – als ein Liebhaber der Menschen, sage ich, besonders wenn sie in Maßen für einige Zeit der einzelnen Zwecke vergessen und sich als Teile des Ganzen fühlen, in dem denn doch zuletzt das Göttliche liegt, ja, der Gott – als einem solchen ist mir jedes Volksfest ein eigentliches Seelenfest, eine Wallfahrt, eine Andacht. (227)[1]

---

[1] It is strange to note how often this grotesque sentence has been taken at face value. Only Politzer appears to have responded to its style: 'Dieser Satz ist nicht nur monströs; sein Gefüge straft auch seine Aussage Lügen' (1967, p. 12). My interpretation here, however, differs from that of Politzer; he believes that the narrator is interested in the people for their vitality, presumably because one with the temperament of 'ein hochnotpeinlich-scharfsichtiger Beobachter', feeling his deficiency, 'sehnt sich nach der Begegnung mit einer Kraft...' (pp. 12–13). This seems to me not to do justice

Both the tone of the passage, and its contradiction by all that the narrator says and does, indicate that this alleged love of the people is a pretentious aristocratic pose; only while safe from them, and feeling superior to them, can the narrator indulge it.

Yet this is only one example of the falseness of the narrator's claims about himself. Consider, for example, his claim to have an 'anthropologischen Heißhunger' (229), or a 'psychologische Neurgierde' (265). Does the narrator show any real curiosity or concern with other human beings, any desire to understand them? Again, his language is interesting. He refers to his meeting with the Spielmann not as something instructive, but as an 'Abenteuer' (229). It is true that he is curious about Barbara and about the Spielmann, but it seems less the intellectual curiosity of the student of human nature, than the kind of curiosity which we think of as prying into other people's affairs. He is always remote from both, and without any of that sympathy for them which would be necessary for him to begin to understand them. I am not here making the point that he is a neutral observer, since I believe that this is not the case;[1] on the contrary, the narrator shows a most unsympathetic attitude. When he leaves the Spielmann for the last time (262) while the old man is still playing his violin, the narrator's remarks are extremely cold: 'Endlich hatte ich's satt, stand auf, legte ein paar Silberstücke auf den nebenstehenden Tisch und ging, während der Alte eifrig immer fortgeigte.' There is no farewell, no expression of sympathy or concern, but instead only the very unsympathetic 'hatte ich's satt', and the cold gesture of leaving some coins, as if to pay for his entertainment. Here, as elsewhere, the narrator never enters into the world of the Spielmann and his violin, instead recording his impatience with it. When going home after his first meeting (234) with the Spielmann, the narrator rather self-righteously

to the element of pretentious self-inflation by the narrator, the only real point of the style of the sentence.

[1] Stern's view that the narrator is aloof, and 'wishes merely to register' (p. 64) cannot be justified by the text. Many other critics have viewed the narrator's unsympathetic attitude as that of a distanced observer without an attitude; cf., e.g., Politzer: 'Er ist die Linse, in der sich die Welt der Erscheinungen spiegelt' (1967, p. 13).

congratulates himself on his (as opposed to the Spielmann's) 'Phantasieren' being something that disturbs no one. That the old man's playing is a disturbance is clear, but the narrator prefers to emphasise this side of the matter rather than that his violin-playing is for the old man something very precious. There are a large number of such ungenerous, impatient responses to the Spielmann and his playing, which grate on the reader for their obsessive denigration of the Spielmann; they gradually become a gratuitous harping on what we already know. Even his report on Barbara – that she could never have been beautiful – concentrates on the ridiculous side of the Spielmann, and unnecessarily, since the old man had told us as much already (243). Likewise, the narrator's off-hand remark on Barbara's tune ('gemütlich, übrigens gar nicht ausgezeichnet', 241) seems, however justified by the nature of the tune, to concentrate on the negative side – it is after all the tune's associations that make it distinctive for the Spielmann. Even against the background of his earlier behaviour, his action at the end of the story is extraordinary. He visits Barbara, as he admits, out of curiosity, but ostensibly to attempt to buy Jakob's violin. Predictably, the request reduces Barbara to tears; and then the narrator goes away, having satisfied his curiosity. He has probed Barbara's response to a considerable provocation, and wounded her in the process. This is wanton self-gratification; a pursuit of entertainment rather than of knowledge of humanity.

The narrator is frequently careless and inconsiderate in his dealing with the Spielmann. His offer of money, to the end, is always as from benefactor to beggar, though the Spielmann had early in the story shown his sensitivity on this score (230 and 233); his pride demands that he accept money only as a fee for his performance. The narrator's attempt to elicit the old man's story is clumsy and demeaning; clumsy, in his baldly announcing that he is 'nach Ihrer Geschichte lüstern' (237), and demeaning, in that his mentioning the Spielmann's display of Latin erudition allows the old man to see that it is his *fall* to the level of a beggar that interests the narrator. Such instances could be multiplied, and together they show that the narrator has no interest in or ability to enter into the world of other people. He refers to the people on occasion as a 'Haufen', or a 'Menschenwall' (229), and even the Spielmann is said, in a phrase whose overtones show his deeper attitudes to lesser categories of human being, to be 'barhäuptig und kahlköpfig...nach Art dieser Leute' (228). His real interests lie in gratifying his idle curiosity, and in projecting a self-congratulatory image greatly at variance with reality.

The question must now arise: how is this personality relevant to the Spielmann? And the answer must surely lie in the fact that the narrator is shown to be the very opposite of the Spielmann. If the Spielmann's outstanding characteristic is his utter sincerity, that of the narrator is his complete lack of it, his incessant posturing and posing, his self-deception and pretence, even pretentiousness. The Spielmann is his opposite in every way, never worrying about social class, and being happy with any human being of whatever rank. He is concerned with other people, and respects them; he is saddened by their unhappiness, and always tries to be helpful, however inefficiently. The narrator, on the other hand, is always distant from everyone in the story, is insensitive to the Spielmann and his world, or to that of the common people around him, gratuitously hurts the feelings of the people he meets, and never shows a sign of regret at having done so. The Spielmann is so generous in his estimate of other people that he even thinks well of his father, in spite of the way his father has treated him. He is even sure that his father meant well, for after his death the Spielmann says that he hopes to find him again 'wo wir nach unsern Absichten gerichtet werden und nicht nach unsern Werken' (250). On neither criterion would the Hofrat have done very well, but it is a touching thing that Jakob ascribes his own well-intentioned inefficiency to his father, whose qualities were in fact the reverse of his. The narrator, by contrast, is very ungenerous to the Spielmann and indeed to everyone else in the story. If at one point he calls the Spielmann his 'Liebling', he quickly undercuts that compliment, for he speaks of the 'Mißklängen meines und, ich fürchte beinahe, nur meines

Lieblings' (235).[1] This underlines the fact that no one else can be expected to have any interest in the old man, which would in turn rob the old man of any *right* to the attention of the narrator too; this is, by implication, an odd quirk of the narrator, not a response to a deservedly interesting person.

It is evidently part of the story's strategy to have the old man introduced by one who is his opposite in certain fundamental characteristics; thus a genuine but incompetent person is introduced by one who is capable but insincere. Yet the most interesting aspect of the contrast between the two lies in their attitudes to their art. The Spielmann's art is consistent with the rest of him: sincere, genuine, but so technically incompetent as to be of value only to him alone. What of the narrator? He, we are told, is a dramatic poet, and we do not experience his dramatic work; however, we do experience his qualities as a storyteller. Some distinct impressions emerge. Consider, for example, his description of the 'Volksfest', and its metaphors:

Und so fort und immer weiter, bis endlich der breite Hafen der Lust sich aufthut und Wald und Wiese, Musik und Tanz, Wein und Schmaus, Schattenspiel und Seiltänzer, Erleuchtung und Feuerwerk sich zu einem pays de cocagne, einem Eldorado, einem eigentlichen Schlaraffenlande vereinigen, das leider, oder glücklicherweise, wie man es nimmt, nur einen und den nächst darauffolgenden Tag dauert, dann aber verschwindet, wie der Traum einer Sommernacht, und nur in der Erinnerung zurückbleibt und allenfalls in der Hoffnung. (226)

The description of the festival hardly matches the image of it as a midsummer night's dream; nothing could be less appropriate. The festival is raucous, while the image is that of a delicate fantasy. Yet this is typical of the narrator's usually forced and pretentious imagery, which always seems to strive for an effect rather than to illuminate a situation. His earlier image of the stream of people is another example:

[1] At this point occurs another of the narrator's unfulfilled protestations, and the discrepancy between what he says and what he does is again instructive. For having said that he will spare his reader any further description of the old man's playing ('dieses höllischen Konzertes') he in fact goes on to give a long description of it. Again, the discrepancy conveys his obsessive denigration of the Spielmann.

Ein wogende Menge erfüllt die Straßen. Geräusch von Fußtritten, Gemurmel von Sprechenden, das hie und da ein lauter Ausruf durchzuckt. Der Unterschied der Stände ist verschwunden; Bürger und Soldat teilt die Bewegung. An den Thoren der Stadt wächst der Drang. Genommen, verloren und wiedergenommen, ist endlich der Ausgang erkämpft. Aber die Donaubrücke bietet neue Schwierigkeiten. Auch hier siegreich, ziehen endlich zwei Ströme, die alte Donau und die geschwollnere Woge des Volks, sich kreuzend quer unter und über einander, die Donau ihrem alten Flußbette nach, der Strom des Volkes, der Eindämmung der Brücke entnommen, ein weiter, tosender See, sich ergießend in alles deckender Überschwemmung. (225)

This time, the narrator has common speech to rely on: he is developing the metaphor inherited from ordinary speech, for in German as in English, we can quite normally speak of a stream of people. But he proceeds to develop this idea at length and in fact *ad nauseam*. He is obviously seeking after literary effect, but eventually mixes the metaphor disastrously. Over several pages the motif recurs: the crowd is 'zuströmend' and 'entegentströmend' (229), it is a 'weiter, tosender See', the fairground is a 'Hafen der Lust', the festival itself constitutes dry land (226), while the German language allows the easy introduction of the embankment as a 'Damm'. The development appears, even on the surface, to be rather forced. But the absurdity of the sequence comes to light when it becomes apparent that the stream is heading for the harbour and land: for a stream reaches its destination when it gets to the sea, not to dry land! The narrator has developed his watery metaphors in a grandiose way, but has confused the different perspectives of a stream running down to the sea, on the one hand, and a ship at sea looking for a harbour and land on the other; and so he has his stream reaching land, as fine an example of a mixed metaphor as one could wish for. The cry should not be 'Land' but 'Meer', and in that the moving stream of people reaches a larger, stationary concentration of people, this would not be inappropriate. What Grillparzer wants to show here is that the narrator is not interested in metaphorical illumination of what he is describing, but only in the creation of impressive language; the metaphor is not a genuine one which springs from the nature of his object, but a false one piled on to increase the appearance of a 'literary' effect. This fact of his artistic performance illuminates his claim to being a student of humanity[1] from another direction. This too is part of the narrator's posture as a literary figure, and of his developing his image as a great writer. Another example of his consciously posing as the poet-dramatist is the much-quoted passage on the common people as literary material:

Wie aus einem aufgerollten, ungeheuren, dem Rahmen des Buches entsprungenen Plutarch, lese ich aus den heitern und heimlich bekümmerten Gesichtern, dem lebhaften oder gedrückten Gange, dem wechselseitigen Behnemen der Familienglieder, den einzelnen, halb unwillkürlichen Äußerungen, mir die Biographien der unberühmten Menschen zusammen, und wahrlich! man kann die Berühmten nicht verstehen, wenn man die Obskuren nicht durchgefühlt hat. Von dem Wortwechsel weinerhitzter Karrenschieber spinnt sich ein unsichtbarer, aber ununterbrochener Faden bis zum Zwist der Göttersöhne, und in der jungen Magd, die, halb wider Willen, dem drängenden Liebhaber seitab vom Gewühl der Tanzenden folgt, liegen als Embryo die Julien, die Didos und die Medeen. (227)[2]

This is a gross and inflated piece of posturing again, noticeable both for the triteness beneath the self-importance and, as usual, for

---

[1] Swales (p. 111) is inclined to see this claim by the narrator as an attempt to excuse his interest in the Spielmann: 'It is almost as if the narrator were ashamed of a moment of weakness for the Spielmann.' But self-inflation seems to me a better explanation than the postulation of a conflict in the narrator's mind; for the narrator has no real personal sympathy for the Spielmann.

[2] Swales alone among recent critics finds this passage suspect: '...do we not detect a certain strain, an element of self-deception in the language – does not our narrator perhaps "protest too much"?' (p. 110). But he draws no broader conclusions from this. It is remarkable how often it has been taken as a true confession by Grillparzer, and even a literary historical manifesto important for the time – as if by 1848 such a thing were necessary; cf., for example, Politzer, p. 6; and von Wiese, p. 138: 'Diese viel zitierte Stelle zeigt einen wichtigen geistesgeschichtlichen Wechsel in der Auffassung vom menschlichen Schicksal.' Yet Seuffert already half a century ago found it an 'etwas gezwungene Wendung', and the juxtapositions it contains a 'gewaltsame Verknüpfung' (p. 292). Seuffert responded very accurately to the tone of these and other phrases early in the story, and it was only his lack of the theoretical distinction between author and narrator which prevented him from proceeding to a better understanding of the story. Having seen so much, he pronounces the 'Dichter' to be Grillparzer himself (p. 296) and proceeds to explain away the interesting material he observes as due to Grillparzer's experiences and character; no more instructive example can be found of a critic whose intuitive response is very fine, but his theory so poor as to waste that advantage.

its irrelevance to what comes after it in the story. There is a pointed contrast between the grand, heroic figures it mentions, and the old, unheroic Spielmann; and the verbs 'durchfühlen' and 'verstehen' are conspicuously inappropriate to the narrator, who makes no attempt to understand the world of the Spielmann's feelings. This is surely stereotype utterance for an author, and more stereotype author behaviour can be found, for example, in his rather crude request for the Spielmann's story.

The old man's incredulity reinforces this impression, and in a sense constitutes a rejection of the resulting unnatural and self-conscious situation: '"Geschichte?" wiederholte er. "Ich habe keine Geschichte... Das also nennen Sie meine Geschichte?"' (237). Grillparzer includes in the text equally self-conscious touches by the narrator when he seems to be taking notes in sentences without verbs; the impression created is that of image-projection on the part of that observant student of the world, the author, e.g. 'Zank, Geschrei, wechselseitige Ehrenangriffe der Kutscher, mitunter ein Peitschenhieb' (226), or 'Voraus die Schuljugend mit Kreuz und Fahne, der Geistliche mit dem Kirchendiener. Unmittelbar nach dem Sarge die beiden Kinder des Fleischers und hinter ihnen das Ehepaar' (265).

Just as his writing strives for effect, his criterion of artistic success is simply public acclaim, and hence his love of the people is, as he admits, greatest when they are applauding him; this is why he finds the 'rückhaltlose Ausbruch eines überfüllten Schauspielhauses' more interesting and even instructive (though one might ask how it could possibly be so), than the judgments of his critics. Taken together with the evidence of his story-telling, this confession confirms that he is concerned with success but not integrity and it also discredits his professed love of the people, for his concern with them seems now to be with their acclaiming him; and this will perhaps explain why it is that he shows no real interest in them for themselves, while claiming that he does. That we have here a more real profession of attitude is shown in the way that it bursts in in an uncontrolled way, overriding the logic and grammatical shape of the sentence. Linguistically and in substance, the attack on the critics is an irrelevant intrusion. Grammatically it is out of place, as a clause having only a precarious link with the main clause by means of an adverbial phrase, and holding up the necessary arrival of the main verb; and as to the substance, it is just as much out of place to justify love of the people by referring to one's being applauded by them, or to express such a violent attack on the critics without any preamble or reported incident from which the attack would spring. In the absence of any reported incident we tend to draw our own conclusions as to the justifiability of the critics' strictures, taking into account the irrational tone of the outburst and the narrator's literary values as we have seen them; but the obsessive nature of the expression leaves no doubt that what the narrator says here is a genuine representation of his concerns, not another pose.

The contrast here with the Spielmann is striking. Rejection as an artist does not cause him to make such a vicious attack on his critics; he is without malice, resigned and forgiving. But this is in part due to another contrast between the two: the Spielmann plays according to his conscience, not to impress other people.[1] He is an incompetent, but not a compromiser. The two display very much the same contrast as artists that they show as men: the Spielmann technically incompetent, yet completely honest and sincere, while the narrator is technically slick and clever, conscious of literary effect, but without integrity, concerned with applause and a shallow kind of impact rather than with real artistic value. There are, to be sure, similarities between the two figures, and yet the main pattern is that of contrast; even these similarities function as common ground on which their differences may emerge in a more subtle way. An example of this is furnished by their both using religious terminology in the context of intensity of feeling. The Spielmann thinks of his music as something sacred:

Als ich nun mit dem Bogen über die Saiten fuhr, Herr, da war es, als ob Gottes Finger mich angerührt hatte... Ich fiel auf die Kniee und betete laut

---

[1] Politzer (pp. 15–16) notes the contrast in the reception given by the public to the art of the Spielmann and of the narrator, and part of their contrasting reactions to that reception, without relating this systematically to the thematic structure of the story.

und konnte nicht begreifen, daß ich das holde Gotteswesen einmal gering geschätzt, ja gehasst in meiner Kindheit, und küßte die Violine und drückte sie an mein Herz und spielte wieder und fort. (241)

As the Spielmann talks of music in these terms, the narrator reports an impression of intense conviction and involvement in what is said: 'Ich kannte meinen Mann beinahe nicht mehr' (242). But the narrator has also spoken of his passions and needs in religious terms too; for him, it is the people who contain 'das Göttliche' and the festival is therefore 'ein eigentliches Seelenfest, eine Wallfahrt, eine Andacht' (227). Later, the narrator speaks of his need for something that will be spiritually uplifting early in the day:

Die Morgenstunden haben für mich immer einen eigenen Wert gehabt. Es ist, als ob es mir Bedürfnis wäre, durch die Beschäftigung mit etwas Erhebendem, Bedeutendem in den ersten Stunden des Tages mir den Rest desselben gewißermaßen zu heiligen. Ich kann mich daher nur schwer entschliessen, am frühen Morgen mein Zimmer zu verlassen... (234)

The Spielmann, too, preserves the morning for an activity that is 'veredelnd':

'Indem ich nun diese Stücke spiele', fuhr er fort, 'bezeige ich meine Verehrung den nach Stand und Würden geachteten, längst nicht mehr lebenden Meistern und Verfassern, thue mir selbst genug und lebe der angenehmen Hoffnung, dass die mir mildest gereichte Gabe nicht ohne Entgelt bleibt, durch Veredlung des Geschmackes und Herzens der ohnehin von so vielen Seiten gestörten und irre geleiteten Zuhörerschaft. Da derlei aber, auf daß ich bei meiner Rede bleibe' – und dabei überzog ein selbstgefälliges Lächeln seine Züge – 'da derlei aber eingeübt sein will, sind meine Morgenstunden ausschließend diesem Exercitium bestimmt.' (232)

Yet the differences are obvious; the Spielmann acts on what he says, while the narrator does not. He gives up his supposedly devotional presence at the 'Volksfest', and also leaves his room in the morning to see the Spielmann; and he seems to believe that what the latter says means nothing too, for though the Spielmann has said that his mornings are taken up exclusively with practising, and that he would wish the narrator to give him advance warning of the day of his visit so that he can accommodate the visit into his round of daily tasks, the narrator ignores both points, and exclaims: 'So werde ich Sie einmal morgens überraschen' (232).

The most interesting of the contrastive parallels of the two characters lies in the narrator's early stream image and the flood through which the Spielmann dies. A precise and comprehensive account of this parallel is given by Walter Silz:[1]

Despite this arithmetical discrepancy, the two frames give the impression of complete balance, and this impression is strengthened by a symmetrical correspondence of motifs, first and last. The public festival of the opening is balanced by the public calamity of the close, the flood of holiday folk at the beginning (a figure carried through at some length) by the flood of destructive waters at the end; a gateway in the park with the joyous living, a gateway in the flooded suburb with the bodies of the dead. Each flood casts its derelicts ashore: the wretched little company of 'Volksmusikanten' at the edge of the park road, and the corpses of the drowned awaiting the coroner.

Papst has correctly observed that what was metaphor in the one case has become reality in the other;[2] but this is in a wider sense the contrast once more of the false and the genuine. The narrator's metaphor is a superficial piece of literary posturing, confused and inappropriate, while the flood and consequent deaths are harshly real.

The involvement of the narrator in the figure of the Spielmann is clearly a complex matter, involving many factors: among them his authorial pose, and the theme of descent in class. Also important here is his compulsive denigration of a man who is his opposite.[3] But the broader reason for the inclusion and juxta-

---

[1] Silz, p. 69. This parallel has been proposed again by later critics, e.g., Swales, p. 109, and Politzer, 1967, p. 10. But it was already noted in 1925 by Seuffert (pp. 293-4) and, as Silz points out, by Alker (pp. 21-2).

[2] Papst, pp. xxx-xxxi.

[3] Unlike Swales, therefore, I do not find the kind of ambivalence which has as one of its sides a wish to identify with the Spielmann: 'He can only – and this in spite of himself

position of the two is that they represent the two sides of the main thematic contrast on which the story is based. This theme is that of integrity in relation to efficiency, and throughout, the narrator and Spielmann are systematically contrasted with each other in terms of it;[1] this is the meaning of the story which gives it a relevance transcending its possible biographical content.[2] The Spielmann, and perhaps even the narrator, may well represent the kind of extremes not met with in everyday life; and yet the issue which is the basis of this contrasting pair is ever-present, and the need to balance the two sides of the contrast inescapable. It is easy to make the judgment that the Spielmann lacks competence in all that he does, and yet it is always possible for the honesty and trustingness which he preserves to become obliterated by the kind of technical expertness manifested by the narrator. The Spiel-mann's trusting nature has reached the point of sheer gullibility, and yet to correct this a wariness is necessary which can bring with it a permanently suspicious nature and a distance from all other human beings. All competence involves an act of emotional distance, and so a move away from the genuineness of the Spielmann's world, which if continued too far lands us in the narrator's world of insincerity and loss of contact with genuine feeling.

The ending of the story brings out the positive side of Jakob more strongly than had hitherto been the case, since we are now shown not the narrator's reactions to Jakob, but those of Barbara and the 'Gärtnerin'; the tears of the former, and the words of the latter, show what an effect Jakob had had on them, while objective signs of his effect on the world are available in the form of his name having been given to Barbara's child, and of his having saved the lives of some children. Thus the story closes by

- offer a personal and instinctive belief, an emotional assent to the person and life of Jakob, the armer Spielmann' (p. 116).

[1] By contrast, Stern says (p. 68) that 'Jacob's devotion to his art (if we are to call it "art"...) emerges as the sole positive value intimated in the *Novelle*.' But it is certainly not his art that wins him people who love or admire him.

[2] Thus Jungbluth's conclusion is both irrelevant and erroneous: 'Die Erzählung *Der arme Spielmann* ist nicht allein eine gnadenlose Abrechnung Grillparzers mit sich selbst, sie ist auch ein Zeugnis für extremen Selbstgenuß' (p. 51).

shifting the balance somewhat in his favour;[1] rightly, since if we have to err on one side or the other, sincerity or technique, gullibility or suspicion, we should all choose to lean to the Spielmann.[2]

[1] To be sure, these positive signs do not occur without something of their opposite; the contrast is maintained by Jakob's actual death coming as a result of his indiscriminately risking his life to rescue what is important (children) and what is unimportant (a small amount of money).

[2] The interpretations of Paulsen and Krotkoff came to hand as this study was completed. Paulsen detects social satire in the story, but only through equating the narrator's attitudes and those of Grillparzer, e.g., referring to the opening of the story, his 'Gerade dadurch, daß Grillparzer das Volk derart mythologisiert...' (p. 284), treats as authorial attitudes to society what should be viewed as part of the characterisation of the narrator. Krotkoff's essay is concerned with the 'Rahmen', but in an unproductive way; 'In den autobiographischen Angaben des Erzählers hat mehr weltanschauliches Gedankangut Grillparzers in dichterischer Gestalt Eingang gefunden als man zuerst annehmen möchte' (p. 365). Thus she takes the narrator's remarks on the 'Volk' as truths for the story's purposes.

6. KELLER: 'DIE DREI GERECHTEN KAMMACHER'

Keller[1] is most often thought of as a pleasantly relaxed writer of an optimistic temperament.[2] Most at home in writing comedy, his choice of the milieu of Seldwyla in the *Leute von Seldwyla* collection, for example, seems to be a commitment to the predominantly sunny landscape of a charming small town, and even the tragic story contained in the collection – *Romeo und Julia auf dem Dorfe* – is far from being emotionally harrowing; it is a rather gently sad tale. The reduced pace of living in the small town allows time, it seems, for his narrator's detailed descriptions of life there, and these digressions also make their contribution to the general effect of an emotional tone being kept down to a level which is never threatening or overwhelming. The narrator's concern with the physical detail of the everyday world is commonly regarded as showing 'Glauben an den Glanz des Diesseits', to use Klein's phrase.[3] Lacking the sheer size of stage which might be needed to produce any really powerful effect, and choosing not to infect his small-scale scene with that pervasive melancholy used so effectively by Storm, for example, it would seem that Keller has committed himself to stories of a fairly lightweight character: enjoyable, interesting, and subtle, yet never really arresting or involving any very deep emotions. Accordingly, his narrator's

---

[1] References are to *Gottfried Keller: Werke* (Zürich, 1965), IV, 201–47. I am much indebted to Mrs. Lilian Hoverland for the stimulus provided by many conversations we have had concerning this story. The only separate essay to have appeared so far is that by D. Pregel, 'Das Kuriose, Komische und Groteske in Kellers Novelle *Die drei gerechten Kammacher*', *Wirkendes Wort*, XIII (1963), 331–45. Pregel's essay is more concerned with categorising aspects of the text than with interpreting it, e.g., 'Zwischen dem belächelbar Geheimnisvollen, dem Lachen erregenden Widersprüchlichen und dem lächerlich Unheimlichen liegen die Grenzen, an denen sich Kurioses, Komisches und Groteskes scheiden' (p. 335).

[2] See, for example, the general assessments of his stories in the standard general works on the Novelle by Klein, *Geschichte der deutschen Novelle von Goethe bis zur Gegenwart*, and Bennett, *A History of the German Novelle*. Significant exceptions to this generalisation are noted below.

[3] Klein, p. 303.

tone and style are pleasantly conversational, avoiding tension and any kind of dramatic concentration. While acknowledging that there are problems in Keller's work, a recent critic maintains: 'Yet the fact remains that he preferred to present these problems and ideas in an amusing and pleasant manner.'[1]

It is easy to see how this kind of view of Keller leads to a view of *Die drei gerechten Kammacher* as an 'entertaining'[2] story, a judgment which tends to imply that its content is slight. Then again, it is understandable that this Novelle should be singled out to exemplify his narrator's digressions and love of detailed description:

Actual material things are a source of pleasure to him, and he will describe a whole catalogue of oddities – such as the collection of Züs Bünzlin in *Die drei gerechten Kammacher* – not merely for its value in the development of the story, but because it is in itself a source of pleasure to him.[3]

And it will naturally seem a good example of Keller's humour, with comic incongruity pervading the text, from such examples as Züs' 'Anleitung zum Kartenschlagen' being sandwiched between pious works for pious young ladies (217), to the mock serious description of Dietrich's discovery of Züs as the act of a Columbus (222). The only difficulty in such a view of the story might be that we were tempted to complain because on occasion the joke goes on too long and becomes tedious; the lists of Züs' possessions, and Züs' own recitations, account for a large part of the text, and might be cut down so that substantially the same joke would not recur so often. Here the narrator, it would seem, has become much too fond of his own joke, and has lost perspective on it.

Yet this view of *Die drei gerechten Kammacher* needs serious qualification; as it stands it misses much of the point of the story,

---

[1] W. Hahn, 'The Motif of Play in Gottfried Keller's *Novellen*', *German Quarterly*, XXXIV (1961), 57.

[2] J. M. Lindsay, 'Gottfried Keller', in *German Men of Letters*, ed. Alex Natan (London, 1961), p. 181.

[3] Bennett, p. 183. Cf. also Pregel, p. 333: 'Der Erzähler hat offensichtlich Freude an der Fülle des Details.'

and of Keller's work in general. While this story is often taken to be a good example of his work according to such an understanding of Keller, I shall try to show that it is especially suited to expose the limitations of this view. For beneath his comic surface, Keller here writes a story that is serious, and even sinister,[1] one whose theme is important and central to human life. The narrator's descriptive digressions provide a strange and oblique, yet highly relevant means of developing his theme, so that the small Swiss setting suddenly and frighteningly becomes a general human one. And once more, it is the narrator's stance which is the key to a better understanding of the story.

Keller's narrator announces his starting-point in a very direct way:

Die Leute von Seldwyla haben bewiesen, dass eine ganze Stadt von Ungerechten oder Leichtsinnigen zur Not fortbestehen kann im Wechsel der Zeiten und des Verkehrs; die drei Kammacher aber, daß nicht drei Gerechte lang unter einem Dache leben können, ohne sich in die Haare zu geraten. (201)

And yet, for all the narrator's directness, it is by no means obvious how we should take this comment. In *Romeo und Julia auf dem Dorfe*, too, the narrator begins by commenting directly on the content of the story he is about to tell, alluding to its being another version of the kind of situation contained in Shakespeare's play (70). Yet it becomes clear later that his opening remarks were not an interpretation of the story; they referred to its superficial plot content rather than to its theme, which has to do with the contrast between the rigid, orderly life of the farmers and the 'wild' life exemplified by the dark fiddler. In *Romeo und Julia* the narrator

---

[1] Lee B. Jennings, 'Gottfried Keller and the Grotesque', *Monatshefte*, L (1958), 9–20, and W. Kayser, *Das Groteske* (Oldenburg, 1957), have both pointed to the sinister quality of some aspects of the *Kammacher*. Jennings' remarks on the story are unfortunately as brief (one short paragraph, p. 12) as they are interesting; but in general he is inclined to see the sinister side of Keller as a suppressed awareness of the darker side of life, still within a predominantly positive attitude. Kayser is more interested in diagnosing the presence of 'das Groteske', than in interpreting the story, and he tends (pp. 117–18) to minimise the impact of the grotesque, for example with the observation that the descriptions of Züs' grotesque 'Hausrat' render it 'vertraut'.

announces the framework within which he will work, rather than the most basic concerns of his story. When we are faced with the direct assertion that *Die drei gerechten Kammacher* 'illustrates Keller's thesis that three just men could not live together under the same roof'[1] we realise that the same holds true of that story too; the initial comment (by the narrator, not by Keller) announces the material of the story rather than its theme. For the actual story the narrator then goes on to tell leaves his initial characterisation of it far behind. Züs is irrelevant to his opening statement, yet she takes up a considerable amount of space in a fairly short story; the comb-makers do not just get in each other's hair – one of them actually commits suicide; and what is most characteristic of the comb-makers is their obsession with a single idea, not their concern with justice. The idea of justice seems to be conspicuously absent from the end of the story: were we prepared for Jobst's death or for Fridolin's virtual destruction by the dominant tone of the story up to that point, and did they deserve to fare so badly? This may well have been the kind of incident which Bennett had in mind when he noted that '... in spite of his much vaunted and usually prevailing human kindliness and charity, there is some-times a little savagery in Keller's treatment of his unsuccessful characters, and more than one instance of lapses from good taste'.[2] And so, the ending of the story would be a blemish.

Yet alleged blemishes turn out not infrequently to be the most interesting parts of literary works, and often to be the critical points at which an element of surprise is used to underline something of crucial importance for the whole text. The fate of the comb-makers may appear unprepared from the standpoint of the narrator's opening remarks, but not so in the light of a more fundamental thematic structure of the story. The narrator's opening remarks establish his framework: he is ostensibly telling a funny story on a trivial subject. But as the suddenly changed

---

[1] Lindsay, p. 181. Cf. also Klein, p. 307, who believes that this story has 'eine ähnlich erzieherische Wurzel, nämlich den Satz, daß ein Staat von Gerechten nicht bestehen kann'. Pregel too (p. 344), thinks that the narrator's opening judgment is reliable for the whole of the story.

[2] Bennett, p. 190.

tone of the ending shows, Keller's purpose throughout is to tell a story of a serious nature, about pathetically vulnerable people unable to manage their lives in a very important respect.

While Züs' conversation is full of comic pretentiousness, and the lists of her possessions are full of comic incongruity, the main thing common to both is that Züs seems unable to exercise much control over what she does; she soon loses the thread, and rambles helplessly without any guiding principle. And though the comb-makers may be termed 'gerecht' by the narrator and by Züs (220) – she seems in fact to be the source of this epithet – the most obvious fact about them is that everything they do is controlled by a single idea, so that they pursue an aim without any deviation from it, shutting out all else from their lives. They are dominated by a single guiding principle, and one that is trivial enough for all emphasis to be put on their subservience to it rather than on its character or inherent value. The clear juxta-position of the comb-makers and Züs in this way shows that in a fundamental characteristic she is their polar opposite; she is indiscriminate and undiscriminating while they are rigidly single-minded. Here, then, must be the relevance of the four to each other and to the story, and here is its most basic theme; beneath the narrator's comic framework Keller has written a fascinating study in aims and aimlessness. Paradoxically, it is given to Züs to enunciate this theme when, before the race, she randomly seeks inspiration from her 'Schatzkästlein', and 'stach mit einer Nadel zwischen die Blätter, und der Spruch, welchen sie aufschlug, handelte vom unentwegten Verfolgen eines guten Zieles' (225). In the contrast between the aimless, indiscriminate nature of her choice, and the single-minded pursuit of an aim recommended by the saying, lies the thematic area which the story explores: it concerns itself with the character of the goals which men set themselves, the degree to which they allow these goals to domi-nate their lives, and to which they then become the prisoners of their goals; with the role of flexibility in pursuit of them, and of adaptability to changing circumstances; with the scope allowed for intelligence by the possibility of change of direction; and with the alternatives to a life with clear goals. At the end of the story the question is raised of how much life itself comes to be dependent on an aim to which an individual has become wholly committed; Jobst's aim may in one sense be worthless, but that only tends to underline its value as something which serves to organise and unify his life. Its objective worthlessness isolates and exposes this other kind of value, and reminds us that choice of a particular goal is arbitrary, but giving one's life purpose (of whatever kind) is an important human need. Here is the point of the narrator's predominantly comic tone: a more serious tone would demand the choice of a more objectively valuable aim, which would give more weight to the intrinsic qualities of that aim. But Keller's study can deal with a ridiculous aim, and so keep in the foreground the irrational nature of the commitment to achieve something, whatever it may be.

All the characters in the story contribute to this thematic study in different ways, not least the people of the town of Seldwyla. They function as an opposite pole to the comb-makers too, but while Züs does so by her being unable to stick to the point, or make any kind of discrimination in what she does, the Seldwylans provide a contrast in their making the absence of any goal into a way of life: they devote themselves to the enjoyment of the moment. Any other coherence to their lives is lacking, and they thus form the perfect background for the comb-makers. But the strange fact is that the Seldwylans' pursuit of what is immediately enjoyable turns out to be an aim of a kind, too, and in the end they are just as inflexible as the comb-makers in their adherence to it. Consider, for example, the inevitability of the bankruptcy of the comb-making business; each owner of the business has taken part in a cycle of prosperity and high living followed by bankruptcy, and each one seems powerless to exercise more prudence than the last. The rigidity of this pattern is emphasised when the current 'Meister', who has more reason to exercise some control than his predecessors in order to retain such a profitable business, and who has more money with which to live a good life anyway, is completely unable to deviate from the pattern already established:

Sie hatten nämlich des Guten zu viel getan und so viel Ware zuweg gebracht, daß ein Teil davon liegen blieb, indes der Meister den vermehrten Erwerb dazu verwendet hatte, das Geschäft, als es auf dem Gipfelpunkt stand, um so rascher rückwärts zu bringen, und ein solch lustiges Leben führte, daß er bald doppelt so viel Schulden hatte als er einnahm. Daher waren ihm die Gesellen, so fleißig und enthaltsam sie auch waren, plötzlich eine überflüßige Last. (223)

The comb-makers are thus able to read the signs and to know with certainty what is to happen next, when the 'Meister' tells them he no longer needs all of them: '...denn die Ankündigung des Meisters war ein sicheres Zeichen, daß er es nicht lange mehr treiben und das Kammfabrikchen endlich wieder käuflich würde' (223). A similar picture, but on a larger scale, is painted when the Seldwylans devote themselves wholeheartedly to the enjoyment of the spectacle of the race. As the suffering of the comb-makers becomes more apparent, the reader begins to find the situation less and less funny. Not so the Seldwylans, who are once more completely unidirectional:

Sie weinten, schluchzten und heulten wie Kinder und schrieen in unsäglicher Beklemmung: 'O Gott! lass los! Du lieber Heiland, lass los, Jobst! lass los, Fridolin! lass los, du Satan!' Dazwischen schlugen sie sich fleißig auf die Hände, kamen aber immer um ein weniges vorwärts. Hut und Stock hatten sie verloren, zwei Buben trugen dieselben, die Hüte auf die Stöcke gesteckt, voran, und hinter ihnen her wälzte sich der tobende Haufen; alle Fenster waren von der Damenwelt besetzt, welche ihr silbernes Gelächter in die unten tosende Brandung warf, und seit langer Zeit war man nicht mehr so fröhlich gestimmt gewesen in dieser Stadt. Das rauschende Vergnügen schmeckte den Bewohnern so gut, daß kein Mensch den zwei Ringenden ihr Ziel zeigte, des Meisters Haus, an welchem sie endlich angelangt. (245–6)

No new development will make the Seldwylans deviate from their goal, their immediate amusement; they pursue that goal relentlessly and without compassion.

Already, we can see that the story's thematic exploration has become complex; for while in one sense the comb-makers and Seldwylans are opposed as the archetypes of a narrow exclusive aim on the one hand, and aimlessness on the other, there is another sense in which both are just as rigidly set in a pattern of pursuing

one thing to the exclusion of all else. But while the comb-makers
sacrifice the present to one single long term goal, the Seldwylans
sacrifice the future to their present enjoyment, whatever the
source of that enjoyment, and whatever its eventual cost to
themselves and others.

This double aspect of the Seldwylans is displayed by the other
characters of the story too: for even Jobst, the most rigid of the
three, has a side to him that is essentially aimless. He spends all
his leisure time doing nonsensical things:

Entschloss er sich aber zu einem Spaziergang, so putzte er sich eine oder zwei
Stunden lang peinlich heraus, nahm sein Spazierstöckchen und wandelte steif
ein wenig vors Tor, wo er demütig und langweilig herumstand und
langweilige Gespräche führte mit andern Herumständern, die auch nichts
Besseres zu tun wußten, etwa alte arme Seldwyler, welche nicht mehr ins
Wirtshaus gehen konnten. Mit solchen stellte er sich dann gern vor ein im
Bau begriffenes Haus, vor ein Saatfeld, vor einen wetterbeschädigten
Apfelbaum oder vor eine neue Zwirnfabrik und düftelte auf das angelegent-
lichste über diese Dinge, deren Zweckmäßigkeit und den Kostenpunkt, über
die Jahrshoffnungen und den Stand der Feldfrüchte, von was allem er nicht
den Teufel verstand. Es war ihm auch nicht darum zu tun; aber die Zeit
verging ihm so auf die billigste und kurzweiligste Weise nach seiner Art,
und die alten Leute nannten ihn nur den artigen und vernünftigen Sachsen,
denn sie verstanden auch nichts. (204)

The contrast between the pointless rambling conversations of
Jobst and his singleminded pursuit of the main idea in his life may
seem strange, but it is thematically the whole point; it raises the
question of the status of Jobst's goal. It is not Jobst's intention to
achieve his goal in order to enjoy his life – he does not know how
to, and does not care to. The goal is something which exists *per se*
for him, and the pursuit of it is what is important in his life. This
pursuit becomes a physical (though still symbolic) race at the end
of the story, and in its being symbolic of the larger issue of the
three men's pursuit of their goal it is able to embody some very
subtle observations on that pursuit. For since Züs has already
decided to marry Dietrich, the race is literally pointless; Dietrich
wins the race by opting out of it; and Jobst and Fridolin having
come to their by now pointless 'Ziel' fail to recognise it anyway!

All of this reflects on the value of the goal, and when Dietrich, having achieved it, is given no happiness by it, we cannot be surprised; that was not the point of the goal. It is clear that Jobst, being even more committed to it than Dietrich, would be even more unhappy to achieve it, and be condemned to a life of 'langweilige Gespräche'. It is evidently dangerous to achieve one's ambitions too completely, though safeguards exist against this happening. To have the organising principle in one's life removed, on the other hand, is fatal for Jobst, and yet he dies with his illusion still intact. Fridolin's commitment to his goal is only slightly less than Jobst's, but the difference is sufficient to allow him to survive. No longer, however, can he expose himself to the suffering of building his life on an aim which may be removed from him, and the only solution for him is to adopt the way of life of the Seldwylans – an aimless life which strives for nothing.

With Dietrich, the role of flexibility and ingenuity comes into the story, for he wins by changing direction, something impossible for his more rigid companions. It is Dietrich who first introduces Züs into the race, and he who eventually wins by marrying her. So far, he appears to be superior to the others in human terms; he is more intelligent, more adaptable. And yet, in another respect, he comes off badly in comparison with the other two. Jobst's narrowness made him both innocent and harmless. His somersaults of joy as he finds himself alone in the bed are all 'in harmloser Lust' (209), and no one, even during his 'langweilige Gespräche', finds him obnoxious. But Dietrich uses and exploits people. His gaining an initial advantage by the introduction of Züs is essentially an exploitation of her, and that pattern continues to the end, becoming intensified to the point where he shrewdly and coldly exploits Züs' femininity. To be sure, she is trying to do exactly the same kind of thing to him, just as ruthlessly, and the resulting mutual exploitation is a grotesque travesty of a human love relationship. Throughout this scene Dietrich's ingenuity is what is stressed, not any feeling for Züs; it is his 'Unternehmungsgeist', and her shortsightedness, which enable him to succeed (243). Nonetheless, he is appropriately punished, as the

narrator makes clear in the last sentence of the story, by simply
being married to Züs; after all, it was a great mistake to try to
exploit one whose whole way of life is an exploitation of others
for her own purposes.

Züs is a sinister figure and in many ways the centre of the story.
She also can be seen in two different ways; on the one hand, she
is the opposite of the comb-makers in being the ultimate example
of aimlessness both in her conversation and in her collection of
things, without ability to discriminate or to keep the thread of any
idea for long. But scarcely beneath the surface of all this is its
underlying point: self-aggrandisement of a completely indiscriminate kind is the aim which rules her life. She collects things
and people without thought of their usefulness in order to aug-
ment what she holds, and so to increase her own stature, to grow
larger. Everything that comes into her hands is carefully hoarded,
with nothing being allowed to slip out of them again:

Sie besaß noch alle ihre Schulbücher seit vielen Jahren her und hatte auch
nicht eines verloren, so wie sie auch noch die ganze kleine Gelehrsamkeit im
Gedächtnis trug, und sie wußte noch den Katechismus auswendig, wie das
Deklinierbuch, das Rechenbuch, wie das Geographiebuch, die biblische
Geschichte und die weltlichen Lesebücher. (216)

Likewise, all the facts that she has ever known or read are all
possessions to be retained in her head, and her collection of
objects is doubly locked away: 'Dies alles war in der lackierten
Lade enthalten, wohl verschlossen, und diese war wiederum in
einem alten Nußbaumschrank aufgehoben, dessen Schlüßel die
Züs Bünzlin allfort in der Tasche trug' (214). Züs' collection of
objects conveys at once both patternlessness and patterns; for
while on one level the indiscriminate hoarding is conveyed by
gold and silver objects being side by side with 'ein Endchen
Marderdreck' (214), there is also in the many miniature things a
suggestion of Züs, witch-like, reducing everything in size in order
to lock it away in her cupboard. This reduction of things in order
to control them certainly seems consistent with her attitude to
people, as Dietrich had to learn, for eventually she 'regierte und

unterdrückte ihn' (247) just as she had always seemed to reduce the stature of her former three admirers, the 'Barbiergeselle', the 'Zeugschmiedgeselle', and the 'Buchbindergeselle', in order to keep them subservient to her. A related pattern in her objects emerges from the special emphasis that is placed on the things given her by the first two admirers and which Züs made special efforts to keep, in the first case by insisting that it was a pledge for a sum of money lent by her, in the second by going to court. It is not difficult to see why they are important objects to her, for the first is 'ein Schnepper zum Aderlaßen' (214), the second 'ein blanker kleiner Gewürzmörser' (215). Again, these objects are suggestive of her treatment of the people with whom she comes into contact: they are crushed and ground up in the one image, and sucked dry in the other.[1] Another sinister image of her dealings with other people is provided later by the narrator's likening her to a kind of one man band, which reduces the comb-makers to instruments that she manipulates:

> Jobst und Fridolin drängten sich hastig herbei und streckten ihre Beine aus; Züs ließ dem Schwaben die eine Hand, gab Jobsten die andere und berührte mit den Füßen Fridolins Stiefelsohlen, während sie mit dem Angesicht einen nach dem andern der Reihe nach anlächelte. So gibt es Virtuosen, welche viele Instrumente zugleich spielen, auf dem Kopfe ein Glockenspiel schütteln, mit dem Munde die Panspfeife blasen, mit den Händen die Gitarre spielen, mit den Knieen die Zimbel schlagen, mit dem Fuß den Dreiangel und mit dem Ellbogen eine Trommel, die ihnen auf dem Rücken hängt. (239–40)

Züs is of course overjoyed to add the three to her possessions: 'noch nie hatte sie mehrere Verehrer auf einmal beseßen' (221), and shows no inclination to choose among them until this is

---

[1] Jennings (p. 12) first noted the suggestion of vampirism contained in Züs' 'blood-letting equipment'. Pregel doubts Jennings' view: 'Aber das erste Verhältnis der Züs zu einem Manne wird nur also eine Episode unter anderen berichtet, und der Aderlaß-schnepper ist ein Andenken neben anderen. Das alles erhält kein episches Gewicht, nichts davon taucht im Verlauf der Novelle später wieder auf. Der Züs fehlen sowohl die äußeren Merkmale einer grotesken Erscheinung wie das bannende einer Zauber-macht' (p. 341). Pregel misses the related 'Mörserchen', and the emphasis given both instruments by Züs' determined retention of them, as well as how the theme of exploitation and grinding down dominates her relations with all her suitors, present and past.

forced upon her; before they leave her she does not miss the opportunity to indulge her passion for self-magnification (the counterpart of her miniature possessions) by proliferating images of herself in her and their imaginations:

Nehmet euch jeder ein Beispiel an mir und denket euch, jeder wäre von drei gleich werten Jungfrauen umblühet, die sein begehrten, und er könnte sich um deswillen zu keiner hinneigen und gar keine bekommen! Stellt euch doch recht lebhaft vor, um jeden von euch buhleten drei Jungfern Bünzlin und säßen so um euch her, gekleidet wie ich und von gleichem Ansehen, so daß ich gleichsam verneunfacht hier vorhanden wäre und euch von allen Seiten anblickte und nach euch schmachtete! Tut ihr dies? (233)

In the last analysis, everything which Züs does has only one aim, self-inflation, whether it be in contemplating her possessions, parading her knowledge, or grinding up and reducing other people; she can appear to be straying from the point and aimless only because her dominant aim is so all-pervasive. Just as in the case with the Seldwylans, there seems to be a contrast of the comb-makers and Züs as between rigid aims and aimlessness; but on closer inspection the aims of Züs (like those of the Seldwylans) turn out to be just as strong a factor in everything she does. The only really aimless behaviour in the whole story, paradoxically, is that of Jobst, in his boring conversations, and in other things he does when not working. But a real and this time irreducible contrast between Jobst and Fridolin, on the one hand, and Züs and the Seldwylans, on the other, is that the former are quite harmless to other people, while the latter are capable of using others cruelly for their own purposes.

It is as this last contrast starts to become clear that the comb-makers begin to gain ground in the narrator's sympathy; during the course of the story they are treated first as animals, but gradually come to be regarded as human beings after all. At the opening of the story occurs the general view of them as embody-ing 'blutlose Gerechtigkeit' (201), and soon the narrator begins the long sequence of animal images used to characterise the three:

Einsmals kam aber ein ordentlicher und sanfter Geselle angereist aus irgend einem der sächsischen Lande, der fügte sich in alles, arbeitete wie ein Tierlein und war nicht zu vertreiben, so daß er zuletzt ein bleibender Hausrat wurde in dem Geschäft und mehrmals den Meister wechseln sah, da es die Jahre her gerade etwas stürmischer herging als sonst. (203)

For some time, such images recur with persistence, e.g., Jobst is a 'Schweinigel' (204), 'wurmisierte er noch ein Weilchen in der Kammer herum' (205), and is like 'ein Fisch im Wasser' (209); Fridolin looks 'wie ein Esel' (211), and the newcomer Dietrich is regarded by the other two 'wie zwei Löwen ein Äffchen, mit dem sie spielen' (211). The implications of these images are stated quite baldly when the narrator says that Jobst's plan to become the 'Meister' is an inhuman one: 'Aber das Unmenschliche an diesem so stillen und friedfertigen Plan war nur, daß Jobst ihn überhaupt gefasst hatte' (206). The early part of the story in general regards the comb-makers as less than human in their rigid adherence to a plan of such a life-impoverishing kind, and as not even qualifying for categorisation among the higher animals:

Auf alle Punkte der Erde sind solche Gerechte hingestreut, die aus keinem andern Grunde sich dahin verkrümmelten, als weil sie zufällig an ein Saugeröhrchen des guten Auskommens gerieten, und sie saugen still daran ohne Heimweh nach dem alten, ohne Liebe zu dem neuen Lande, ohne einen Blick in die Weite und ohne einen für die Nähe, und gleichen daher weniger dem freien Menschen als jenen niederen Organismen, wunderlichen Tierchen und Pflanzensamen, die durch Luft und Wasser an die zufällige Stätte ihres Gedeihens getragen worden. (207)

The motif of ecology introduced here has importance beyond the mere characterisation of Jobst as an animal. It provides the terms in which humanness is to be thought of. At the one end of the scale is the amoeba-like creature with its very simple needs, while humanness consists in the increase in the complexity of the demands made by human beings on their environment. By this standard Jobst is subhuman. When Jobst wakes early on the morning of the race, the 'Wanze' (228–9) which had hibernated beneath the fresh blue paint is another explicit ecological symbol, this time of the comb-makers having to leave the comfortable niche in which they have been in a semi-conscious state for so long. Further, subtle ecological touches in this early part of the story can be seen in Jobst's thriving in an environment containing other 'Gesellen' who give him 'Rippenstöße' (209) in the narrow bed, but being so upset that he cannot sleep because the next one to arrive sleeps as quietly as he usually does; already he realises that they are two of a kind, unable to survive together for long in the same place because of their identical needs. Their weapon of aggression against each other is, characteristically, patience; they are 'beflissen, einander aus dem Bett und dem Haus hinaus zu dulden' (212). But here something interesting begins to emerge, for at last the comb-makers in their competition for the coveted little niche no longer seem bloodless, free of all human feelings and passions, or like vegetables:

Aber dies war ein strenges Leben für die armen Kammacher; so kühl sie von Gemüt waren, gab es doch, seit einmal ein Weib im Spiele, ganz ungewohnte Erregungen der Eifersucht, der Besorgnis, der Furcht und der Hoffnung; sie rieben sich in Arbeit und Sparsamkeit beinahe auf und magerten sichtlich ab; sie wurden schwermütig... (222)

Here they begin to look like ordinary human beings, and for that reason begin too to earn the sympathy of the narrator in his calling them 'die armen Kammacher'. Their fears break out in a dream from which all three awake in terror: 'Sie glaubten, völlig erwachend, der Teufel wolle sie holen, oder es seien Räuber in die Kammer gebrochen; sie sprangen schreiend auf... Zitternd vor Furcht, Groll und Scham zugleich krochen sie endlich wieder ins Bett und lagen lautlos nebeneinander bis zum Morgen' (222–3). This attribution to the comb-makers of normal human emotions increases until it evokes from the narrator an expression almost of incredulity: '...denn die äußerste Lage der Dinge, der schöne Frühlingstag, der ihren Auszug beschien, und Züsis Putz mischten in ihre gespannten Empfindungen fast etwas von dem, was man wirklich Liebe nennt' (231). It is almost as if he were surprised to find that he was compelled to describe the comb-makers in human terms, so inhuman did they look earlier. From the very moment of their coming together in the same room, however, the comb-makers had appeared human above all in their pathetic dependence on an ideal, however absurd that ideal might seem. It was when they first appeared frightened and vulnerable that they no longer seemed like animals or automatons; and interestingly enough, from this point of the story the narrator transfers the animal imagery largely to Züs, who comes to seem less feeling or comprehending, in fact less human than they.

When Jobst's remark that he 'konnte nie ein Tierlein leiden sehen' (235) begins a competition between the three as to who is most loved by animals, Züs breaks in to say that she too is well-loved by them, but the mention of animals touches off one of her rambling lists of facts about them:

Der Affe ist ein menschenähnliches Wesen und tut alles, was er die Menschen tun sieht, und der Papagei versteht unsere Sprache und plaudert mit uns wie ein Alter! Selbst die Schlangen lassen sich zähmen und tanzen auf der Spitze ihres Schwanzes; das Krokodil weint menschliche Tränen und wird von den Bürgern dort geachtet und verschont. (236–7)

There is much here that refers conspicuously to Züs herself; *she* reproduces, parrot-like, everything which she has read or heard, without understanding. In a subtle touch, Keller makes her mis-report the abilities of parrots; they can of course reproduce human speech, but not intelligently, a distinction which might well escape one such as Züs. The monkey who is like a human being but can only imitate what human beings do carries that theme further; the crocodile's apparent display of human emotion, underneath which is of course a lack of any, is comparable to Züs again, while the notion of a tame snake seems also not irrelevant to her. In case we are in any doubt as to the import of these references to animals, Züs closes the subject with an explicit statement relating them to herself:

Was aber mein Verhältnis zu ihnen betrifft, so ist dies zu bemerken: Die Katze ist ein schlaues und listiges Tier und ist daher nur schlauen und listigen Menschen anhänglich; die Taube aber ist ein Sinnbild der Unschuld und Einfalt und kann sich nur von einfältigen, schuldlosen Seelen angezogen fühlen. Da mir nun Katzen und Tauben anhänglich sind, so folgt hieraus, daß ich klug und einfältig, schlau und unschuldig zugleich bin, wie es denn auch heißt: Seid klug wie die Schlangen und einfältig wie die Tauben! Auf

diese Weise können wir allerdings die Tiere und ihr Verhältnis zu uns
würdigen und manches daraus lernen, wenn wir die Sache recht zu betrachten
wissen. (237–8)

After this, there is no longer any doubt that the animal imagery
refers primarily to Züs herself. We may be sure, too, that her
criticism of the flowers around her for being 'unwissend und
geistlose Geschöpfe' has the effect of questioning whether she is
in any way superior to the vegetable world, a point which had
until now been made against the comb-makers:

Wie viele Blumen stehen hier um uns herum, von allen Arten, die der
Frühling hervorbringt, besonders die gelben Schlüsselblumen, welche einen
wohlschmeckenden und gesunden Tee geben; aber sind sie gerecht oder
arbeitsam? sparsam, vorsichtig und geschickt zu klugen und lehrreichen
Gedanken? Nein, es sind unwissende und geistlose Geschöpfe, unbeseelt und
vernunftlos vergeuden sie ihre Zeit, und so schön sie sind, wird ein totes Heu
daraus, während wir in unserer Tugend ihnen so weit überlegen sind und
ihnen wahrlich an Zier der Gestalt nichts nachgeben; denn Gott hat uns nach
seinem Bilde geschaffen und uns seinen göttlichen Odem eingeblasen. (232)

But not only do these passages now link Züs, rather than the
comb-makers, with the animal and vegetable imagery; they tend
also to change the notion of what it is that distinguishes human
beings from other forms of life. Previously, this difference was
found in relative complexity of needs; now the emphasis is more
on feeling and understanding as marks of humanness.

The ending of the story, in which Züs and Dietrich embrace
and resolve to marry, might well have served to show the emergence of the essential humanity of the two, especially in Züs' case,
since she has seemed to turn away from her earlier strict calculation of her personal financial advantage to the more human motive
of feeling attracted to Dietrich. But the narrator makes quite sure
that the situation will not enhance her stature as a human being.
From the beginning there is an unscrupulous battle of wits
between the two: 'Züs schmunzelte falsch und freundlich,
Dietrich schmunzelte schlau und süßlich' (239). And as Dietrich
succeeds, the narrator leaves us in no doubt that he does so by

taking up Züs' game of ruthlessly exploiting human emotions and outmanoeuvring her in it, not through his calling forth in her an answer to a genuine feeling of love:

> Züs [verlor] endlich den Kompaß, als ein Wesen, dessen Gedanken am Ende doch so kurz sind als seine Sinne; ihr Herz krabbelte so ängstlich und wehrlos wie ein Käfer, der auf dem Rücken liegt, und Dietrich besiegte es in jeder Weise. Sie hatte ihn in dies Dickicht verlockt, um ihn zu verraten, und war im Handumdrehen von dem Schwäbchen erobert; dies geschah nicht, weil sie etwa eine besonders verliebte Person war, sondern weil sie als eine kurze Natur trotz aller eingebildeten Weisheit doch nicht über ihre eigene Nase wegsah. (243)

The animal image here again relegates Züs to a much lower form of life, just as among the comb-makers only her eventual husband Dietrich had been compared to an animal during their outing; when Züs had sighed at him, 'sein Herz hüpfte wie ein Häschen im Weißkohl' (242).

While Züs and Dietrich are thus being devalued by the narrator, Jobst and Fridolin are treated in the opposite way; they ascend from their former subhuman status to become only too human.[1] The narrator gives them his sympathy completely in their suffering, which is the more pathetic in that we already know how pointless it is, as he tells us that 'dicke Tränen rollten den armen Männern über die Gesichter' (244). Now the narrator refers to them as both 'gerecht und ehrbar', no longer merely as 'gerecht', and as 'die zwei armen Gesellen' (245) while they run on amid the dreadful laughter of the crowd.[2] The ending of the story is dominated not by the marriage of Züs and Dietrich, but by the other two being 'halbtot vor Scham, Mattigkeit und Ärger', by the despairing thoughts of 'die beiden armen Teufel',

---

[1] Contrast Klein's view of the relative value in the story of the comb-makers and the Seldwylans: 'Die drei Kammacher heben sich unvorteilhaft gegen ihn [Seldwyla] ab', and 'Es ist eine Bosheit Kellers, daß die Kammacher keine Schweizer sind; er verspottet die deutsche Arbeitswütigkeit. Der wenigst Dumme von den Dummen ist der Schwabe, der dem Alemannen am nächsten steht' (pp. 308–9). Both statements underestimate the change which takes place towards the story's end.

[2] Pregel views the narrator differently: 'In der Kammacher-Novelle lassen sich die Meinungen des Erzählers nicht relativieren, die eingenommene Haltung ist fest und klar, zum Teil sogar absolut' (p. 344).

at which 'wollte ihnen das Herz brechen' (246–7), and finally by the fates of first Jobst and then Fridolin: 'Ganz schwermütig zog er vor Tag wieder aus der Stadt und hing sich an der Stelle, wo sie alle gestern geseßen, an einen Baum. Als der Bayer eine Stunde später da vorüberkam und ihn erblickte, fasste ihn ein solches Entsetzen, dass er wie wahnsinning davonrannte...' (247). The whole race is suddenly a harrowing picture of very human suffering.[1]

Over the last half of the story even the trivial goals which the comb-makers had set themselves are gradually granted some dignity by the narrator; their longed-for position as 'Meister' is 'ein himmlisches Jerusalem' (223), the room they sleep in a 'Paradies' (228), and the reward for the race is a 'Palme' (225). These evaluations are evidently those of the comb-makers, with the narrator reporting from their perspective; yet even by making us see how the comb-makers feel about their goals, the narrator raises the question of the quality of their involvement in those goals, where previously he had only spoken dismissively of them. More importantly, these are the first examples of a biblical motif that becomes at the end of the story a means of making the sufferings of Jobst and Fridolin representative of the suffering of humanity, and which marks the endpoint of the development of the narrator's attitudes away from his regarding them as inhuman. Through a number of motifs, the combination of which may well appear bizarre, the end of the story shows many echoes of the story of Christ. There is a kind of last meal together; a time in the wilderness; the cheering crowd whose good humour gives way to cruel taunting; and the triumphal entry into the town followed by a lonely death outside it.

From the standpoint of the opening paragraph of *Die drei gerechten Kammacher*, it would certainly seem odd that there should now appear these overtones of the death of Christ in the death of Jobst. But this is because Keller, though using the convention of the narrator who feels free to comment and judge what

---

[1] Klein's view of the tone at the end of the story differs from my own: 'Das lächerliche Ereignis ist der Wettlauf' (p. 308).

is happening, does not use that convention to offer an interpretation of his story at its very beginning, but instead to register an initial rather superficial view which then develops in a different direction as the story forces it to do so. And so during the course of this story which had at first seemed to be a light-weight anecdote poking fun at some caricatured and subhuman characters, Keller has gradually introduced a serious undertone which at the end comes fully to the surface. Initially, his narrow-minded comb-makers had seemed to fall short of an ideal of humanity which was essentially concerned with a breadth of horizon, a complexity of response to the world, and a perspective on life which produced, among other things, the good humour of the Seldwylans. But gradually, the notion of being human has changed, until at the end it is not narrowness but unfeelingness and cruelty which are most obviously men's worst side, a standard by which the Seldwylans, Züs and to a lesser extent Dietrich are now the despised characters. On the other hand, it is in their suffering that men seem most human, and this is what can make his eccentric caricatures suddenly so typical of humanity that they can evoke Jesus Christ, the archetype of all sufferers. Keller's framework of a comic anecdote is a vehicle for a serious underlying theme which emerges in a tragic form only at the end; the apparently uncontrolled and easy-going narrative was in fact a very careful and subtle study of the way people necessarily live by their aims, and of the disasters which befall them both in their achieving and in their failing to achieve the arbitrary goals which are their guiding stars.

7. STORM: 'DER SCHIMMELREITER'

The narrative framework of Storm's *Der Schimmelreiter*[1] is notoriously complex, and involves at least four visible or implied story-tellers; but though some recent criticism of Storm's narrative technique has been very interesting, it is surprising that no detailed examination of the narrative framework of his most popular Novelle has yet appeared.[2] The brief and undeveloped remarks on the question to be found in criticism of the *Schimmelreiter* do not generally consider it to be an important aspect of the story, and at best think of it as a technical matter which is unimportant from an interpretative point of view. Burroughs says that here 'Storm elaborates his favourite technical device', but that it is unimportant and quickly forgotten as the story moves

[1] References are to *Theodor Storms Sämtliche Werke in acht Bänden*, ed. A. Köster (Leipzig, 1920), VII, 252–377. Most of this chapter has already appeared as 'Narration in Storm's *Der Schimmelreiter*', in *Germanic Review*, XLIV (1969), 21–30. There are separate essays by J. C. Blankenagel, 'Tragic Guilt in Storm's *Schimmelreiter*', *German Quarterly*, XXV (1952), 170–81; W. Silz, 'Theodor Storm's *Schimmelreiter*', *Publications of the Modern Language Association of America*, LXI (1946), 762–83, much of which was reprinted as 'Storm, *Der Schimmelreiter*', in his *Realism and Reality*, pp. 117–36; A. Burchard, 'Theodor Storms *Schimmelreiter*. Ein Mythos im Werden', *Antaios*, II (1960–1), 456–69; L. Wittmann, 'Theodor Storm: *Der Schimmelreiter*', in *Deutsche Novellen des 19. Jahrhunderts. Interpretationen zu Storm und Keller* (Frankfurt a. Main, 1961), pp. 50–92; E. Loeb, 'Faust ohne Transzendenz: Theodor Storm's *Schimmelreiter*', in *Studies in Germanic Languages and Literatures. In memory of Fred O. Nolte.* (St. Louis, 1963), pp. 121–32; J. Hermand, 'Hauke Haien. Kritik oder Ideal des gründerzeitlichen Übermenschen?', *Wirkendes Wort*, XV (1965), 45–50; D. S. Artiss, 'Bird Motif and Myth in Theodor Storm's *Schimmelreiter*', *Seminar*, IV (1968), 1–16. I find Silz's essay the best of these by far.

[2] Two valuable books on Storm's narrative art have appeared recently: C. A. Bernd, *Theodor Storm's Craft of Fiction. The Torment of a Narrator*, 2nd ed. (Chapel Hill, 1966; 1st ed. 1963); and E. A. McCormick, *Theodor Storm's Novellen. Essays on Literary Technique* (Chapel Hill, 1964). Both authors wisely prefer to conduct a searching analysis of a few selected Novellen, rather than a more superficial survey of his whole oeuvre; in neither case is *Der Schimmelreiter* one of the Novellen selected for this treatment. Bernd, however, includes brief, but perceptive remarks on the story in his 'Das Verhältnis von erlittenem und überwundenem Vergänglichkeitsgefühl in Theodor Storms Erzählhaltung', *Schriften der Theodor Storm Gesellschaft*, X (1961), 32–8. Even R. M. Browning's 'Association and Disassociation in Storm's Novellen: A Study on the Meaning of the Frame', *Publications of the Modern Language Association of America*, LXVI (1951), 381–404, contains less than a page on *Der Schimmelreiter*.

on,[1] while another common view of the framework is that it is designed to achieve greater objectivity and credibility. Mainland[2] has recently sharply and convincingly criticised the view that this is in fact achieved by Storm's framework; he has pointed out that once we accept the convention of fiction, as we must, we do not need such artificial props as the narrator's telling us that he has not made up the story by himself, but that he was given it by someone else who assured him it was true. Mainland is surely right; the need to accept the fictional convention is not lessened by this device.

Discussion of the meaning of the story has almost invariably been carried on without reference to narrative perspective; Hauke's character is discussed as though it were given to us directly, and not indirectly through a number of different speakers. Take, for example, a recent comment by Schumann: 'Hauke Haien überragt seine Mitmenschen. Er ist "ihnen um Kopfeslänge überwachsen", – Storm scheut sich nicht, den Vergleich mit Sokrates und Christus anzubringen – ...'[3] But this is not *Storm*'s view of Hauke, it is the schoolmaster's, and so it cannot even be attributed to 'der Erzähler' as Hermand[4] does.

[1] E. H. Burroughs (ed.) *Der Schimmelreiter, by Theodor Storm* (London, 1953), p. xiii. Burroughs somewhat inconsistently goes on to say that there are interruptions by the schoolmaster which serve as 'breathing space', i.e. the frame is apparently not forgotten after all.

[2] W. Mainland, 'Theodor Storm', in *German Men of Letters*, ed. Alex Natan (London, 1961), p. 162. To be sure, Mainland condemns the framework in general ('the subtlety of the device is suspect') because he does not consider any other view of its function than that which he criticises. (Cf. Bernd's comments, p. 132.) I do not follow him in this, as is evident from the rest of my argument. But in my view he performs a great service in demonstrating the inadequacy of this very common view of Storm's narrative frameworks.

[3] Cf. his essay on Storm in the collection of essays edited by W. Schumann and J. Gearey entitled *Einführung in die deutsche Literatur* (New York, 1964), p. 291. This view clashes oddly with that stated two pages later, where Schumann notes that the use of two narrators leaves open the boundary between what is credible and what is incredible; it seems that Schumann probably has in mind here only the question of the existence or non-existence of ghosts, and not the wider question of the values of the story. W. J. Lillyman has pointed out to me that even the schoolmaster does not directly compare Hauke with Christ and Socrates, but only the treatment received by the three.

[4] Hermand, p. 46. Hermand views the frame as a technical matter of the author's distancing himself from his 'Stoff'; and Hauke 'soll nicht von nah betrachtet werden, sondern

Silz, writing some time before these two critics, pointed out that the comparison must be taken in the light of the schoolmaster's personal interest in championing the 'Aufklärer' in Hauke.[1] And yet if we take this fact seriously then the whole frame with all its narrators needs to be examined; between us and the 'real' events of the story or the 'real' people there is a broad barrier involving many different perspectives. How do these all affect the view we must take of the meaning of the story? A systematic analysis of the perspectives of the various narrators is unavoidable.

It is a striking feature of the story that it employs a number of devices which, far from making the story more objective and credible, do exactly the reverse: they both render it less credible, and also remove the *need* for us to believe the account which we are given of the life of Hauke Haien. This is done by giving us a series of unreliable narrators. Some of them are unreliable because of their retelling a story from memory after a considerable lapse of time, others because they have a distinct bias and an axe to grind. We first see the story taken back in time by successive narrators, and get a sense of its being handed on from one to the next, with the distortion that this process must involve; the first narrator takes the story back from the date of its composition (1888) to a time 'vor reichlich einem halben Jahrhundert' (252), the second to a time 'im dritten Jahrzehnt unseres Jahrhunderts', and the third (the schoolmaster) another seventy years or more as he begins his narrative with the phrase 'In der Mitte des vorigen Jahrhunderts' (257). But it is made clear that the third narrator is relying on other accounts which he has heard and which have been passed on from one person to the next during the time which has elapsed. At the time of the schoolmaster, it is evidently already a story with a life of its own, with differing versions preferred by different people: 'es ist viel Aberglaube darin, und eine Kunst, es ohne diesen zu erzählen' (257). The three narrators that we see

aus respektvoller Entfernung, durch Rahmen und Historie ins Monumentale gesteigert' (pp. 42–3). The thematic relevance of the frame is largely ignored here, and in fact the frame is by no means full of respect for Hauke.
[1] W. Silz, *Realism and Reality*, p. 118.

are only part of a larger process in which the story has been handed down from one generation to the next. This is the way a legend is made, and we are by virtue of the narrative framework persuaded to view it as such. This will mean, as far as the interpretation of the story goes, that the question of the original basis of the legend (who really was Hauke Haien and what did he do?) is not necessarily all-important; the attitudes of the people who have allowed this original material to become a legend will be woven into it, and will be an important element in themselves. It will also mean, therefore, that categorical statements about Hauke's qualities will be less possible and less useful for criticism of the story than an attempt to investigate such questions as: What is the relationship between this legendary figure and the people for whom he has become a legend? What role does the legend play in their lives?

These questions may be illuminated by reference to the attitudes and biases of the various narrators of the story. The first narrator's attitude consists merely in his having found the story very striking, so that he has not forgotten it after fifty years. From this we gather at least that it will involve important human issues. The first narrator's function is also to add to the blurring process: he tells the story from memory after fifty years, and cannot 'die Wahrheit der Tatsachen verbürgen...' (252), which implies once more that facts will be less important than attitudes. The second narrator appears in the role of the neutral outsider, who can see all sides of the legend. He thinks he sees the ghost; he likes folk-stories with superstition in them (257); yet on the other hand he judges the schoolmaster positively both before and after the story, first with his remark 'Der Alte sah mich mit verständnisvollem Lächeln an' (257) and later with the more direct 'Er scheint mir ein verständiger Mann' (377). His final attitude is noncommittal, and avoids the acceptance or non-acceptance of any of the conflicting views he has heard: 'das muß beschlafen werden!' (377). His importance in the story, therefore, consists in his emphasising that no objective version of the events is possible; though his closing words reassert the one undeniable fact of the story, the continued existence of Hauke's dyke after nearly a century.

The third narrator is the first of them to be a member of the community in which the legend of Hauke Haien has developed. His general bias in Hauke's favour is very clear and his identification with Hauke is brought out in many ways. Silz[1] has pointed out that the physical leitmotif of being 'hager' connects Hauke, his father, wife, and horse. But there is another person who is described as 'ein kleiner hagerer Mann' (256) – the schoolmaster. The identification of the two is further developed by their both being men of book-learning unlike the rest of those who surround them, by their being champions of reason against superstition, by their being devoted to the improvement of their fellow men (even against the wishes of the latter) and by their consequent isolation from their fellows, who view them with suspicion. It is against this background that the schoolmaster's view of Hauke must be seen:

Der Dank, den einstmals Jewe Manners bei den Enkeln seinem Erbauer versprochen hatte, ist, wie Sie gesehen haben, ausgeblieben; denn so ist es, Herr: dem Sokrates gaben sie ein Gift zu trinken, und unsern Herrn Christus schlugen sie an das Kreuz! Das geht in den letzten Zeiten nicht mehr so leicht; aber – einen Gewaltsmenschen oder einen bösen stiernackigen Pfaffen zum Heiligen, oder einen tüchtigen Kerl, nur weil er uns um Kopfeslänge überwachsen war, zum Spuk und Nachtgespenst zu machen – das geht noch alle Tage. (376)

This passage is in praise of people like the schoolmaster, educators and saviours, who aim to improve human life but get no thanks for what they do.

That the story is told by a man who thinks of himself as being in the same category as Hauke, and is therefore distinctly sympathetic to him, is a point which is stressed and developed in the mention of the hypothetical other version of the story by Antje Vollmers. The positions in which this motif occurs are a guide to its importance: Storm makes sure that it occurs both immediately before, and immediately after, the schoolmaster's story. In the former instance, the *Deichgraf* is anxious to tell the traveller-narrator that the schoolmaster will tell the story 'freilich nur in seiner Weise und nicht so richtig, wie zu Haus meine alte Wirtschafterin Antje Vollmers es beschaffen würde' (256); and at the end the schoolmaster himself returns to the issue and says 'Freilich, die Wirtschafterin unseres Deichgrafen würde sie Ihnen anders erzählt haben' (375). The reason for this stress on another version of the story, which the *Deichgraf* even insists would be a more correct one, is not difficult to see; just as the schoolmaster is the counterpart of Hauke, Antje Vollmers as a superstitious old woman of the people is the counterpart of Trin Jans, and it is from Trin Jans' perspective that we could expect the other version to be told. It is not the old, but the young to whom the schoolmaster's version appeals: '"Erzählt, erzählt nur, Schulmeister", riefen ein paar der Jüngeren aus der Gesellschaft', – another motif linking him with Socrates (257).

The two possible versions of the story, then, are separated, and it seems that we are to be given only one of them. But now there are further complications, and the two factors emerge which tend to indicate that we do get elements of Antje Vollmers' version after all. First, it becomes less certain how completely the schoolmaster identifies with Hauke. A motif occurs which gives this relationship more than one dimension when we are told by the *Deichgraf* that the schoolmaster has only remained in this district 'einer verfehlten Brautschaft wegen' (256). In the schoolmaster's life, as in Hauke's, marriage and rise in social position are related, though in both cases in ways which are difficult to assess; and in the schoolmaster's case we must take into account the fact that the source of information is at least mildly hostile to him. Yet what is certain is that the schoolmaster's being involved thematically in Hauke's life in this way is another limitation on the objectivity and credibility of his narrative, and another reason for us to conceive of other versions of the story by less interested parties. But the most interesting thing about this piece of information concerning the schoolmaster is that it can point in both directions. The schoolmaster's engagement was broken, Hauke's was not.

His attitude to this issue in Hauke's life cannot be presumed with certainty to be sympathetic or not. This is the first of a number of pointers to the fact that the schoolmaster's narrative may well be a mixture of attitudes identifying with Hauke, and attitudes which do not. There is a contrast between Hauke's being tall and the schoolmaster's being small, a striking one in view of the latter's spatial metaphor for Hauke's value: he is 'uns um Kopfeslänge überwachsen'. And the schoolmaster, unlike Hauke, has achieved nothing; he has no dyke which will last a century. If, then, the schoolmaster is like Hauke in many ways, Storm takes care to make him an insignificant and unsuccessful version of Hauke. His bias is therefore not likely to be completely in Hauke's favour.

The second and even stronger factor which indicates that the actual narrative is not purely told from a perspective like that of Hauke consists simply in the schoolmaster's agreeing to attempt to tell a compromise version. Before his story he admits that 'es ist viel Aberglaube dazwischen und eine Kunst, es ohne diesen zu erzählen' (257). The traveller-narrator then urges him not to leave out the superstition and reassures him: 'traut mir nur zu, daß ich schon selbst die Spreu vom Weizen sondern werde!' This assurance stresses once more the need to read the story in the light of the narrative framework, and the need to interpret, not merely to accept the version of Hauke and his life given there. The schoolmaster tacitly agrees to do as he is asked: 'Der Alte sah mich mit verständnisvollem Lächeln an: "Nun also!" sagte er.' That the schoolmaster agrees explains the unexpectedness of his final juxtaposition of Hauke to Christ and Socrates, which strikes us as inconsistent with what he has told us: Hauke seemed there to be most unlike either of the two. We must remember that this judgment by the schoolmaster is based on his own version of the story, not the one he has told; and this clash serves to remind us of the status of the actual narrative just as it has ended. Another reason why his narrative cannot exclude superstition lies in its being already a folk-tale; as such it must have been passed on mainly by word of mouth among the people, and it is this repository of superstition which is the schoolmaster's chief source for his story. To the bias of the rationalist narrator, then, a bias which is in any case not inherently consistent, we must add the bias of his anti-rationalist sources; whether or not he wishes that he could cut this bias out, it would be impossible for him to do so completely. We really have not three narrators, but four: the implied fourth is the people of the district.

There are, then, two hypothetical stories of Hauke: that which might have been told by the schoolmaster, if left to himself and if his own life had allowed a more complete identification with Hauke, and the popular version which Antje Vollmers would have given. The former would have been much more, the latter much less, sympathetic to Hauke than the schoolmaster's actual narrative, which contains elements from both. Apart from this distortion by two opposing biases, the narrative is also blurred and eroded by its having been told and retold over a long period of time, a process we see at work in its first two frame narrators. And a result of the whole sequence of narrators is that attention is deflected from the real person, Hauke Haien, onto the more important issue of what he represents in the minds of those who contribute to the survival of the legend. All this is achieved by the narrative framework; it remains to relate this narrative framework to the issues of Hauke's life to come to a more complete interpretation of the story.

It is obviously a misinterpretation of the text either to accept the schoolmaster's final judgment of Hauke, or to abstract the opposite view from his narrative.[1] But it is also misinterpreted if we try to achieve a 'balanced' judgment of Hauke which does

---

[1] Wittmann, for example, interprets the story in a way which is very hostile to Hauke Haien; it is not difficult to do this if all elements hostile to him are abstracted and no others. His attempts to avoid the latter are instructive; he writes 36 pages before coming to the question of the narration, and having already interpreted the story then discusses separately in 3 pages (86–9) 'Die Form der Rahmenerzählung'. This section is almost entirely devoted to the schoolmaster's judgment at the end of the story, difficult to account for on Wittmann's interpretation, and he attempts to show that the schoolmaster must be completely disregarded. But this suggests the rather obvious question: why then does the schoolmaster occur in the story at all? Browning (pp. 402–3) suggests that Storm dissociates himself from Hauke by linking him with the schoolmaster; but this too is a partial and selective view of a situation which is much more complex.

justice to both perspectives. Storm could have achieved this with only one narrator. What he has done instead is to write two contradictory and irresolvable views of Hauke into his story, which cannot be reduced to a compromise between them. To the schoolmaster's juxtaposition of Hauke and Christ there corresponds the people's view that he is in league with the devil.[1] The report of his saving the dog from the cruel superstition of the people is in opposition to that of his killing Trin Jans' cat. We cannot therefore make any statement about what Hauke was really like; we can only recognise two attitudes to a shadowy legendary figure.[2]

The two attitudes to Hauke emerge not only in conflicting views of his personality, but also in different perspectives on the ideas for which he stands. Hauke is, on any interpretation, a lone figure, isolated from his fellow men; but the text shows traces of two different ways of completing the image we have of him. Some aspects of the text show that he is genuinely intellectually superior to others and wishes to use this capacity to help them; he is a born leader, and because of this becomes *Deichgraf*. But other parts of the story make him appear pathetically insecure, ambitious to build a monument to himself, and impatient with and intolerant towards those whom he considers inferior to himself. Hauke's marriage is another factor which must be weighed against his natural abilities when his career is judged; in the strange lack of emphasis in the narrative on any emotional warmth or romance

[1] A view similar to that of Wittman (e.g., p. 72). The opposite attitude to Hauke's place in the story's value system is taken by Loeb, whose rationalistic interpretation is on the same lines as that of the schoolmaster. Both Wittmann and Loeb, in spite of their opposing orientations, tend to see any negative side of Hauke as coming towards the end of the story and so postulate a change in him as a way of dealing with the different attitudes to Hauke. The text, however, has both sides of Hauke from the very beginning.

[2] Cf. Bernd, 'Das Verhältnis von erlittenem und überwundenem Vergänglichkeitsgefühl in Theodor Storms Erzählhaltung', pp. 37–8. Here Bernd also (though for a different purpose and as a result of a different argument) emphasises that the story of Hauke is a 'Volkssage', that two versions of it exist, and that therefore 'das Leben und Lebensglück des Hauke Haien nicht mehr getreu in der Sagenerinnerung aufbewahrt bleiben konnten'. Blankenagel's interpretation of Hauke is a balanced account of one man with good and bad sides to him, as if seeing beyond the prejudices of the narrators to the real Hauke. Significantly, however, he ignores the narrative framework in giving this account. Loeb's Faustian interpretation makes a similar omission.

in his relationship to Elke, and in Hauke's own vulnerability to the suggestion that he became *Deichgraf* by marrying Elke, there is a hint at the marriage being motivated by ambition.

More important, however, than attitudes towards Hauke's personality are those towards what he represents. Once more, two quite different abstractions from the text seem equally possible: on the one hand, he stands for reason, knowledge, and progress as against prejudice, ignorance and refusal to change; on the other hand, he seems to be a force working against nature (including human nature) and upsets its balance with his short-sighted and arbitrary intervention in its ways, misunderstanding it because of his narrow and over-simplified rationalism. Interpretations have, in general, tended to favour the first of these to the detriment of the second; the text, however, balances the two very carefully. Since the first attitude has been stressed most hitherto, I shall begin with the second, and consider these features of the text which convey the attitude that Hauke is against nature, even unnatural.

The people of the district all fear that the dyke is an interference with nature, and that this interference must have bad consequences. By itself this tends to make us sympathetic to Hauke. But Hauke's killing Trin Jans' cat is a detail of the story which works in the opposite direction. Hauke kills birds and usually gives them to the cat. When he finally goes past the cat without giving it the bird he is carrying, the cat attacks him for it. This natural reaction is something which Hauke does not understand or have any sympathy for, and he throttles the cat. Apart from demonstrating his own limitations, he has upset the balance of nature, and also the balance of Trin Jans' life; the cat killed and ate rats which would otherwise have preyed (and now do prey) on Trin Jans' ducks. This disturbance of the ecological system of Trin Jans and her ducks is analogous to his disturbance of the ecological system of sea and people through the dyke. The two even seem to be connected; before the dyke finally collapses, Hauke sees that it has been undermined with mouseholes (357), which harks back once more to his removal of the cat. This episode portrays Hauke as a man whose vision is narrowly turned towards his own goal, without any consideration of the possible side-effects of any of his actions. He introduces a change which in a limited sense seems easy enough, but without realising that this one change will cause a chain of others, and that he is in effect demanding an entire change of system of both the animals and the people. Trin lives at peace with nature and her animals because there is a balance and mutual interdependence between them all. Her animals are part of her way of life, as the old dyke is part of the people's way of life, a domestication of nature of long standing; Hauke has no concept of how much he is disturbing.

The harshest representation of Hauke's attitude to nature is in his shout at the sea and the gulls: '"Ihr könnte nichts Rechtes... so wie die Menschen auch nichts können!"' (261), and in his throwing stones at, and killing the sandpipers (265). The game of 'Eisboseln' also contains an incident which makes Hauke appear as being in opposition to nature. After Hauke has aimed and thrown at the goal, a gull momentarily (289) obscures his throw. The game thus gives a smaller version of the larger action; Hauke has his eye firmly on a distant goal, which is obscured momentarily by a part of the natural scene.[1] His daughter has a tame gull, but she is feeble-minded (263), another detail of the text which opposes nature and intelligence; and at the end of the story (369) Hauke tramples the tame gull because his vision is directed far ahead of him, towards his dyke. Both before and after

[1] There is an echo of this in the frame, as the long wings of the birds brush against the traveller-narrator and his horse (253). Artiss' recent essay on the bird-motif contains interesting material, but his misinterpretation of this episode (Hauke's victory is linked by it with 'the forces of the other world', p. 8) should remind us that the introduction of material from folk-lore does not bring with it an interpretation of the story; on the contrary, it must be strictly subordinated to the thematic structure of the text. Artiss' interpretative comments are mostly limited to the identification of figures in the story (the gulls, crows, cat, dog, bird-wings, kingfisher, osprey, lapwing, and horse) as agents of death, ill omens, messengers from the other world of chaos, representatives of the other demonic world, and so on, and do not justify his claim that 'A closer study of the birds in the story reveals the author's "grand design"' (p. 1). The basis of this view of the story is less to do with the text than with such mystic beliefs as: 'Birds are in a sense at one with the mysterious force which controls the world. They are therefore related to the spheres of infinity and eternity and thus symbolize the two dimensions of space and time' (p. 14).

this Hauke cries '"Vorwärts"' to his horse; his relentless drive forward neither allows him to see the gull, nor to stop after the damage is done. Here, as in the game of 'Eisboseln', the character of Hauke's ambition is symbolised. That eyes are made much of in the story has been shown by Silz,[1] and this must be related to the theme of vision: Hauke sees far, but his vision is narrow. This kind of vision, efficient in one way yet not in another, is analogous to the concept which is frequently used, as Silz[2] also showed, to refer to the intellectual superiority of Hauke: 'rechnen'. There is something insufficient about such a concept, if it is to sum up the intelligence of a human being. It is a bloodless and abstract kind of intelligence, inadequate for dealings with people or nature. Hauke can calculate how much earth a dyke needs in order for it to contain a given amount of water; but the calculation fails to take the mice into account. This significantly small natural species is allowed to show the inadequacy of Hauke's 'rechnen', its over-simplicity and inability to take into account issues other than mechanical ones. The quality of Hauke's intelligence corresponds to descriptions of him, and of his behaviour; lack of fullness characterises all three. He is frequently described as 'hager', whereas the old *Deichgraf* eats well (272), and the newest one is 'besonders stattlich' (255). He is always serious, and cannot easily take part in a dance (291). These details all stress the gulf between him and nature, and the basis of the gulf in his calculating rationality. But this is even more evident in his and Elke's waiting to get married until her father's death; they both here seem bloodless, unnatural and calculating (300). It seems that Hauke expects only reason to govern his own behaviour, and in this context it seems as inappropriate to do so as it did when he killed the cat for its acting on its instincts. The episode of Hauke's killing the cat is also illuminating for his attitude to the people. The people have certain habits, beliefs and customs which are part of their nature, as the cat had a natural set of habits; any plan involving either cat or people must take their natures into account. In both cases Hauke acts in a way which violates those habits and

[1] Silz, pp. 135–6.   [2] Silz, p. 131.

produces a sense of unbearable departure from them; and this leads directly to violent reactions against Hauke. In both cases Hauke himself then acts unreasonably and aggressively because he does not understand what has produced those reactions. Hauke also fails to come to terms with his own nature and limits. He is by nature unable to stand constant opposition and the strain of hard work which he imposes upon himself; and so in addition to fighting the sea and the people, he has to fight his own psychological and physical constitution. Both break down towards the end of the story. He first becomes very ill, and is physically weakened; and then he yields to an instinctive and natural human desire, one which he had disregarded much as he disregarded the cat's and the people's emotions: the need to be liked. His compromise at the end is thus the result of his misjudging himself and his own nature.

Within the narrative which we are given, then, numerous details invite this interpretation of Hauke's limitations. But equally numerous details give us a different version, and either set of details can be ascribed to the elaboration of the story by a teller with a given attitude to it. This other version has been discussed more often by critics and frequently accepted as the attitude of the story in general, and it therefore needs less exposition here. In this view, Hauke is a man who stands for reason against superstition, for progress and a better life. He uses human skill and understanding to tame the elements and provide more living space for the people; and he is successful in that his dyke is still standing almost a century later. His battle with the sea is analogous to his battle with superstition; his lot, like that of any great progressive figure in any society, is to be hated and given no thanks, but his contribution to society remains. His antagonist Ole Peters is shown in a very unpleasant light, and so by implication his enemies are envious, malicious trouble-makers, who mislead the people and stir them up against him, where they would otherwise naturally acclaim him as their leader.

The narrative framework excludes the possibility that we can ask which event really happened, or that we might reduce the story to a consistent one. For the focus of the story is on the life of the community and the legend within it, rather than on the life of the actual Hauke. Reactions to his story have become almost inseparable from it, and the narrative embodies an orderly scheme of these reactions. The reaction of the first narrator is one of fascination with the story of Hauke, which establishes its human significance. The excitement of the first narrator is balanced by the calm and objectivity of the second, whose function is to establish the need for an overall perspective which refuses to identify with either one of the two main judgments of Hauke, and which will accept all impressions of the story without attempting to discount any of them. The function of the new *Deichgraf* at the end of the narrative is largely to allow the second narrator to announce his attitude: 'Das muß beschlafen werden.' These two 'frame' narrators therefore form a complementary pair; through them Storm indicates that his reader is to be engaged by his story, but neutral; excited by it, but objective. The reactions to Hauke's life story of the schoolmaster, and those which would hypothetically emanate from Antje Vollmers, or from the common people, form similarly a complementary pair, though there must be some ambiguity in both. Hauke can be seen as a highly intelligent man, or an inhuman one, as being above the people or against them, as being an innovator or one who destroys. The legendary figure of Hauke is important for the community because he embodies the most challenging idea that any community has to deal with: the idea of change. The idea is double-edged,[1] and Storm's intricate narrative frame enables this to be built into his story.

[1] An interesting feature of the text from this point of view is the setting of the story in the mid-eighteenth century – the 'Aufklärung'. Hermand's emphasis on the contemporary background of Storm's own lifetime is an unnecessary limitation of the story's meaning; the schoolmaster's final judgment of Hauke introduces a broader perspective which cannot be overlooked. Critics who have compared *Der Schimmelreiter* with *Faust*, while they have commonly taken the comparison so far that the great difference between the two works has been obscured, have at least tended to emphasise the human rather than merely historical significance of the story.

8. HAUPTMANN: 'BAHNWÄRTER THIEL

With Hauptmann's *Bahnwärter Thiel*[1] we return to a narrative in which the story-teller neither figures as a character in the story nor presents himself as an identifiable man telling it, but remains as the unidentified epic narrator. His story is, in outline, a fairly simple one, but his descriptions of the settings in which it takes place are often outlandish. The forest, for example, has a strange appearance: 'Die Stämme der Kiefern streckten sich wie bleiches, verwestes Gebein zwischen die Wipfel hinein, die wie grauschwarze Moderschichten auf ihnen lasteten' (62). The moon appears as a 'riesige purpurglühende Kugel' (65), and the sun on a fine Sunday morning has a weird effect on the landscape: 'Die Sonne goß, im Aufgehen gleich einem ungeheuren, blutroten Edelstein funkelnd, wahre Lichtmaßen über den Forst...Von Wipfeln, Stämmen und Gräsern floß der Feuertau. Eine Sintflut von Licht schien über die Erde ausgegoßen' (54). The description of the train is no less grotesque: 'Zwei rote, runde Lichter durchdrangen wie die Glotzaugen eines riesigen Ungetüms die Dunkelheit. Ein blutiger Schein ging von ihnen her, der die Regentropfen in seinem Bereich in Blutstropfen verwandelte. Es war, als fiele ein Blutregen vom Himmel' (53). In fact, the word 'description' fails to do justice to what can more accurately be thought of as the evocation of an apparition. There is clearly a

[1] References are to *Gerhart Hauptmann: Sämtliche Werke*, ed. Hans-Egon Hass (Frankfurt a. Main/Berlin, 1963), VI, 37–67. There are separate essays by M. Ordon, 'Unconscious Contents in Bahnwärter Thiel', *Germanic Review*, XXVI (1951), 223–9; P. Requadt, 'Die Bilderwelt in Gerhart Hauptmanns *Bahnwärter Thiel*', in *Minotaurus. Dichtung unter den Hufen von Staat und Industrie*, ed. A. Döblin (Wiesbaden, 1953), pp. 102–11; W. Silz, 'Hauptmann: *Bahnwärter Thiel*', in *Realism and Reality*, pp. 137–52; B. von Weise, 'Gerhart Hauptmann: *Bahnwärter Thiel*', in *Die deutsche Novelle*, I, 268–83; F. Martini, 'Gerhart Hauptmann: *Bahnwärter Thiel*', in *Das Wagnis der Sprache*, (Stuttgart, 1954), pp. 56–98; W. Zimmermann, 'Gerhart Hauptmann: *Bahnwärter Thiel*', in *Deutsche Prosadichtungen unseres Jahrhunderts, Interpretationen für Lehrende und Lernende*, I (Düsseldorf, 1966), 69–87, first published as *Deutsche Prosadichtungen der Gegenwart*, I (Düsseldorf, 1956), 39–61.

pattern, running through all of these examples, of an idiosyncratic and exaggerated language, and this kind of language is the most interesting and immediately arresting feature of the narration; to consider how it functions in *Bahnwärter Thiel* must surely be an important part of interpreting the story. But oddly enough, critics have often described the narrative as though its most central feature did not exist. Bennett[1] said that this work exhibited 'a detached transcription of reality...the transcription of reality is more meticulous, less artistically elaborated, than is usual with Saar'. This seems remote from Hauptmann's very unreal, and highly elaborate descriptions; yet its general direction is fairly typical. Martini, too, emphasises objective, realistic description:

> Wir müßen wiederholen: dem Realismus der Aufnahme entspricht die Haltung des Erzählers. Er bewahrt die Objektivität der Distanz, er steht dem geschilderten Gegenstande gegenüber, nimmt ihn beobachtend entgegen und verhält sich empfangend zu ihm. Realistisches Erzählen benötigt diesen Abstand des Erzählers...[2]

And so, too, does von Wiese: 'Die liebevolle Beschreibung des Kleinen und Dinglichen erinnert noch an die Prosa des Realismus.'[3] As for the stance of the story-teller, Martini believes that 'Hauptmann wählt den Standpunkt des Zuschauers.'[4]

There is little doubt that these views of the narration in *Bahnwärter Thiel* derive from the literary historian's awareness that the story stands between Realism and Naturalism, rather than from its text; for the text itself will not support the judgment that the narrator is an objective and distanced spectator who transcribes passively received impressions from the outside world, or who describes simply and realistically without any artistic elaboration. To be sure, there is little direct comment by the narrator on the sequence of events, but it would be misleading to note this fact without also noting that he colours his descrip-

---

[1] Bennett, p. 238.   [2] Martini, p. 74.   [3] Von Wiese, p. 268.
[4] Martini, p. 68. Once more, author and narrator are not distinguished.

tions of those events in a highly idiosyncratic way.[1] Nor can the absence of direct comment be thought of as an absence of attitudes on the narrator's part;[2] on the contrary, his attitudes and evaluations are conveyed very strongly by his grotesque descriptions and by his choosing to dwell on and elaborate certain aspects of the events. Selection and emphasis can be just as expressive of attitude as direct comment.

If we conclude that the narrator of *Bahnwärter Thiel* is by no means 'objective', then the next step is to consider his distinctive characteristics and concerns in the story. We have already seen that he often produces strange, exaggerated and unreal descriptions in which, for example, colour is an obtrusive feature. But before considering the place of these passages in the thematic structure of the text, it is necessary to consider in more general terms the way in which the narrator tells his story. It is true that direct comment on and interpretation of the events and characters is not common, but it is not entirely absent; his attribution of 'brutale Leidenschaftlichkeit' to Lene (38), for example, is interpretation and expression of attitude rather than mere description. We are offered the interpretation *ex cathedra*, and thus accept it as fact, but it is no less a conclusion of the narrator for that. Yet for the most part his presence is indeed felt in less direct though scarcely less forceful ways. On the contrary: he exercises control over the narrative in a very blatant way, allowing it to become very obvious that he includes in or omits from his narrative whatever he thinks fit, without regard for the expecta-

---

[1] E.g. von Wiese: 'Jede reflektierende Stellungnahme des Dichters ist vermieden' (p. 268), and Martini: 'Bewußt wird jede subjektive Identifikation mit dem Erzählten, jede direkte oder indirekte Selbstäußerung in ihm vermieden' (p. 65). At another point in his essay, von Wiese writes in a somewhat different vein: '...es geht hier keineswegs um eine beliebige Wirklichkeitsnachahmung, der irgendwo anfängt und irgendwo aufhört, sondern um eine bestimmte Art künstlerischer Verwandlung, die sich zwar an die wirklichen Objekte hält, an die gegenständliche Umwelt oder an psychologisch erfassbare Seelenvorgänge, aber ihnen durch eine bestimmte Weise des Verknüpfens und Wiederholens eine durch das Sicht-und Meßbare weit hinausweisende Bedeutung verleiht' (p. 271). But it is still insufficient to see in this 'Verknüpfen und Wiederholen' the text's only deviation from or development of realism.

[2] Silz (pp. 142–3) points to some of the theoretical inadequacies of the term 'Naturalism' which relate to this point.

tions of the reader; and his manner of telling the story can change abruptly, too. The reader is constantly reminded of his sovereign, almost dictatorial, control over the content and manner of the narrative. Some examples will illustrate this.

At a key point in the story, the narrator changes into the present tense from the preterite which he had used hitherto. But the change occurs in mid-paragraph: 'Thiel keuchte; er mußte sich festhalten, um nicht umzusinken wie ein gefällter Stier. Wahrhaftig, man winkt ihm – "Nein!"' (58). The present tense continues for two more pages, then is replaced by the past once more, again in mid-paragraph: 'Er meint sich zu erwecken; denn es wird ein Traum sein, wie der gestern, sagt er sich. – Vergebens. – Mehr taumelnd als laufend erreichte er sein Häuschen' (60). This might seem an arbitrary use of narratorial control, and yet while in one sense the entrance and exit of the present tense are equally unexpected, not occurring at natural breaks in the narrative, in another sense there is a logic to these transitions; both occur as Thiel is struggling to grasp what is happening to him. The change of tense functions as a switch to an unreal present scene, and we thus experience the whole episode of Tobias' accident in the present tense of what is before Thiel's eyes. Thiel's wondering whether it is all real signals an end to this unreal mode of experience, and a return to the more comfortable world of the story-teller's preterite, with its air of referring to credible past events. While the narrator's moving from one tense to another is definitely a ruthless and sudden shift, it is certainly functional – a point which must be borne in mind when the other examples of his apparently arbitrary procedure are examined. Take his relating the facts of Thiel's first and second marriages, for example; the sequence in which the information is given is again idiosyncratic. We see Thiel alone in church, then together with a wife, then alone again; and only after the last pseudo-fact are we told the important real fact, which would seem to overshadow the mere fact of his being alone in church by a long way: 'An einem der vorangegangen Wochentage hatte die Sterbeglocke geläutet; das war das Ganze' (37). But it is *not* 'das Ganze'; we still know only half the story. Only when Thiel wishes to marry again do we learn, as if by chance, what actually happened. The priest then asks Thiel why he wishes to remarry so quickly, and we are told that Thiel wants someone to look after his son. At last we find out, almost by a chance remark, that Minna died in child-birth, and the child lived (38). Now this withholding of informa-tion and subsequent introduction of it in a curiously accidental way is not indicative of a general tendency to be sparse in the provision of the detail of events; on the contrary, on the first page of the story, just as we are conspicuously not being told how Minna died, or of Thiel's child, we are instead told of his having been hit by objects thrown from the train, at a length which is dispropor-tionate to the brevity of the account of the more important events. Again, a very arbitrary attitude to what deserves a further explanation, and what does not, seems to be shown.

Equally indicative of the narrator's blunt assertion of his prerogative is his brusque beginning of the second section of the story: 'An einem Junimorgen gegen sieben Uhr kam Thiel aus dem Dienst' (42). After the general and somewhat remote charac-ter of the narration up till now, this has an immediate effect, as if to announce through its determined and precise insistence on a definite time, place and occasion: now we are getting down to business! This closing in to definite events gives the impression that the narrator intends to select an important occasion from Thiel's daily life. All narration must be selective; but this narrator makes an issue of his selectivity, and draws our attention to it by his sudden switch from general comments about Thiel's house-hold to this highly specific beginning.

Perspective can change in the same drastic way, as at the end of the story when the narrator stops seeing the whole story from the point of view of Thiel's presence. Throughout the story, for example, he gives us a view of only those actions of Lene which Thiel experiences, the others being hidden from us; now, instead of following Thiel to his murder of Lene and on the last journey through the forest, we switch to the perspective of outsiders: 'Nach Verlauf von einigen Stunden, als die Männer mit der

Kindesleiche zurückkehrten, fanden sie die Haustüre weit offen' (66). We then follow the men in their searching for Thiel and Lene, and so learn of what has happened through a radically different perspective to that chosen by the narrator hitherto.

Even in its style, the story shows the same decisive narratorial control in its alternating between terse, short sentences and long expansive ones; apparently, when the narrator wishes to expand he does, and otherwise the simplest and barest statement of a fact will suffice. The grotesque and unreal descriptions of natural objects fall into this same pattern; they are highly individual visions, in which the uniqueness of the way the narrator sees things is always uppermost.[1]

Taken together, all of this gives a strong impression of the narrator's being ever-present, dominating the narrative with obtrusive decisions and sudden changes in any of its aspects: how much information and of what kind, the balance of generality and detail, and the kind of perspective, style, or imagery. The narrator makes it very obvious that we experience everything through his mediation; though not obtrusively present in the classic manner of the explicitly moralising and interpreting narrator, he is in his own way just as evident, and a presence of which we cannot fail to be conscious. So much, then, for the extent of his presence; but what are the concerns shown in this presence, and how do they contribute to the meaning of the story? The best way into these questions is by means of his descriptions which link Thiel and the train, by showing Thiel in terms reminiscent of the train, and the train in terms reminiscent of Thiel. When describing either Thiel or the train the narrator often shows a sequence of events in which an initial calm is followed by the sudden onrush of a disturbance, which then gives way to a state of quiet once more. The first such description of the train is the fullest portrayal of the pattern. The

---

[1] These highly individual descriptions are on occasion thought of as stylistic defects; e.g., by Martini (p. 96), and by the array of early critics cited, apparently with sympathy, by S. D. Stirk in his introduction to the Blackwell edition of *Bahnwärter Thiel* and *Fasching* (Oxford, 1952), p. xxviii. This is a natural consequence of the assumption that the story is a 'realistic' or 'naturalistic' one; all that will not fit that assumption must be viewed as inconsistency and error.

feeling evoked by this sequence is important for the whole story, and I therefore cite it in full:

Ein dunkler Punkt am Horizonte, da wo die Geleise sich trafen, vergrößerte sich. Von Sekunde zu Sekunde wachsend, schien er doch auf einer Stelle zu stehen. Plötzlich bekam er Bewegung und näherte sich. Durch die Geleise ging ein Vibrieren und Summen, ein rhythmisches Geklirr, ein dumpfes Getöse, das, lauter und lauter werdend, zuletzt den Hufschlägen eines heranbrausenden Reitergeschwaders nicht unähnlich war. Ein Keuchen und Brausen schwoll stoßweise fernher durch die Luft. Dann plötzlich zerriß die Stille. Ein rasendes Tosen und Toben erfüllte den Raum, die Geleise bogen sich, die Erde zitterte – ein starker Luftdruck – eine Wolke von Staub, Dampf und Qualm, und das schwarze, schnaubende Ungetüm war vorüber. So wie sie anwuchsen, starben nach und nach die Geräusche. Der Dunst verzog sich. Zum Punkte eingeschrumpft, schwand der Zug in der Ferne, und das alte heil'ge Schweigen schlug über dem Waldwinkel zusammen. (49–50)

The train begins as 'Punkt', and ends that way, but meantime has built up to a frightening climax of noise, vibration and smoke, to the point where it can not inappropriately be called a monster. Both before and after this frightening apparition there is silence. Now this climactic pattern is very characteristic of Thiel himself.[1] When, for example, he arrives home to find Lene illtreating Tobias, there is the following description of the rise and fall of Thiel's emotions:

Der Wärter fühlte, wie sein Herz in schweren, unregelmäßigen Schlägen ging. Er begann leise zu zittern. Seine Blicke hingen wie abwesend am Boden fest, und die plumpe und harte Hand strich mehrmals ein Büschel naßer

---

[1] Klein's (Geschichte der deutschen Novelle, p. 436) brief and undeveloped comment is certainly to the point here: 'Die Stille und die Stürme des Forstes, die unheimlichen Eindrücke, wenn ein Zug heranbraust – all das ist zugleich Ausdruck von Thiels Seele und Erlebnisweise. Stilles Grübeln und stürmische Erregung wogen ähnlich in ihm auf und ab.' Cf. also Martini: 'Die Antinomie dieser Mächte ist das Symbol der Antimonie in Thiel selbst, in jenem Manne, aus dessen gelassener Ruhe und beseelter, stiller Innerlichkeit die wilde Gewalt vernichtend aufsteigen und ihn selbst zerstören wird' (p. 88). But a systematic development of this idea would necessitate his taking, for example, the later phrase 'spannten sich seine Muskeln' not as the poor attempt at theatrical effect which he believes it to be, but as part of the opposition of tension and relaxation which is to do with the sudden onrush of 'wilde Gewalt', in the train and Thiel. Requadt (pp. 105–6) also notes the connection of Thiel and the train, but thinks of this as showing Thiel's 'Verfallensein an das Maschinenwesen'.

Haare zur Seite, das immer von neuem in die sommersproßige Stirne hineinfiel.

Einen Augenblick drohte es ihn zu überwältigen. Es war ein Krampf, der die Muskeln schwellen machte und die Finger der Hand zur Faust zusammenzog. Es liess nach, und dumpfe Mattigkeit blieb zurück. (46)

The same trembling begins the growing intensity, there is the same climax in a moment when something threatens to overwhelm him, and then the gradual disappearance of the tension. The same thing happens to him again a page later, as he looks at Tobias this time with a more explicit monster inside him which needs restraining: 'Einen Augenblick schien es, als müße er gewaltsam etwas Furchtbares zurückhalten, was in ihm aufstieg; dann legte sich über die gespannten Mienen plötzlich das alte Phlegma, von einem verstohlnen begehrlichen Aufblitzen der Augen seltsam belebt'. (47) This link between Thiel and the train is so well developed that the interpretation of the whole story depends on it. Its details radiate out into the rest of the text; the train becomes a complex symbol of Thiel himself, and even an interpretation of him. When Tobias is hit by the train, for example, Thiel 'reißt sich auf mit gewaltiger Anstrengung. Siene schlaffen Muskeln spannen sich...' (59). This is a subtle allusion to the earlier passage; the tensing of the muscles goes back to the previous occasion on which Thiel was nearly overwhelmed by something rising up within him, with its more explicit suggestion of danger, and so gently suggests the loss of control, the going berserk, which will result in his killing Lene and her child. Yet it also refers forward, for when the train starts off again it too 'stößt weiße, zischende Dämpfe aus ihren Zylindern und streckt ihre eiserne Sehnen' (60).

This anatomical and temperamental analogy between the two is extended into their being creatures of habit, governed by the strictest timetable. The train arrives on time, strictly according to the clock, but Thiel's life is no less ruled by time and order. Here is the point of the narrator's strangely incomplete and haphazard introduction of the events of Thiel's marriages. There is a logic to this haphazardness after all, for the whole of the first page of the story behaves as if Thiel were a mechanical thing that appeared at a certain place at a recurring time, just as his trains reach his part of the line at the same time each day. He is in church at exactly the same time, 'allsonntäglich' each week, like a train in a station. And just as Thiel's experience of the train is of things which he sees in the same place at the same time, irrespective of what has happened to them in the meantime, so we experience Thiel first of all in the same way; we wait for him to arrive week by week at the church, and only then learn what has happened since his last arrival there. The story's opening words refer to Thiel's appearance in church every Sunday as if reading from his timetable.[1] This is followed up by constant references to the rigidity of his behaviour; a 'peinlich gepflegte Uhr' (60) is among his few possessions, he is described as 'militärisch gescheitelt' (37) and as moving 'mit langsamem, fast militärisch steifem Schritt' (64), does things mechanically (48 and 58), and even his conversations with his little son are given much the same kind of appearance: '"Was willst du werden?" fragte ihn der Vater und diese Frage war stereotyp wie die Antwort des Jungen: "Ein Bahnmeister"' (43). His leisure time is spent in a highly regular pattern, for 'Der ganze Ort hatte sich gewöhnt, ihm bei nur irgend erträglichem Wetter an dieser Stelle zu erblicken' (43), while his packing up his things to go off to his post is similarly automatic: 'Er brauchte dazu, wie zu allen seinen Verrichtungen, viel Zeit; jeder Handgriff war seit Jahren geregelt; in stets gleicher Reihenfolge wanderten die sorgsam auf der kleinen Nußbaumkommode ausgebreiteten Gegenstände: Messer, Notizbuch, Kamm, ein Pferdezahn, die alte eingekapselte Uhr, in die Taschen seiner Kleider' (44).

Taken together, this series of motifs linking Thiel and the train add up to an interpretation of him by the narrator. Both are regular of habit, and channelled, but also intrinsically very powerful; the train is a giant and a monster, while Thiel too, with his

---

[1] The word 'allsontäglich' occurs twice in the first two pages; but the repetition cannot be considered a stylistic flaw in view of the importance here of the notion of similar actions repeated in a similar way. Cf. Requadt, p. 104.

'herkulische Gestalt' (37), is also a giant of a man. In both, a great natural force is channelled and put onto narrow rails, which make it predictable and harmless. Yet in spite of this domestication the primitive power seems always dangerous and about to erupt; the train as it passes by is a frightening apparition, while the threat of Thiel's being 'überwältigt' is just as ominous. With both, the danger is of their leaving the rails and bursting the inhibiting bonds which hold them in check.[1]

It is Thiel's allegiance to two very different women, representing different forces in his life, which is at the root of the imbalance in his mind, and makes his control at times seem precarious; but at those moments when his control is threatened, a restraining force seems to operate, and this restraining force finds its expression in another of the metaphors which link Thiel and the train. After Thiel's avoidance of a confrontation with Lene over her treatment of Tobias, he returns to his post in the wood. The scene there is then made the subject of one of the narrator's grotesque descriptions:

Die schwarzen, parallellaufenden Geleise darauf glichen in ihrer Gesamtheit einer ungeheuren eisernen Netzmasche, deren schmale Strähne sich im äußersten Süden und Norden in einem Punkte des Horizontes zusammenzogen.

Der Wind hatte sich erhoben und trieb leise Wellen den Waldrand hinunter und in die Ferne hinein. Aus den Telegraphenstangen, die die

---

[1] Many critics, in talking of the forces unleashed here, are tempted to use rather generalised metaphysical and mythological language. For K. S. Guthke, the trains are 'Dämonen, Chiffren eines Unfasslichen', and in the outcome '...bricht denn das Dämonische unaufhaltsam auf ihn [Thiel] herein' ('Gerhart Hauptmann', in *Einführung in die deutsche Literatur*, ed. J. Gearey and W. Schumann, New York, 1964, pp. 329–30). Von Wiese also invokes 'das Dämonische' (p. 280), and views the death of Tobias as the symbolic expression of 'das übermenschlich Chaotische' (p. 273). Martini speaks of 'überpersönliche Lebensmächte' (p. 73), finds in the descriptions of nature 'eine schaffend-zerstörerische Allmacht' (p. 83), and in those of the technological objects a 'nicht vom Menschen gelenkte und beherrschte, sondern aus sich selbst lebende Gewalt, als ein Elementares, welches das Elementare im Naturvorgang ablöst und überdonnert' (p. 86). My own view here is that notions such as 'das Dämonische' or 'das Elementare' are admittedly weighty but not very useful; they are too vague to say anything specific about this specific text, and they tend to inhibit further analysis by their grandiose air of finality. To talk of 'überpersonliche Mächte' in connection with Thiel, for example, does not help us to understand what he is or what happens to him, since the source of his personal catastrophe seems to be located elsewhere.

Strecke begleiteten, tönten summende Akkorde. Auf den Drähten, die sich wie das Gewebe einer Riesenspinne von Stange zu Stange fortrankten, klebten in dichten Reihen Scharen zwitschernder Vögel. (49)

The scene appears as a giant spider's web. But the key to this metaphor lies in its having been used to describe Thiel's feeling of helplessness with Lene shortly before: 'Eine Kraft schien von dem Weibe auszugehen, unbezwingbar, unentrinnbar, der Thiel sich nicht gewachsen fühlte. Leicht gleich einem feinen Spinngewebe und doch fest wie ein Netz von Eisen legte es sich um ihn, fesselnd, überwindend, erschlaffend. Er hätte in diesem Zustand überhaupt kein Wort an sie zu richten vermocht...' (47).[1] The railway and telegraph lines form a net, a spider's web, which surrounds the train, just as there is a net around Thiel which restrains him. The way in which repression and inhibition work here is unusual in its direction, for it is Lene's sexual power and Thiel's response to it that inhibits any direct expression of allegiance to Minna and to the other side of his personality. The eventual breakdown comes from his obsession with his dead wife, his visions of her and a sense of guilt at his betrayal of her and her child. Lene's unattractive qualities are, of course, dwelt upon and there is nothing positive in the narrator's tone as he reports that Thiel 'geriet durch die Macht roher Triebe in die Gewalt seiner zweiten Frau' (39). Yet these forces also inhibit his madness.

It is Thiel's physical dependence on Lene which shows most clearly that susceptibility to visual impressions which is a recurring theme in the story and the source of yet another motif linking Thiel with the train. As Lene undresses, Thiel watches her: 'Plötzlich fuhr sie herum, ohne selbst zu wissen, aus welchem Grunde, und blickte in das von Leidenschaften verzerrte, erdfarbene Gesicht ihres Mannes, der sie, halbaufgerichtet, die Hände auf der Bettkante, mit brennenden Augen anstarrte' (55). Earlier, it was his looking at Lene which had quietened his anger over her mistreating Tobias: 'Sekundenlang spielte sein Blick

[1] Von Wiese (p. 273) notes this parallel (following Ordon, p. 226, and Requadt, p. 105), and comments: 'Alles Unheimliche und Unbegreifliche verdichtet sich in dem Dingsymbol...' But it is less helpful to call something a symbol than to say what it symbolises.

über den starken Gliedmaßen seines Weibes...' (47). But equally, it was his looking at Tobias that had threatened to produce an outburst: 'Seine Blicke streiften flüchtig das heulende Tobiaschen. Einen Augenblick schien es, als müße er gewaltsam etwas Furchtbares zurückhalten...' (47). In both these examples, a rather studied use of 'Blick' with a tactile verb gives an unusual aura and an extra importance to visual impressions; and the same kind of formulation is used when Thiel is about to enter the house, and wants to avoid the issue by not *looking* at anything: 'Seine Blicke hingen wie abwesend am Boden fest...' (46). When Thiel is said not to notice what is happening with Tobias and Lene, 'er schien keine Augen für sie zu haben' (42). It is after this introduction of the motif of Thiel's eyes and his 'Blicke' that the grotesque visual images in the text occur, and it is to this motif that these extraordinary descriptions must be related; but the description of the eyes themselves eventually becomes grotesque too. As he waits for news of his son 'seine gläsernen Pupillen bewegten sich unaufhörlich' (62), and Lene, after Thiel sees Tobias is dead, is afraid of 'ein unstetes Licht in seinen Augen' (64). As is usual with Thiel, any outstanding characteristic of his is matched by the train in dramatic fashion: 'Zwei rote, runde Lichter durchdrangen wie die Glotzaugen eines riesigen Ungetüms die Dunkelheit. Ein blutiger Schein ging vor ihnen her, der die Regentropfen in seinem Bereich in Blutstropfen verwandelte. Es war, als fiele ein Blutregen vom Himmel' (53). The monster engine has the same 'Glotzaugen' as Thiel has, the same staring and vacant eyes, which at one point (62) even give the impression of blindness. These 'eyes' produce the blood-red appearance of the rain, which is part of the riot of unnatural colour in the story, and of the series of highly unreal descriptions. The unreal visual images suggest in general not only something of Thiel's distorted vision, but also the extent to which he is attacked by and sensitive to visual impressions; this is the point of the impressionistic style[1] in the thematic structure of the story.

The variety and strangeness in its impression of colour are one

---

[1] Stirk (p. xxv) also thinks the style of the story impressionistic.

of the story's most striking features. In the space of a paragraph of twenty-two lines (44–5) for example, we have 'die Wanduhr mit dem langen Pendel und dem gelbsüchtigen Zifferblatt', the pine forest 'dessen Nadelmaßen einem schwarzgrünen, wellenwerfenden Meere glichen', 'die rostbraunen Säulen des Hochwaldes', 'ein bläulicher, duchsichtiger, mit allerhand Düften geschwängerter Dunst', 'ein schwerer milchiger Himmel', and 'schwarze Wasserlachen'. These colours are almost all complex, and suggestive of a very strange light in which there can be black-green, transparent bluishness, and water that can look black. The unusual features of the colours – their unlikely compounding, colours unnatural for a particular object, and above all the obsession with blackness – all occur also in the first description of the train, where in a similarly short space there are a 'schwarzweiße Sperrstange', and 'der rötlichbraune kiesbestreute Bahndamm', 'die schwarzen parallellaufenden Geleise', 'das schwarzgrüne Wipfelmeer', 'Ströme von Purpur', and 'Die Geleise begannen zu glühen, feurigen Schlangen gleich...' (48– 9). This colouring finds its eventual climax in the sight of Tobias after the accident:

Vor seinen Augen schwimmt es durcheinander, gelbe Punkte, Glühwürmchen gleich, unzählig. Er schrickt zurück – er steht. Aus dem Tanze der Glühwürmchen tritt es hervor, blaß, schlaff, blutrünstig. Eine Stirn, braun und blau geschlagen, blaue Lippen, über die schwarzes Blut tröpfelt. Er ist es. (59)

These visual impressions overload Thiel's brain and bring him to the point of madness; as he waits at his post after the little boy is taken away for medical treatment, he is obsessed with the colour of Tobias, and repeats over and over again 'braun und blau geschlagen' (62). Thiel's direct speech now contains the same kind of colours, which emphasises that the narrator's descriptions are to be taken as projections of his vision.

Consistent with the story's concern with grotesque and grim colour, and with the power of visual effects, is its series of images of light, and their seeming always to be destructive. The train spreads a light that looks like a rain of blood; the same unnatural redness was present in the 'Ströme von Purpur' of the sun during the first description of the scene at Thiel's post, and there too as the sun sets it leaves the trees 'in kaltem Verwesungslichte' (49). On the next morning the sun is blood-red: 'Die Sonne goß, im Aufgehen gleich einem ungeheuren blutroten Edelstein funkelnd, wahre Lichtmaßen über den Forst... Eine Sintflut von Licht schien über die Erde ausgegoßen' (54). Flood, devastation and fullness of light occur together again in the last of the natural descriptions: 'Die Sonne goss ihre letzte Glut über den Forst, dann erlosch sie. Die Stämme der Kiefern streckten sich wie bleiches, verwestes Gebein...' (62). This sequence of connected light imagery not only suggests the coming disaster, but also stresses the literally devastating character of visual impressions.

Much the same kind of pattern can be seen in other details of the story, among which the pattern of sounds is the most developed. The sound of the train is always given prominence: 'Ein Keuchen und Brausen schwoll stoßweise fernher durch die Luft. Dann plötzlich zerriß die Stille. Ein rasendes Tosen erfüllte den Raum...' (49). Contrasted with this noise is 'das alte heil'ge Schweigen', which returns as the train recedes into the distance. At the end, we have similar noises from the train, but a rather more personal image of it as Thiel hears: 'Das Keuchen einer Maschine, welches wie das stoßweise gequälte Atmen eines kranken Riesen klang...' (63). The last phrase suggests the breathing of the sick giant Thiel after Tobias' death: 'das schwere, aber gleichmäßige Atemholen' (66); but even without this more direct link, the verbal motif of 'keuchen' once more connects the two, for when Thiel witnesses the accident, his first response is: 'Thiel keuchte...' (58), just as he answers only with 'ein Röcheln' (59) when told there may be a chance for Tobias.

Apart from their more specific functions which I have already discussed, the light and sound imagery contribute to a much more general pattern of textual details which harp on the coming disaster and so help to create the effect of strain and impending breakdown of Thiel's world. A bird appears at the railway line early in the story: 'Ein Specht flog lachend über Thiels Kopf weg, ohne daß er eines Blickes gewürdigt wurde' (49). It reappears at the time of the disaster, but so does the final phrase of this sentence, in a different context; 'Das Hämmern eines Spechts durchdrang die Stille' (62), is followed shortly by 'Thiel würdigte sie [this time Lene] keines Blickes' (64). The signal bell is heard frequently throughout the early part of the story (48, 52, 58, 61), but eventually is transformed into a metaphor of the approach of madness, not the train: 'Aus dem nahen Birkenwäldchen kam Kindergeschrei. Es war das Signal zur Raserei' (63). Once more, the approach of the train and the approach of madness are juxtaposed. Even Thiel's madness has ironic pointers early on. First his wife is said to be 'rein närrisch' because of her joy over the new field (43), then Tobias is called 'närrischer Kerl' by Thiel himself in reply to Tobias' pointing to the squirrel and asking 'Vater ist das der liebe Gott' (57). Both wife and son having been lightly called 'närrisch', it is next Thiel's turn; but the third time is serious, and it is precisely the repetition of what Tobias had said at the sight of the squirrel that makes Thiel exclaim 'Aber mein Gott, das ist ja Wahnsinn' (63). The early mention of the accident involving a 'Rehbock' is another example: 'In einer Winternacht hatte der Schnellzug einen Rehbock überfahren' (41). This introduces the notion of the train's running over something living, and the figure of the 'Rehbock' returns to remind us of this: 'Ein Rudel Rehe setzte seitab auf den Bahndamm. Der Bock blieb stehen mitten zwischen den Geleisen' (64–5).[1] But the animal escapes, as if to emphasise that he is not the victim this time.

And so the impressionistic descriptions and the many forward-pointing details of the text build up a kind of pressure and create the sense of an overload of experiences and impressions in Thiel's mind. But perhaps 'overload' is not quite the right notion here

[1] Silz (p. 139) notes that 'the "recall" has an artistic effect', and he discusses possible meanings of it; von Wiese also notes the recall, but instead of interpreting it, sees 'Dämonie': 'Ist nicht alle Kreatur durch die Dämonie des Eisenbahnnetzes bedroht?' (p. 282).

to describe precisely what happens to Thiel, for the text provides its own idea: a slow fermentation. An apparently inconsequential detail of the story is its early account of how Thiel found and then later lost a bottle of wine near the railway-line:[1]

An einem heissen Sommertage hatte Thiel bei seiner Streckenrevision eine verkorkte Weinflasche gefunden, die sich glühend heiß anfasste und deren Inhalt deshalb von ihm für sehr gut gehalten wurde, weil er nach Entfernung des Korkes einer Fontäne gleich herausquoll, also augenscheinlich gegoren war. Diese Flasche, von Thiel in den seichten Rand eines Waldsees gelegt, um abzukühlen, war von dort auf irgendwelche Weise abhanden gekommen, so daß er noch nach Jahren ihren Verlust bedauern mußte. (41)

Yet this passage has many echoes in the text. When, for example, Thiel overhears Tobias being illtreated by Lene, and then returns to his post, he is troubled: 'Thiel riss die Mütze vom Kopf. Der Regen tat ihm wohl und lief vermischt mit Tränen über sein Gesicht. Es gärte in seinem Hirn' (52). The fermentation is now in Thiel's brain and it too is cooled by water. As we might expect, Thiel's madness at the end of the story recalls this idea of fermentation: 'Alte, erfahrene Leute hatten kalte Umschläge angeraten, und Lene befolgte ihre Weisung mit Eifer und Umsicht. Sie legte Handtücher in eiskaltes Brunnenwasser und erneuerte sie, sobald die brennende Stirn des Bewußtlosen sie durchhitzt hatte' (66). This, then, is the story's own way of seeing the effects of Thiel on the impressions which attack him. If one image of his going mad is the sudden interruption of calm and control by a monster which overwhelms him (the train image), the other, complementary image is that of slow ferment; the impressions received by his brain react together like the ingredients of a wine, until they build up so much pressure that the container erupts and overflows 'einer Fontäne gleich'. Within the framework of this notion of Thiel's development, some occasions seem to indicate sudden shifts, or distinct stages

[1] Ordon (p. 229) does not interpret this motif in the light of its context in the story, but derives its significance directly from Jungian psychology: 'Mythology refers to it as the "waters of life" or the "rebirth" archetypal experience'. She concludes that the motif is not well worked out in the story, for otherwise it would mark 'rebirths' of Thiel's psyche.

in the fermenting process. As Thiel begins to throttle the baby, for example, he suddenly comes to himself: 'Da fiel etwas in sein Hirn wie Tropfen heißen Siegellacks, und es hob sich wie eine Starre von seinem Geist' (63). This, and the shortly preceding 'Ein Lichtschein fiel in sein Hirn', both suggest sudden movements within Thiel's mind, its physical instability, but it is the verbal link with 'Sein Hirn gärte' that gives them their full meaning. A similar shift occurs immediately after the first train description: 'Und plötzlich zerriß etwas wie ein dichter, schwarzer Vorhang in zwei Stücke, und seine umnebelten Augen gewannen einen klaren Blick' (51). The process of 'gären' has moved on a stage. The other image of Thiel's madness is present here too, as the train's violence ('plötzlich zerriß die Stille') is suggested.

When we think of Thiel's final madness, it is easy to treat it as something caused by the experience of seeing his son's accident; but the text presents it as a process of mental ferment beginning much sooner. Very early in the story the slow reaction in Thiel's mind is hinted at in a slightly menacing way:

Wohl wahr! Im Verlauf des Tages glaubte Lene mehrmals etwas Befremdliches an ihm wahrzunehmen; so im Kirchstuhl, als er, statt ins Buch zu schauen, sie selbst von der Seite betrachtete, und dann auch um die Mittagszeit, als er, ohne ein Wort zu sagen, das Kleine, welches Tobias wie gewöhnlich auf die Straße tragen sollte, aus dessen Arm nahm und ihr auf den Schoß setzte. Sonst aber hatte er nicht das geringste Auffällige an sich. (54)

This passage already suggests that something is evolving in Thiel's mind. And although he is said not to notice how Tobias is suffering at Lene's hands (42), his forgetting his lunch and consequently returning at an unusual time, suggests that at some level of his mind he is concerned about it; for it is the breakdown of his regular routine of packing his things that allows him to experience Tobias being ill-treated, and the possible connection between this highly uncharacteristic behaviour and its result cannot be ignored. Thiel is otherwise never late and always meticulous in his preparations to go to work. The disturbance of his equilibrium is reflected in more deviations from his clockwork habits; he is late for work, then falls asleep and awakens believing that he has missed the signal-bell. Thiel's precarious balance between Lene and Minna is evidently in danger. The accident finally brings on his breakdown, but only finishes a process which began long before that,[1] by providing the final ingredient in the fermentation. One last detail of the story remains to be considered, for it introduces another wine-bottle in the first paragraph:

Im Verlaufe von zehn Jahren war er zweimal krank gewesen; das eine Mal infolge eines vom Tender einer Maschine während des Vorbeifahrens herabgefallenen Stückes Kohle, welches ihn getroffen und mit zerschmettertem Bein in den Bahngraben geschleudert hatte; das andere Mal einer Weinflasche wegen, die aus dem vorüberrasenden Schnellzuge mitten auf seine Brust geflogen war. Außer diesen beiden Unglücksfällen hatte nichts vermocht, ihn, sobald er frei war, von der Kirche fernzuhalten. (37)

This might seem a lengthy digression, especially in view of its position in the text; but its relations with the rest of the text establish its importance. The two objects are contrasted, the one a rough piece of natural stone, the other a product of civilisation and culture. The first attacks Thiel by smashing his leg, the other hits him in the chest; here there are connotations of physical, as opposed to emotional attack. The contrast seems similar to that of the two wives: one rough, coarse and making a physical appeal to Thiel, the other more refined and the object of a 'eine mehr vergeistigte Liebe' (39). And yet, Minna's is the more dangerous attack on Thiel. It is she who is associated with the mental ferment of the wine-bottle, and a broken leg is less dangerous than a blow 'auf seine Brust'. In a curious way, it seems that she actually becomes synonymous with the wine-bottle; for Thiel's finding the bottle which becomes the source of the fermentation image, his hiding it in the wood, and his regretting years later his loss of it, is all suggestive of his lasting sorrow over Minna's death and his secret dedication of his woodland retreat to her. The literal story makes Tobias' death an accident but the symbolism of the story makes it seem otherwise. It is when Lene

---

[1] Cf. Silz's accurate comment that '...things that do affect him, without outward sign, tend to "go down" and accumulate, and erupt later' (p. 146).

visits the place dedicated to Minna that Thiel's world breaks down. He can no longer keep the two forces in his mind in equilibrium by separating them. As we have seen, the train and Thiel are constantly juxtaposed, so that the train provides an interpretation of Thiel. But nowhere does the train seem more completely to be a symbolic expression of Thiel's mind than in this opening paragraph, for here the train throws out the emblems of the two different women, and it only destroys Tobias, on whom the harmonising of the two women in Thiel's mind depends, when that harmony is breaking down.

Bahnwärter Thiel is a more complex story than it would appear to be. It is only superficially the story of an accident told in vivid language. The impressionism of its descriptions is part of the bombardment of Thiel by experiences which he cannot digest and which must cause him more and more inner turmoil; the dominant symbols of the work, the wine-bottle and the train, bring out the slow process of fermenting of these impressions on the one hand, and the abruptness of the final eruption of violence on the other. Both images suggest a containment and inhibition of natural force. Thiel's outer calm and orderliness is a repression of the dangerous ferment of his mind, with its two opposing forces, which must be kept in strict control.[1] Meanwhile the narrator both creates this thematic network with his impressionistic and symbolic descriptions, and contributes to the theme of rigid control and its loss with his conspicuous domination of every aspect of his narrative.

[1] Garten's view, shared in essence by many commentators, that Thiel is 'driven, by inexorable circumstances' (in 'Gerhart Hauptmann', *German Men of Letters*, ed. A. Natan, London, 1961, p. 240) is therefore not a useful view of his motivation.

9. KAFKA: 'DAS URTEIL'

From a critical point of view, Kafka's[1] strange but compelling style has been to some extent the victim of its own success: critics have become familiar with this bizarre and unfamiliar idiom, and what was outstanding for its unpredictability has now begun to be treated as if it were, predictably, 'Kafkaesque'. But such epithets leave unexplained the expressive power of what Kafka writes, nor do the commonly used words 'nightmarish' or 'dream-like' carry understanding further forward; still to be investigated is the characteristic quality and content of this, rather than any other kind of dream or nightmare. Kafka's strange narrative convention is evidently an important part of his meaning, but it is all too easy to treat it in terms that are too general, or to discuss the characters and events in his work as if they were given to us not by Kafka's narrator, but by the more familiar realistic narrator. Consider, for example, this characterisation of Georg:

Georg ist keiner echten Kongruenz fähig: die Braut ist ihm Objekt der Lust und Mittel zur weiteren Sicherung seines materiellen Daseins...[2]

---

[1] References are to: *Franz Kafka: Gesammelte Werke*, ed. M. Brod, 'Erzählungen', pp. 53–68. There are separate interpretations by E. Edel, 'Franz Kafka: *Das Urteil*', *Wirkendes Wort*, IX (1959), 216–25; W. Zimmermann, 'Franz Kafka; *Das Urteil*', in *Deutsche Prosadichtungen unseres Jahrhunderts. Interpretationen für Lehrende und Lernende*, I (Düsseldorf, 1966), 189–208, revised version of *Deutsche Prosadichtungen der Gegenwart*, III (Düsseldorf, 1960), 93–110; K. H. Ruhleder, 'Franz Kafka's *Das Urteil*. An Interpretation', *Monatshefte*, LV (1963), 13–22; J. J. White, 'Franz Kafka's *Das Urteil* – an Interpretation', *Deutsche Vierteljahrsschrift für Literaturwissenschaft und Geistesgeschichte*, XXXVIII (1964), 208–29. General treatments of Kafka are by now numerous, but they do not as a rule give *Das Urteil* a great deal of space or critical attention. A recent example is H. Politzer's *Franz Kafka, Der Künstler* (Gütersloh, 1965), where the view is expressed that: '*Das Urteil* vermittelt keine klarere Lehre als eine unbestimmte Warnung vor dem Verlust des Junggesellentums' (p. 102). Beissner in his 'Kafka the Artist' (translated from his *Kafka der Dichter*, Stuttgart, 1958, and included in R. Gray's anthology *Kafka. A Collection of Critical Essays*, Englewood Cliffs, 1962) gives this story special attention, but he finds in it the 'portrayal of a "dream-like inner life"' (p. 25), a conception general enough to apply to many other works by Kafka and by other writers. An unusually full treatment of the story, on the other hand, is that in W. Sokel's *Franz Kafka: Tragik und Ironie* (Vienna/Munich, 1964), pp. 44–76.

[2] Edel, p. 217.

188

Or the following summary of the story:

Georg Bendemann wird von seinem alten, verwitweten Vater wegen seiner Heiratspläne und seiner Erfolge im väterlichen Geschäft zum Ertrinkungstod verurteilt und vollstreckt die Strafe an sich selbst.[1]

This seems reasonable enough; but is this really the kind of story in which one can say that the father has two perfectly ordinary reasons – Georg's intent to marry and his business success – for his judgment? Any summary falsifies what is summarised to a degree, but that is not the issue here; the point is that what is characteristic of a Kafka story may vanish when the motivation of the characters is spoken of in this way.

Part of the trouble lies in a misdirected response to the mysterious quality of Kafka's texture. Instead of treating this as a means of expression, and instead of examining the meaning and function of this enigmatic quality, critics have tended to want a kind of translation into a more normal mode. This would imply that Kafka's meaning is not radically different from anyone else's but that it is expressed in a kind of private code;[2] one goes to the diaries and letters to get the code, uses it to decode the works, and is then left with a meaning which is now independent of Kafka's style of writing and freed of its former bizarre trappings. Throughout Kafka criticism there occurs the telling phrase: 'for Kafka, x means...' According to von Wiese,[3] for example, one must know that the notion of 'Nahrung' has 'für Kafka eine chiffrenhafte Bedeutung.' Edel gives another entry for the Kafka lexicon: 'Kind und Kindlichkeit sind für Kafka nicht

---

[1] Sokel, p. 44. As my analysis will show, what is at issue in the story is not two actions by Georg, but a whole mode of thought.

[2] Nobody has put this critical attitude more clearly than Politzer: 'Kafka war sein bester Kritiker. Er erkannte seine Schwächen als erster und erkannte sie unumwunden an. Darum produzierte er auch eine ganze Abfolge von Aufschlüsselungen, die das Unentzifferbare entziffern sollten' (pp. 102–3). Though his title refers to the artist Kafka, Politzer thus relies heavily on biographical material. Beissner, too, chooses a title *Kafka der Dichter*, but also makes much use of letters and diary entries in a critical approach that is still biographical to an important degree; e.g., we should read Kafka 'with a delicate and exact regard for his ability to portray his dream-like inner life' (p. 26).

[3] Von Wiese, 'Franz Kafka: *Die Verwandlung*,' in *Die deutsche Novelle*, II, 327.

eindeutig Signa im positiven Sinne.'[1] The critic mediates between reader and work by supplying the key to the code, and the story has been made less challenging; no longer is it the strange thing it was before. Kafka did not say all that he meant, and the critic supplies what is necessary. But this is a most paradoxical position. Can the source of Kafka's powerful and original effects be even in part a failure of expression? This is inherently most unlikely. The biographical information often supplies what is already available; for example, both English and German allow negative and positive values to the concept of a child (*childish* and *childlike*, *kindisch* and *kindlich*). Only an illusion of deciphering the enigma has been given. But in the process an important assumption has been made: it is that Kafka has a standard use of 'the child' (or 'Russia', and so on) which is constant throughout his work. And this must involve the further assumption that one can state the meaning and value of such a notion in *Das Urteil* without examining its use in the story. But that use must always be regarded as the primary source of its meaning; the possibility must always exist that in any given context a motif may be used by Kafka in a way which is different from any of his previous uses of that motif, and for a different purpose. And once that is conceded, it follows that looking at his uses elsewhere of motifs which occur in *Das Urteil* produces only the knowledge they are or are not used differently in this text, not any determination of their meaning here.[2]

It is evidently the temptation to simplify Kafka that leads to criticism which proceeds in this way. The simplification may seem to provide a way of dealing with the baffling quality of Kafka which substitutes for the pursuit of more appropriately complex answers. To produce an equation of a concept in the

[1] Edel, p. 219.
[2] Critical arguments of this kind can always be settled by a dilemma: *either* the element of meaning diagnosed by means of a diary entry is already provided by common linguistic usage and associations, the context of the word or idea in the story, or a combination of both, *or* there is no evidence that the meaning so diagnosed is relevant to the story at all, in which case an intent which was incompletely executed has to be assumed without any evidence for that assumption.

story with a phrase from a diary is a tempting escape for a reader in that floundering condition that Kafka obviously *wants* him to be in, but to offer that escape is to do the reader a disservice. Kafka obviously saw some purpose in his bizarre narrative convention, and his readers have responded with a fascination which confirms that its purpose is indeed achieved, though they know nothing of his possible private code. It is surely with this public effect, not Kafka's private world, that the critic should concern himself.

The main weight of *Das Urteil* lies in the interview between Georg and his father, to which there is a prelude (Georg's thoughts about his friend in Russia) and an epilogue (the judgment and its fulfilment). The central episode, unlike the first part of the story, is highly unrealistic and 'absurd'; and yet, as we shall see, much of that effect is derived from its being slowly prepared in the earlier part of the story. The story's opening is worth close attention:

Es war an einem Sonntagvormittag im schönsten Frühjahr. Georg Bendemann, ein junger Kaufmann, saß in seinem Privatzimmer im ersten Stock eines der niedrigen, leichtgebauten Häuser, die entlang des Flußes in einer langen Reihe, fast nur in der Höhe und Färbung unterschieden, sich hinzogen. Er hatte gerade einen Brief an einen sich im Ausland befindlichen Jugendfreund beendet, verschloss ihn in spielerischer Langasmkeit und sah dann, den Ellbogen auf den Schreibtisch gestützt, aus dem Fenster auf den Fluß, die Brücke und die Anhöhen am anderen Ufer mit ihrem schwachen Grün. (53)

This is apparently a realistic description, demanding to be evaluated as such, and yet it is in many ways a strange one.[1] The reference to the row of houses, for example, seems oddly phrased.

---

[1] Zimmermann (p. 191) comments appropriately: 'In der zunehmenden *Verfremdung* der *Wirklichkeit*, die dadurch erreicht wird, daß der Autor mit den Mitteln der realistischen Erzählkunst das Absurde in ein alltägliches Geschehen integriert, erkennen wir die charakteristische Signatur Kafkaschen Erzählens'. I am not entirely in agreement, however, with his view (p. 192) that the story until Georg's entry into his father's room presents 'eine Welt, der nichts Ungewöhnliches anhaftet', that this world follows 'den ihm [dem Leser] vertrauten Gesetzen der Kausalität und Psychologie', and that Georg's thoughts seem 'von zwingender Logik wie von menschlicher Rücksichtnahme bestimmt'. The early part of the story does have its disturbing signs.

The emphasis of 'fast nur in der Höhe und Färbung unter-schieden' suggests that there is a general effect of sameness, only slightly relieved. And yet if the houses are all of different size and colour, only their design can be similar, and this would create an overall impression of difference, not of sameness; design would be the least striking of the three factors, for the design of adjacent houses is very commonly similar. The descriptive phrase at first seems reasonable, until we see its internal contradiction; the houses could only seem that way to an onlooker who was con-centrating on the one factor (design) to the exclusion of the others. Now in so doing he would, though in one sense seeing what is there, nevertheless be viewing it in such a selective way that it became distorted and unreal. The quality of Georg's vision is already apparent here: he seems in touch with reality, and yet he focuses on things around him in such a way that they become, through his emphases, quite unreal. Throughout the following train of thought concerning his friend in Russia he focuses sharply on some issues and ignores everything else, in the process distorting even what he sees by getting the proportions of the whole scene quite wrong. Another peculiar detail here is the colour of the 'Anhöhen am anderen Ufer mit ihrem schwachen Grün'. 'Schwach' is unusual as a qualifier of 'grün'; more nor-mally German uses lightness rather than weakness to indicate intensity of colour. The reference to weakness, then, seems out of place. Again, this is a prefiguration of something characteristic of Georg, namely his obsession with strength and weakness. The adverb 'spielerisch', too, adds to the unreality of the scene, as if suggesting that Georg is in fact remote from what he is doing.

All of this cannot fail to put the reader on his guard; the introduction is mainly realistic, and yet there is something wrong with it, a suggestion that the whole scene is slightly out of focus. This raises the question of the perspective of the narrator. It may not be quite precise to say that we experience the story through Georg's eyes,[1] for Georg is not the first person narrator. But it is true to say, more precisely, that almost all of the story is narrated

[1] Sokel, p. 45.

through the medium of Georg's thoughts, and a series of comments on them. During the interview between father and son, for example, we have only impressions of the exterior of the former, what he says and does, but with the latter we also have what he is thinking. Thus the strangeness of the narration throws doubt on the adequacy of Georg's relation to what is going on outside himself. As yet, however, this doubt is no more than a subdued hint, and it is counterbalanced by a contrary development: the reader is gradually drawn into Georg's version of what is going on around him by a lengthy, very explicit and at first sight reasonable train of thought concerning his friend in Russia. Yet even this sequence of thoughts has its disturbing side. It appears at first to be sensible and well-intentioned, but it can also seem obsessive, over-subtle and fundamentally self-congratulatory too. We can think of it in the first of these two ways if we accept Georg's own point of reference; he is concerned for his friend, and would like to help him or at least to spare him the unhappiness which might result from his becoming too aware of the discrepancy between his current pitiable state and Georg's good fortune. And yet the obsessive length of this train of thought makes it questionable; Georg seems to be using his friend's life to dwell on his own successes, so that his thoughts seem to be more concerned with his own feelings of self-satisfaction than with his friend's welfare. Georg's reflections are in fact very largely concerned with the contrast between his own successes and his friend's failures. The friend's business in Russia 'seit langem aber zu stocken schien' (53) while Georg's family business in the last two years had doubled its personnel and quintupled its turnover, with even better prospects (55). While his friend had seemed to be preparing himself for 'ein engültiges Junggesellentum' (53), Georg was about to make a marriage with 'einem Mädchen aus wohlhabender Familie' (56). While his friend was isolated and in exile in Russia, Georg still enjoyed an existence at home and among his family. The reader may well get the impression that Georg is rehearsing his own successes with some satisfaction. And the superficial impression of the breadth of his human sympathy for his friend is overshadowed by a contrary impression of narrowness in Georg's judgments of value, for judgments of his friend's life are made rigidly on the basis of Georg's values. 'Junggesellentum' may well be a *choice* for his friend,[1] but Georg insists that only a failure to achieve marriage can be involved, which then must lead him to envy Georg. This narrowness of judgment corresponds to a narrow view of marriage which emerges when Georg persistently calls Frieda a 'Mädchen aus wohlhabender Familie'; in thinking of a successful marriage Georg evidently thinks more of the success than the marriage.

Georg's geographical views are similarly narrow; home is an ultimate value and any other place is automatically undesirable, so that leaving home can only be taking flight and not a positive choice. No value is allowed by Georg to leaving home in a spirit of enterprise and adventure, for example: the only associations which he allows for such a journey are those of danger, loneliness, and so on. In this connection, there are interesting discrepancies between Georg's judgment of his friend's wretchedness and what he reports as fact. His friend had tried to persuade him, too, to leave home, which is not consistent with his unhappiness abroad, but Georg quickly dismisses the possibility:

Früher, zum letztenmal vielleicht in jenem Beileidsbrief, hatte er Georg zur Auswanderung nach Rußland überreden wollen und sich über die Aussichten verbreitet, die gerade für Georgs Geschäftszweig in Petersburg

---

[1] The text does not allow the opposite assumption, that bachelorhood and asceticism are positive values for the story. Cf. Politzer: 'In gleichem Maße jedoch, in dem Georg seinem Junggesellentum untreu geworden war, ist der Freund im Geist des alten Bendemann zur Verkörperung all jener Junggesellentugenden angewachsen, die der Sohn verraten hatte' (p. 94). This deviates from the text in that Georg's father was apparently happily married, in that we know almost nothing of the friend's life, and in that the story in general contrasts egocentricity unfavourably with communication and relationships; the self sufficiency of asceticism and bachelorhood would clash with this value system. The text by itself would provide no occasion for the perception of these values, which are evidently derived from biographical concerns (Kafka the ascetic and bachelor). The widowed father can scarcely be seen as being in and valuing a second 'Junggesellentum' without *his* expressing a sense of having betrayed the first; to the contrary, he expresses a positive attitude to his late wife.

bestanden. Die Ziffern waren verschwindend gegenüber dem Umfang, den
Georgs Geschäft jetzt angenommen hatte. (55–6)

In like manner, Georg refuses to take seriously his friend's
excuses for not returning home in the last three years:

Der Freund war nun schon über drei Jahre nicht in der Heimat gewesen und
erklärte dies sehr notdürftig mit der Unsicherheit der politischen Verhältnisse
in Rußland, die demnach also auch die kürzeste Abwesenheit eines kleinen
Geschäftsmannes nicht zuließen, während hunderttausende Russen ruhig in
der Welt herumfuhren. (54–5)

His friend, then, insists that he stays away because his business is
demanding, and argues that Georg should follow him; Georg
interprets this as a flight from home, and a fear of feeling small if
he returns. We know little if anything about Georg's friend and
his real personal or commercial position;[1] but it seems possible
that Georg converts all that he hears from his friend to his own
version of life, in which his own values are paramount, and his
success by those standards unquestioned. Now this is the same
selective vision that occurs in the story's first paragraph, and the
same ability to project emphases onto a situation which are
Georg's, but not those of the situation itself. In the light of this,
we cannot avoid suspecting that Georg's pity for his friend is
possibly misplaced, and that it may be primarily a defensive
stratagem on his part. It could well be that for Georg constantly
to tell himself that his friend is unhappy is essential to his own
well-being. There is, after all, something destructive in Georg's
'considerateness' towards his friend; it seems to provide the
opportunity for an orgy of denigration of him, a very full series
of imaginings of his helplessness, wretchedness and even disgrace
which are very congenial and flattering to Georg, as though he

---

[1] Georg's view of his friend is often taken to be reliable, e.g.: 'Der Unterschied zwischen
Georg und dem Freund ist fundamental...Denn Georg hat die wahre Unschuld
gekannt, die er verloren, der Freund aber besaß sie nie... Er war zu feig, um im Leben
der Heimat durchzuhalten. Ja, nicht genug damit, ist er auch zu feig zurückzukehren'
(Sokel, pp. 64–5).

were savouring the thought that he had completely defeated someone who was his main competitor:

> Was wollte man einem solchen Manne schreiben, der sich offenbar verrannt hatte, den man bedauern, dem man aber nicht helfen konnte. Sollte man ihm vielleicht raten, wieder nach Hause zu kommen, seine Existenz hierherzuverlegen, alle die alten freundschaftlichen Beziehungen wiederaufzunehmen – wofür ja kein Hindernis bestand – und im übrigen auf die Hilfe der Freunde zu vertrauen? Das bedeutete aber nichts anderes, als daß man ihm gleichzeitig, je schonender, desto kränkender, sagte, daß seine bisherigen Versuche misslungen seien, dass er endlich von ihnen ablassen solle, dass er zurückkehren und sich als ein für immer Zurückgekehrter von allen mit großen Augen anstaunen lassen müße, daß nur seine Freunde etwas verstünden und daß er ein altes Kind sei, das den erfolgreichen, zu Hause gebliebenen Freunden einfach zu folgen habe. (53–4)

Scarcely beneath the surface of the 'considerateness', Georg is mentally destroying his friend. It is unnecessary to conjure up this vision of his friend's disgrace, of his being a public spectacle, of his being abjectly forced to listen to the denunciation of his errors and his childishness; all this is for Georg's own delight, a confirmation that of his contemporaries he has achieved most and proved wisest. Georg even reflects, with twisted logic, that all this must be mercilessly explicit in order not to be even more injurious! Does Georg really want his friend to return at all? For having said that there is 'kein Hindernis' to this return, he then goes on to make it impossible by the shameful vision of his friend's fate. The real 'Hindernis' must be Georg himself, if this is the welcome he has in mind.

The parable of the prodigal son is implicit in the situation of Georg's having stayed at home while his friend, a kind of sibling rival ('Er wäre ein Sohn nach meinem Herzen', says Georg's father, 63) has ventured afield. Georg interprets that venture negatively: it is for him a running away from home, to loneliness and failure. But the parable interprets it more positively, stressing the adventurous spirit of those who brave new country, and insists that they are worthy of a splendid welcome – not a disgrace. And so we can neither rule out the positive side of going abroad[1] (e.g., enterprise, adventure, and standing on one's own feet) nor ignore the negative side of staying at home (opting for safety and the comfort which has been the result of the work of one's father). In the parable the stay-at-home sons are angered by their more adventurous brother's reception, and betray their own insecure feeling that he did what they dared not do; Georg's hostility to his friend is less overt, but his 'considerateness' seems to be a defensive reaction to one who has chosen a harder course than owing everything to his father. The friend's return might well provoke the welcome envisaged in the parable, not the abject position which Georg imagines (and wishes) for him, and this once more arouses the suspicion that Georg would not himself welcome this return.

At the beginning, Georg's negative attitude towards his friend appears only in certain implications of the text, but it slowly becomes more explicit. For example, Georg's initial intent is to prevent his friend's learning of his engagement. But he afterwards admits that 'Das kann ich allerdings nicht verhindern' (57), which reminds us of his earlier protestation that there was no 'Hindernis' to his friend's return. And meanwhile Georg does everything he can to get the news to his friend without seeming to do so. Thus he tells his friend obsessively of 'die Verlobung eines gleichgültigen Menschen mit einem ebenso gleichgültigen Mädchen dreimal in ziemlich weit auseinanderliegenden Briefen' (56). Having thus caused his friend to become interested in this repeated information 'ganz gegen Georgs Absicht', (!) and having raised with his friend the issue of engagements, he then takes up the matter with Frieda and allows himself very quickly to be convinced that he should in fact tell all. There is a very strange sequence of statements which introduces this conviction:

[1] Thus 'Russia' in *Das Urteil* is primarily a symbol of openness, as opposed to the closedness of an existence at home. Home and Russia are contrasted as places of safety and unenterprisingness on the one hand, as opposed to danger and opportunity on the other. Both sides of the opposition have positive and negative aspects. Kafka's diary entries cannot therefore be allowed to limit the meaning of 'Russia' in this text to loneliness (Sokel, p. 66) or the Infinite (White, p. 211), a pair of readings which well shows the pitfalls of assuming that Kafka always had one thing in mind whenever he thought of Russia.

'Wenn du solche Freunde hast, Georg, hättest du dich überhaupt nicht verloben sollen.' 'Ja, das ist unser beider Schuld; aber ich wollte es auch jetzt nicht anders haben.' Und wenn sie dann, rasch atmend unter seinen Küßen, noch vorbrachte: 'Eigentlich kränkt es mich doch', hielt er es wirklich für unverfänglich, dem Freund alles zu schreiben. (57)

This is a sudden conversion indeed. It is much shorter than his initial series of thoughts which led in the opposite direction; his scruples are brushed aside in an exchange that is less convincing than anything in the story up to this point. But the final demonstration of Georg's underlying motives comes in the letter which he writes; after all his thoughts of sparing his friend's feelings, the letter could scarcely be more injurious:

Ich habe mich mit einem Fräulein Frieda Brandenfeld verlobt, einem Mädchen aus einer wohlhabenden Familie, die sich hier erst lange nach Deiner Abreise angesiedelt hat, die Du also kaum kennen dürftest. Es wird sich noch Gelegenheit finden, Dir Näheres über meine Braut mitzuteilen, heute genüge Dir, daß ich recht glücklich bin und daß sich in unserem gegenseitigen Verhältnis nur insofern etwas geändert hat, als Du jetzt in mir statt eines ganz gewöhnlichen Freundes einen glücklichen Freund haben wirst. Außerdem bekommst Du in meiner Braut, die Dich herzlich grüßen lässt, und die Dir nächstens selbst schreiben wird, eine aufrichtige Freundin, was für einen Junggesellen nicht ganz ohne Bedeutung ist. (57)

Georg is at pains to identify Frieda as being 'aus wohlhabender Familie', he alludes to his friend's still being a bachelor in a way which is condescending (as usual, under the guise of talking about what is good for his friend) and stresses his own improved status as someone no longer 'gewöhnlich', again under the guise of talking of his friend's gain from the changed situation. It is now no longer a suspicion, but clearly a fact that the point of Georg's earlier train of thought was to gloat over his successes; for the letter makes it clear that Georg has no real concern for his friend's feelings. Having said that he wanted to do one thing, Georg does precisely the reverse. His exhortation to his friend to attend the wedding, and 'alle Hindernisse über den Haufen zu werfen', is undermined by the final sentence 'Aber wie dies auch sein mag, handle ohne alle Rücksicht, und nur nach Deiner

Wohlmeinung' (58). Even if it were not becoming more and more clear that 'Hindernis' is Georg's favourite word for masking his self-deception, these final words of the letter would still indicate that Georg is very ready to contemplate his friend's non-arrival.

After six pages the story turns to Georg's interview with his father, which, though increasingly grotesque and unreal in character, is basically a continuation of the same themes in a different context. As the disturbing factors below the surface of the prelude are progressively revealed, the story slides more and more into a fantastic mode. The central feature of the whole interview is his father's questioning Georg's version of reality. When Georg tells his father what he proposes to do – to tell his friend of his marriage – he begins to sound even more obsessive as he repeats his former words: '... von anderer Seite kann er von meiner Verlobung wohl erfahren, wenn das auch bei seiner einsamen Lebensweise kaum wahrscheinlich ist – das kann ich nicht hindern –, aber von mir selbst soll er es nun einmal nicht erfahren' (59). By now, these protestations have a rehearsed and fixed quality. But the whole house of cards[1] which Georg has built in his mind is attacked when Georg's father says quite directly: 'Hast du wirklich diesen Freund in Petersburg?' (60). This thrust is the beginning of the end for Georg; his response to it consists of a retreat into a way of speaking and thinking which matches exactly that of his earlier reflections on his friend, but the context of this response in the conversation with his father sheds more light on the first pages of the story. Georg's earlier train of thought was given no context, for his friend never appeared. But now we see much more clearly that Georg's long and elaborate considerations concerning his father's need for help and

---

[1] Sokel thinks of the father's question in narrower terms: 'Mit seiner Frage scheint der Vater die Existenz eines Freundes Georgs in Petersburg zu beweifeln... Fällt aber die Betonung auf das Wort *Freund*, dann bezieht sich die Frage auf die Natur, das Wesen des Objekts. Dann heißt die Frage: Hat Georg einen *Freund* in Petersburg, oder nicht vielleicht einen *Feind*' (p. 53). It seems preferable to take the thrust of the question in the broadest way; Georg's father is questioning not just the existence or the friendliness of the friend, but the whole edifice of Georg's version of his own life in relation to his friend's.

sympathy are a retreat following an attack by his father; Georg retires into a cocoon of words and logical arguments which he spins out to provide a protective covering for the private version of the world which he must defend against a threat to question it. Here is surely the key to the air of unreality of Georg's thoughts on his friend. The content of his speech is similar to the earlier thoughts too. There is the same concern for the other's welfare which puts Georg into a superior position in the relationship, and allows him to avoid the issues raised by his father, since the implication is that everything he says can be attributed to infirmity or sickness; and there is the same shutting out of communication in order to expand a version of what is happening that is obsessively reasonable in tone:[1]

Lassen wir meine Freunde sein. Tausend Freunde ersetzen mir nicht meinen Vater. Weißt du, was ich glaube? Du schonst dich nicht genug. Aber das Alter verlangt seine Rechte. Du bist mir im Geschäft unentbehrlich, das weißt du ja sehr genau, aber wenn das Geschäft deine Gesundheit bedrohen sollte, sperre ich es noch morgen für immer. Das geht nicht. Wir müssen da eine andere Lebensweise für dich einführen. Aber von Grund aus. Du sitzt hier im Dunkeln und im Wohnzimmer hättest du schönes Licht. Du nippst vom Frühstück, statt dich ordentlich zu stärken. Du sitzt bei geschlossenem Fenster, und die Luft würde dir so gut tun. Nein, mein Vater! Ich werde den Arzt holen, und seinen Vorschriften werden wir folgen. Die Zimmer werden wir wechseln, du wirst ins Vorderzimmer ziehen, ich hierher. Es wird keine Veränderung für dich sein, alles wird mit übertragen werden. Aber das alles hat Zeit, jetzt lege dich noch ein wenig ins Bett, du brauchst unbedingt Ruhe. Komm, ich werde dir beim Ausziehn helfen, du wirst sehn, ich kann es. Oder willst du gleich ins Vorderzimmer gehn, dann legst du dich vorläufig in mein Bett. Das wäre übrigens sehr vernünftig. (60–1)

All of this evidently aims to reduce the stature of Georg's father until he is no longer a threat; and we can infer that Georg's pitying his friend has the same purpose of preserving his self-centred and self-satisfied view of his life against a possible challenge. In spite of Georg's benevolent tone, he is on both occasions making a counter-attack of a deeply aggressive nature, its aim being the

[1] Politzer views this as Georg's attempt 'das Thema zu wechseln' (p. 90), missing the thematically more important aspects of his returning to the mode of thought with which the story began.

subtle destruction of the opponent. It is because we see this defence mechanism spring into action against an attack by his father that we can assume that it was a response to a need to defend against his friend, and it is easy to see where the need arises; his friend has acted on a set of values very different to Georg's, and Georg may well feel this alternative to his own actions as a pressure on him needing to be relieved by preserving the belief that his friend is in error, wretched and childish. But Georg is in even more danger from his father, who as a father is the ever-present censor of what Georg is doing, the original critic of Georg's life, and the one man above all before whom Georg feels he must always justify himself.[1] For one so concerned with justifying himself to himself, practising much self-deception in the process, his father is a constant threat to Georg's precarious mental world. Georg had felt himself compelled to present his action in relation to his friend for his father's scrutiny, and the story is much concerned with Georg's experience of his father as a powerful force. As Georg enters his father's room his instinctive reaction is: 'Mein Vater ist noch immer ein Riese' (59), and his father's later emergence from his state of being nearly 'zugedeckt' is conspicuous as above all a display of power:

'Sei nur ruhig, du bist gut zugedeckt.' 'Nein!' rief der Vater, daß die Antwort an die Frage stieß, warf die Decke zurück mit einer Kraft, daß sie einen Augenblick im Fluge sich ganz entfaltete, und stand aufrecht im Bett. Nur eine Hand hielt er leicht an den Plafond. 'Du wolltest mich zudecken, das weiß ich, mein Früchtchen, aber zugedeckt bin ich noch nicht. Und ist es auch die letzte Kraft, genug für dich, zuviel für dich.' (63)

Within the convention of the story, the judgment of his father is so strong as to compel Georg's death.

Throughout the conversation with his father, it is evident that Georg is attempting to refuse communication and to avoid answering what his father says. But the issue of communication has been present from the beginning of the story; Georg raises it

---

[1] The meaning of the figure of Georg's father in the story is of course an abstraction from what he does and says as well as his effect on others, and is neither to be derived from Kafka's other works nor from Freud.

as he thinks over his friend's reports: 'Wie er erzählte, hatte er keine rechte Verbindung mit der dortigen Kolonie seiner Landsleute, aber auch fast keinen gesellschaftlichen Verkehr mit einheimischen Familien und richtete sich so für ein endgültiges Junggesellentum ein' (53). After these thoughts on his friend's lack of communication with other people, Georg then goes on to reflect that he too finds it impossible to communicate with him: 'Aus diesen Gründen konnte man ihm, wenn man noch überhaupt die briefliche Verbindung aufrechterhalten wollte, keine eigentlichen Mitteilungen machen, wie man sie ohne Scheu auch den entferntesten Bekannten machen würde' (54).

Yet another impression of separateness and lack of communication emerges from Georg's thoughts as he enters his father's room. He reflects that he has not entered the room for months: 'Es bestand auch sonst keine Nötigung dazu, denn er verkehrte mit seinem Vater ständig im Geschäft.' In any case, he thinks, they often sat together 'jeder mit seiner Zeitung, im gemeinsamen Wohnzimmer' (58). In protesting to himself that he really does have contact with his father, Georg gives us an odd picture of both sitting physically near each other but mentally separate, their newspapers providing a convenient barrier between their mental worlds. Georg had complained that his friend made separateness inevitable, but here it seems to be Georg who does it – another hint at a reinterpretation of Georg and his friend – while his father may be seeking to avoid the barrier by peering round the edge of his newspaper: 'Der Vater saß beim Fenster in einer Ecke, die mit verschiedenen Andenken an die selige Mutter ausgeschmückt war, und las die Zeitung, die er seitlich vor die Augen hielt, wodurch er irgendeine Augenschwäche auszugleichen suchte' (58). Does he really want to read it at all? But by the middle of the interview it has become clear why communication is such an issue. His father speaks very directly, and Georg avoids what he says, because communication is the great danger to Georg's mental world; it can only stay intact if everyone else is kept out of it. Real communication would subject it to the test of a different view of the world, which might sweep away all Georg's defences, and with them his delusion of being both a great success and a kind, considerate person. For this reason Georg is extremely busy in his avoidance of communication, trying one means after another. The first, as we have noted, is his normal flight into an elaborate monologue, kind and considerate to his father, yet with the unspoken implication that the old man's mind is wandering too much for him to be taken seriously. His father counters the long monologue with a single syllable: '"Georg", sagte der Vater leise, ohne Bewegung' (61).[1] The rejection of all that Georg has said is subtle; it is achieved by the formal contrast of the monosyllable with Georg's copious speech, the former simple, direct and with much unspoken force, the latter weak and evasive in its fullness. Faced with this accurate answer to and rejection of his first line of defence, Georg immediately makes another attack on his father, this time a wordless one; he kneels beside him, 'hob den Vater vom Sessel und zog ihm, wie er nun doch recht schwach dastand, den Schlafrock aus' (61–2). Now he treats him as a child, undresses him, and puts him to bed, resolving to take care of his father in future in terms which are as condescending as they are hopeful of failure: 'Doch jetzt entschloss er sich kurz mit aller Bestimmtheit, den Vater in seinen künftigen Haushalt mitzunehmen. Es schien ja fast, wenn man genauer zusah, daß die Pflege, die dort dem Vater bereitet werden sollte, zu spät kommen könnte' (62–3).

As Georg's attitude to his father emerges more clearly, a fresh assessment of what has happened in the family business is called for. Georg's view (55) was that he had produced a great expansion since his mother's death and his father's subsequently taking less part in the business; but his father's complaint (60 and 65) is that Georg has attempted to exclude him from knowledge of what is happening while profiting from his father's preparation of the direction to be taken by the business. The outline of the situation is by now familiar; Georg's success and someone else's failure,

---

[1] Ruhleder (p. 15) says that this single word 'seems to express neither support nor reproach', and thus misses the point of the contrast of Georg's length with his father's monosyllable.

with the suggestion that both are brought about by Georg's subtle undermining of the other.

Georg's putting his father to bed is an attempt to pretend that he is senile, weak and bedridden,[1] and thus no longer one whose power must be feared; but his father emerges stronger than ever, throwing off the bedclothes and the position which Georg has assigned to him. Now he is a giant again, and Georg's second attack on him has failed, as has his second line of defence against his father's understanding of him. Increasingly desperate attempts now follow; he cannot reduce his father's stature by pity or condescension, and so tries to avoid the awareness of his own plight by pitying his friend once more, a move which by now seems a pathetically inadequate attempt to shore up his crumbling position: 'Georg sah zum Schreckbild seines Vaters auf. Der Petersburger Freund, den der Vater plötzlich so gut kannte, ergriff ihn wie noch nie' (64). Georg's formerly well-polished defensive system has here degenerated to a feeble and automatic response, a despairing attempt to divert his attention from his own plight to that imagined for another. The retrospective reinterpretation of the early pages of the story continues; Georg's dwelling on his friend's inadequacy is there too to be regarded as an avoidance of his own problems. But this defence now becomes useless as his father assures him '"Aber der Freund ist nun doch nicht verraten!"' (65), and reveals that '"Ich war sein Vertreter hier am Ort."' At this Georg's very last instinctive defence appears: '"Komödiant!" konnte sich Georg zu rufen nicht enthalten, erkannte sofort den Schaden und biß, nur zu spät – die Augen erstarrt – in seine Zunge, daß er vor Schmerz einknickte' (65). Though he regrets it, it is all he has left, and so he now deliberately tries to make fun of his father. His father tells him that his friend in Russia already knows the circumstances of Georg's present life '"tausendmal besser"', and his response is: '"Zehntausendmal", sagte Georg, um den Vater zu verlachen, aber noch in seinem Munde bekam das Wort einen todernsten Klang' (66). These two instances link with his father's calling

---

[1] That there is here an overtone of actual burial is pointed out by White, p. 221.

Georg a 'Spassmacher' (61), and the story's opening with Georg sealing his letter 'spielerisch'; joking and playing are also part of Georg's defensive armoury of devices for keeping reality at arm's length, by not taking things seriously which would damage his version of it.[1]

That the narration has been from Georg's point of view has allowed us to be drawn into his world and to get a sense of its inner logic and persuasiveness, though to be sure we also get an uneasy feeling of its unreality.[2] We therefore experience the challenge to that world by Georg's father from within it. Georg's father brings reality into Georg's unreal world, but from our vantage point and that of Georg it appears as a sudden eruption of irrationality, terror and unreality; sanity appears as insanity, and fantasy has become so ordered that what interrupts it seems the thing that is fantastic. Yet at the same time, we also begin to see floating to the surface of Georg's mind reactions which begin to acknowledge that his father's version of events is the real one, an acknowledgment eventually to be made openly to his father. The first of these is his ' " " Mein Vater ist noch immer ein Riese " " ', an instinctive reaction not consistent with the fantasy about his infirmity. But the first really explicit crack in Georg's view of his life comes after his father has refused to co-operate in Georg's attempts to ignore what he is saying by treating him as a senile person in need of care; at last, the truth begins to emerge:

Vor einer langen Weile hatte er sich fest entschlossen, alles vollkommen genau zu beobachten, damit er nicht irgendwie auf Umwegen, von hinten

---

[1] Sokel views the word 'spielerisch' differently: 'Am Wort "spielerisch" fällt das Unernste auf. Indem Georg den Brief spielerisch versiegelt, drückt er mit dieser Geste seine unernste und unentschlossene Einstellung zur Verlobung und somit zum Erwachsensein aus' (p. 73). It appears to me not seriousness of purpose that Georg lacks; on the contrary, he is quite ruthless in his pursuit of what he wants. There is no evidence to support the view that Georg is not serious about the marriage to Frieda; once more, the biographical parallel with Kafka and his fiancée is not helpful.

[2] Beissner's view is that for the sake of 'unity of meaning' the narrator has 'completely transformed himself into the lonely Georg' (p. 25). This statement of the purpose of the narrative scheme appears to me too vague and general to catch its specific purpose, and the description of the scheme blurs the distinction between narration by Georg and narration from his point of view.

her, von oben herab überrascht werden könne. Jetzt erinnerte er sich wieder an den längst vergeßenen Entschluss und vergaß ihn, wie man einen kurzen Faden durch ein Nadelöhr zieht. (64–5)

This feeling becomes more and more explicit, after a curious projection of the kinds of connections and inferences that are made in Georg's mind: '"Sogar im Hemd hat er Taschen!" sagte sich Georg, und glaubte, er könne ihn mit dieser Bemerkung in der ganzen Welt unmöglich machen. Nur einen Augenblick dachte er das, denn immerfort vergaß er alles' (66). Thoughts float around in Georg's mind without any secure point of reference, once that provided by his well-ordered mental world has been shaken; other visions of safety then need to be seized on, and much needs to be forgotten. His attempts to create reality by his own language and reasoning are stripped to their essentials here in a fantasy wish that is a kind of reduction to absurdity of his tactics so far; he now suffers openly from the delusion that his thought about his father's shirt-pockets can achieve the reduction of his father that has escaped him until now. The absurdity of the inference highlights the need for the conclusion, and is a comment on all previous sequences of thoughts leading to a similar conclusion; their logic was just as spurious, under a much better covering. Full awareness of the danger from his father, and an explicit wish for his destruction, emerge at last in Georg's '"wenn er fiele und zerschmetterte"' (65), and '"Du hast mich also aufgelauert!"' (67). His real feelings of being threatened by his father's presence break through into the open at last, as does the awful fact of the conspiracy against him, when his father announces that he has been writing to the friend in Petersburg. It was fear of others uniting against him that led him to attempt to destroy the relationships between them, to insist that his father really did not like his friend: '"Ich konnte ja deine Abneigung gegen ihn ganz gut verstehn, mein Freund hat seine Eigentümlichkeiten. Aber dann hast du dich doch auch wieder ganz gut mit ihm unterhalten. Ich war damals noch so stolz darauf, dass du ihm zuhörtest, nicktest und fragtest"' (62). Here Georg was trying to lead his father into his own negative attitude towards the friend, and then a condescending one in which nothing which his friend says is taken seriously. The final judgment pronounced by Georg's father ties together many of the threads of the story: '"Jetzt weißt du also, was es noch außer dir gab, bisher wußtest du nur von dir! Ein unschuldiges Kind warst du ja eigentlich, aber noch eigentlicher warst du ein teuflischer Mensch! – Und darum wisse: Ich verurteile dich jetzt zum Tode des Ertrinkens!"' (67). Georg's father is not drawing a distinction between Georg's knowledge of himself as against his ignorance of the alliance against him,[1] but between his living in his own mental world as opposed to the world in which people exist outside himself. Georg allows others no independence of his values, and they are forced to exist as satellites in a system of which he is the centre. If by nature they tend to threaten this system, they are subtly undermined and destroyed. This self-centredness is in one way the innocence of the child – it contains no explicit malice – but it is devilish in its destructiveness. Thus it is not inconsistent that Georg cries, as he falls into the river to his death, '"Liebe Eltern, ich habe euch doch immer geliebt"' (68); this childish love existed but was never outgrown. Yet his father, since Georg behaved as if everything were a potential danger to him unless crippled or destroyed, can also cry, without inconsistency: '"Glaubst du, ich hätte dich nicht geliebt, ich, von dem du ausgingst?"' (65). For Georg has behaved as if all the world were hostile to him, and he could trust nobody. He has said that his friend is an 'altes Kind', but this seems rather to refer to Georg, whose childish egocentricity has survived after his childhood is over.

The last words of the story are a comment on what has gone wrong with Georg: 'In diesem Augenblick ging über die Brücke

<hr>

[1] Contrast Sokel: 'Was ist aber die Erkenntnis, die Georg zufällt? Bisher wußte er nur von sich, jetzt weiss er, "was es noch außer (ihm) gab!" Was aber gab es "ausser ihm"? Die Allianz zwischen Freund und Eltern, die als Rache an Georgs Verrat zustande kam, seine trostlose Isolierung offenbart und seinen Untergang besiegelt' (p. 54). But the point on which the meaning of the whole story depends, is that Georg's father is attacking Georg's egocentric refusal to allow for the existence of people separately from himself. Thus his increased awareness at the end need not be narrowed down to the awareness of the conspiracy against him.

ein geradezu unendlicher Verkehr' (68). The end of Georg's lonely, isolated and unreal world is accompanied by a vision of the enormous activity around him that was separate from but ignored by him. Its ceaselessness and diversity are its health while Georg's sickness lay in the uniformity and isolation of his outlook; and in the taking up once more of the motif of 'Verkehr',[1] there is a suggestion of the movement to and fro, the communication, which was absent from Georg's shut-off private world. In these final words the narrative perspective changes abruptly. No longer are we looking at the world with Georg; he has dropped to the river below, and is gone, while the narrator describes the scene above. At last, Georg is part of the scene rather than its centre. And as part of the scene, he is now no longer noticeable, as the noise made by everything outside of him makes the noise of his fall inaudible. Georg's father has sentenced him to death to pay for his egocentricity,[2] but the narrator sentences him to be removed from occupying the centre of the narrative; in death he will no longer be central to what happens in the real world, and we are suddenly made to see the scene in its true perspective, rather than in Georg's.

An element of the meaning of the story often overlooked is its network of biblical and Christian imagery, which on the surface appears to be contradictory. The sequence of such images includes the maid's cry of 'Jesus' as Georg rushes out to his death, and her covering her face as if the sight were one arousing dread (67);

---

[1] The word 'Verkehr' may well have overtones of sexual communication, (cf. White, p. 229) but only insofar as that too is communication; the dominant meaning of 'Verkehr' here must be communication in general, since its meaning must be determined by its place among other occurrences in the text (e.g., pp. 53 and 58). Ruhleder cites Kafka's well-known comment on the last line ('Ich habe dabei an eine starke Ejakulation gedacht') and makes the comment that this 'true meaning' of the last sentence would have been rejected as 'far-fetched' if not pronounced by Kafka (p. 13). Cf. Politzer, p. 97. There is, of course, no reason to allow an off-hand comment by the author to determine absolutely the meaning of a word in preference to the determining factors within the text of other occurrences of the same word.

[2] By contrast, Politzer finds the judgment unjustified, and this lack of justification a 'technical' flaw: 'Wenn wir genauer zusehen, läßt sich im Text der Geschichte von Georgs Leben keine Schuld entdecken, die ein Urteil von solcher Härte rechtfertigte. Zumindest ein Teil des Rätsels, das diese Erzählung dem Leser aufgibt, entspringt disem technischen Mangel' (p. 102).

Georg's father announcing that he is the 'Vertreter' of the friend in Russia (65), with the latter's living in the town of Petersburg itself being a link with the word 'Vertreter'; the implicit situation of the parable of the prodigal son; Georg's denial 'wenigstens zweimal' of his friend in his father's presence (62); the story of the priest in Russia who cuts a cross of blood in his hand (62); and finally Georg's own hanging from the bridge as if crucified.

Even without these explicitly Christian motifs, it is clear that *Das Urteil* is concerned with ideals that play an important part in the ethos of Christianity, e.g., loyalty and betrayal, meekness and childish innocence, and the sacrifice of one who was (apparently) meek and childlike. But the explicitly Christian motifs underline the fact that in *Das Urteil* the values of Christianity are thrown up in the air, and come down in an unfamiliar shape. For one thing, the positions occupied by Georg, father and friend within the Christian scheme seem to change all the time. At one point, Georg seems to the maid to be Jesus, and fulfils that role with his being condemned to death for his 'meekness' and hanging as if crucified from the bridge.[1] But at another time, his friend is the Christ-figure, denied by Georg, and with Georg's father as his 'Vertreter'. It may seem puzzling that both Georg and his father play Peter to the friend's Christ, albeit different stages of Peter, but the confusion is increased by the friend himself being Peter of Petersburg, and telling stories of how the gospel is preached with blood in Russia. But this uncertainty as to who occupies the centre of the system of values here is a mirror of the uncertainty of the system itself, for the story explores the ambiguous and dark side of the Christian ethic. Christ was crucified because his humility was felt to be arrogance, his meekness to be aggressive and his advocacy of childlike innocence to be devious and insidious. But in Kafka's story, the ethic of peace and good-will towards men really *is* an expression of arrogance and aggression, Goerg's innocence is devilish, his sympathetic concern for others is aggressive and destructive, his lack of self-assertion is at a

[1] Cf. Ruhleder, p. 17.

deeper level highly assertive and selfish, and his self-criticism is a means of maintaining a high degree of self-satisfaction. Kafka can thus make Georg analogous to Christ to bring out this darker side of the Christian ethic, can make him seem dreadful to the servant-girl, and deserving of his crucifixion. The assignment to Georg of the 'wrong' place in the Christian scheme has something profoundly right about it; and the rest of Kafka's jumbling the roles likewise has much point. For the same kind of turning the Christian ethic upside down is visible in Georg's denial of his friend; Peter's loyalty to Christ wavers at the moment of his denial because of his wish to save himself, while Georg's very 'loyalty' to his friend is the means of his preserving himself, so that his denial is only a final emergence of his more fundamental disloyalty. The priest's spreading the gospel with blood on his hands is in the same vein; it brings to the surface the violent basis of the ethic of love, just as Georg's father links the ideal of childish innocence with devilishness.

Kafka's story is evidently a tightly-knit piece of narration, small in compass, but dense in texture. Its bizarre surface must not be removed and discarded by a process of decoding,[1] but considered seriously as part of its meaning. It draws us slowly into the world of Georg, at first comfortable enough apart from an odd hint of its artificiality, and from this position we experience the nightmare, fantastic quality of his father's challenge to it, and its final disintegration into utter disjointedness. And by this technical achievement Kafka can then do what is the point of the story; he can turn upside down the values we start with, and which are apparently Georg's – loyalty, concern for and protection of others, unselfishness, sympathy and love – and allow the final emergence of their selfish, aggressive, destructive, self-aggrandising basis. The familiarity and unquestioned nature of these values adds to the comfortable quality of Georg's world in which we enter the story, and the increasingly fantastic character of the

[1] The most elaborate decoding attempt is that of Ruhleder, who assigns various elements of the story to a mythological system including Chronos, Uranos, Aphrodite, and so on. The translation is systematic, but no less distorting for that.

narrative as they become reversed is consistent with the fact that seeing their other side is indeed strange. Kafka's narrative is very much part of his theme; the aggressive nature of love is a paradoxical idea, and a paradoxical narrative is the result.

BIBLIOGRAPHY

A full bibliography of all the critical literature containing interpretative comments on the eight stories I have discussed (biographies, histories of literature, general works of reference), or a full list of all works bearing on the theory of narration, would be both impossibly large and unnecessary. A very full bibliography on the latter subject is contained, for example, in Wayne Booth's *The Rhetoric of Fiction*; the *Wege der Forschung* volume *Novelle*, edited by Josef Kunz, contains a full bibliography of writings on the Novelle since 1915; and on the individual authors of the eight stories I have discussed there are already adequate bibliographies in the more recent biographies, or in some cases separately produced bibliographies. Since, for example, Tieck's *Der blonde Eckbert* is practically his best known work, almost anything written on Tieck will have something to say about it. I list, therefore, only the most central works on the theory of the Novelle and on narration, and on the stories work devoted exclusively to the particular text, together with any other titles of especial significance for that text (e.g., Klussmann for *Der blonde Eckbert*).

HISTORY AND THEORY OF THE NOVELLE, AND COLLECTIONS OF
INTERPRETATIONS

Bennett, E. K. *A History of the German Novelle.* 2nd ed., revised and continued by H. M. Waidson. Cambridge, 1961. (1st ed.: 1934.)

Himmel, Hellmuth. *Geschichte der deutschen Novelle.* (Sammlung Dalp, 94.) Berne & Munich, 1963.

Klein, Johannes. *Geschichte der deutschen Novelle von Goethe bis zur Gegenwart.* 4th ed. Wiesbaden, 1960. (1st ed.: 1954.)

Kunz, Josef. *Die deutsche Novelle zwischen Klassik und Romantik.* (Grundlagen der Germanistik, 2.) Berlin, 1966.

Kunz, Josef, (ed.). *Novelle.* (Wege der Forschung, 55.) Darmstadt, 1968.

Kunz, Josef. *Die deutsche Novelle im 19. Jahrhundert.* (Grundlagen der Germanistik, 10.) Berlin, 1970.

Lockemann, Fritz. *Gestalt und Wandlungen der deutschen Novelle.* Munich, 1957.

Malmede, Hans Hermann. *Wege zur Novelle. Theorie und Interpretation der Gattung Novelle in der deutschen Literaturwissenschaft.* (Sprache und Literatur, 29.) Stuttgart, 1966.

Polheim, Karl Konrad. *Novellentheorie und Novellenforschung. Ein Forschungsbericht 1945–1964.* Stuttgart, 1965.

Polheim, Karl Konrad, (ed.). *Theorie und Kritik der deutschen Novelle von Wieland bis Musil.* Tübingen, 1970.

Silz, Walter. *Realism and Reality. Studies in the German Novelle of Poetic Realism.* (University of North Carolina Studies in German Language and Literature, 11.) Chapel Hill, 1954.

Wiese, Benno von. *Die Deutsche Novelle von Goethe bis Kafka: Interpretationen.* 2 vols. Düsseldorf, 1956 & 1962.

Wiese, Benno von. *Novelle.* (Sammlung Metzler, M. 27.) 3rd ed. Stuttgart, 1967. (1st ed.: 1963.)

Zimmerman, Werner. *Deutsche Prosadichtungen unseres Jahrhunderts. Interpretationen für Lehrende und Lernende.* 2 vols. Düsseldorf, 1966–9. Revised version of: *Deutsche Prosadichtungen der Gegenwart.* 3 vols. Düsseldorf, 1953–60.

THEORY OF NARRATION

Booth, Wayne. *The Rhetoric of Fiction.* Chicago, 1961.

Brinkmann, Richard, ed. *Begriffsbestimmung des Literarischen Realismus.* (Wege der Forschung, 212). Darmstadt, 1969.

Brinkmann, Richard. *Wirklichkeit und Illusion. Studien über Gehalt und Grenzen des Begriffs Realismus für die erzählende Dichtung des neunzehnten Jahrhunderts.* 2nd. ed. Tübingen, 1966. (1st ed.: 1957.)

Friedemann, Käte. *Die Rolle des Erzählers in der Epik.* Berlin, 1910.

Hamburger, Käte. *Die Logik der Dichtung.* Stuttgart, 1957.

Kayser, Wolfgang. 'Wer erzählt den Roman?' in *Die Vortragsreise. Studien zur Literatur.* Berne, 1958.

Lämmert, Eberhard. *Bauformen des Erzählens.* Stuttgart, 1955.

Lubbock, Percy. *The Craft of Fiction.* London, 1921.

Stanzl, Franz K. *Typische Formen des Romans.* Göttingen, 1964.

EDITIONS

Heinrich von Kleist. Sämtliche Werke und Briefe, ed. Helmut Sembdner. 3rd. ed. 2 vols. Munich, 1964.

Ludwig Tieck's Schriften. 28 vols. Berlin, 1828–54.

E. T. A. Hoffmann. Sämtliche Werke, ed. Walter Müller-Seidel. 5 vols. Munich, 1960–5.

Grillparzers Sämtliche Werke, ed. August Sauer. 5th ed. 20 vols. Stuttgart, 1892–3.

Gottfried Keller. Werke. 5 vols. Zürich, 1965.

Theodor Storms Sämtliche Werke, ed. Albert Köster. 8 vols. Leipzig, 1920.

Gerhart Hauptmann. Sämtliche Werke, ed. Hans Egon-Hass. 10 vols. Frankfurt a. Main/Berlin, 1963.

BIBLIOGRAPHY

Franz Kafka. Gesammelte Werke, ed. Max Brod. 8 vols. Frankfurt a. Main, 1946–58.

KLEIST: *Das Erdbeben in Chili*

Aldridge, Alfred. 'The Background of Kleist's *Das Erdbeben in Chili*', *Arcadia*, IV (1969), 173–80.

Blankenagel, John C. 'Heinrich von Kleist: *Das Erdbeben in Chili*', *Germanic Review*, VIII (1933), 30–9.

Conrady, Karl O. 'Kleists *Erdbeben in Chili*. Ein Interpretationsversuch', *Germanisch-Romanische Monatsschrift*, N.F., IV (1954), 185–95.

Ellis, John M. 'Kleist's *Das Erdbeben in Chili*', *Publications of the English Goethe Society*, XXXIII (1963), 10–55.

Gausewitz, Walter. 'Kleist's *Erdbeben*', *Monatshefte*, LV (1963), 188–94.

Kayser, Wolfgang. 'Kleist als Erzähler', in *Die Vortragsreise*. Berne, 1958, pp. 169–83; also *German Life and Letters*, N.S., VIII (1954–5), 19–29.

Klein, Johannes. 'Kleists *Erdbeben in Chili*', *Der Deutschunterricht*, VIII (1956), 5–11.

Kunz, Josef. 'Die Gestaltung des tragischen Geschehens in Kleists *Erdbeben in Chili*', in *Gratulatio: Festschrift Christian Wegner*. Hamburg, 1968, pp. 145–70.

Lucas, R. S. 'Studies in Kleist, II: *Das Erdbeben in Chili*', *Deutsche Vierteljahrsschrift für Literaturwissenschaft und Geistesgeschichte*, XLIV (1970), 145–70.

Modern, Rodolfo E. 'Sobre *El Terremoto en Chile*, de Kleist', *Torre*, X (1962), XXXIX, 151–5.

Ossar, Michael. 'Kleist's *Das Erdbeben in Chili* and *Die Marquise von O.*', *Revue des Langues Vivantes*, XXXIV (1968), 151–69.

San Juan, Epifanio Jr. 'The Structure of Narrative Fiction', *Saint Louis Quarterly*, IV (1966), 485–502.

Silz, Walter. '*Das Erdbeben in Chili*', *Monatshefte*, LIII (1961), 210–38; also a chapter of his *Heinrich von Kliest. Studies in his Works and Literary Character*. Philadelphia, 1961, pp. 13–27.

Wiese, Benno von. 'Heinrich von Kleist: *Das Erdbeben in Chili*', *Jahrbuch der deutschen Schiller-Gesellschaft*, V (1961), 102–17; also a chapter in his *Die deutsche Novelle*, II, 53–70.

Wittkowski, Wolfgang. 'Skepsis, Noblesse, Ironie: Formen des Als-ob in Kleists *Erdbeben*', *Euphorion*, LXIII (1969), 247–83.

TIECK: *Der blonde Eckbert*

Atkinson, Margaret (ed.). *Tieck: Der blonde Eckbert. Brentano: Geschichte vom braven Kasperl und dem schönen Annerl*. (Blackwell's German Texts.) Oxford, 1951.

NARRATION IN THE GERMAN NOVELLE

Gellinek, Janis. '*Der blonde Eckbert*: A Tieckian Fall from Paradise', *Festschrift für Heinrich Henel*, eds. J. L. Sammons and E. Schürer. Munich, 1970, pp. 147–66.
Hahn, Walter. '*Tiecks blonder Eckbert* als Gestaltung romantischer Theorie', *Proceedings of the Pacific Northwest Conference on Foreign Languages*, 1967, pp. 69–78.
Häuptner, Gerhard. '*Tiecks Märchen Der blonde Eckbert*', in *Verstehen und Vertrauen. Otto Bollnow zum 65. Geburtstag*, eds. J. Schwartländer, M. Landmann and W. Loch. Stuttgart, 1969, pp. 22–6.
Hubbs, Valentine C. '*Tieck, Eckbert, und das kollektive Unbewußte*', *Publications of the Modern Language Association of America*, LXXI (1956), 686–93.
Immerwahr, Raymond. '*Der blonde Eckbert* as a poetic confession', *German Quarterly*, XXXIV (1961), 103–17.
Klussmann, Paul G. 'Die Zweideutigkeit des Wirklichen in Ludwig Tiecks Märchennovellen', *Zeitschrift für deutsche Philologie*, LXXXIII (1964), 426–52.
Lillyman, William J. 'The enigma of *Der blonde Eckbert*: the significance of the end', *Seminar: A Journal of Germanic Studies*, VII (1971), 144–55.
Northcott, Kenneth J. 'A Note on the Levels of Reality in Tieck's *Der blonde Eckbert*', *German Life and Letters*, N.S., VI (1952–3), 292–4.
Rippere, Victoria L. 'Ludwig Tieck's *Der blonde Eckbert*: a Psychological Reading', *Publications of the Modern Language Association of America*, LXXXV (1970), 473–86.

HOFFMANN: '*Rat Krespel*'

Hewett-Thayer, Harvey W. *Hoffmann: Author of the Tales*. Princeton, 1949, pp. 207–13.
Segebrecht, Wulf. *Autobiographie und Dichtung. Eine Studie zum Werk E. T. A. Hoffmanns*. Stuttgart, 1966.
Wiese, Benno von. 'Ernst Theodor Amadeus Hoffmann: *Rat Krespel*', in *Die deutsche Novelle*, II, 87–103.

GRILLPARZER: *Der arme Spielmann*

Alker, E. 'Komposition und Stil von Grillparzers Novelle *Der arme Spielmann*', *Neophilologus*, XI (1925), 15–27.
Brinkmann, Richard. 'Franz Grillparzer: *Der arme Spielmann*. Der Einbruch der Subjecktivität', in *Wirklichkeit und Illusion*, pp. 87–145.
De Cort, J. 'Zwei arme Spielleute: Vergleich eine Novelle von F. Grillparzer und von Th. Storm', *Revue des Langues Vivantes*, XXX (1964), 326–41.
Gutmann, Anna. 'Grillparzers *Der arme Spielmann*: Erlebtes und Erdich-

216

BIBLIOGRAPHY

tetes', *Journal of the International Arthur Schnitzler Research Association*, VI (1967), 14–44.

Jungbluth, Günther. 'Franz Grillparzers Erzählung: *Der arme Spielmann*. Ein Beitrag zu ihrem Verstehen', *Orbis Litterarum*, XXIV (1969), 35–51.

Krotkoff, Hertha. 'Über den Rahmen in Franz Grillparzers Novelle *Der arme Spielmann*', *MLN*, 85 (1970), 345–66.

Papst, Edmund E. (ed.). *Grillparzer: Der arme Spielmann and prose selections*. London and Edinburgh, 1960.

Paulsen, Wolfgang. 'Der gute Bürger Jakob. Zur Satire in Grillparzers *Armem Spielmann*', *Colloquia Germanica*, 1968, 272–98.

Politzer, Heinz. 'Die Verwandlung des armen Spielmanns. Ein Grillparzer-Motiv bei Franz Kafka', *Jahrbuch der Grillparzer-Gesellschaft*, IV (1965), 55–64.

Politzer, Heinz. *Franz Grillparzers 'Der arme Spielmann.'* Stuttgart, 1967.

Seuffert, Bernhard. 'Grillparzers Spielmann', in *Festschrift August Sauer zum 70. Geburtstag des Gelehrten am 12 Oktober 1925.* Stuttgart, 1925, pp. 291–311.

Silz, Walter. 'Grillparzer, *Der arme Spielmann*', in *Realism and Reality*, pp. 67–78.

Stern, J. P. 'Beyond the Common Indication: Grillparzer', in *Reinterpretations*. London, 1964, pp. 42–77.

Straubinger, O. Paul. '*Der arme Spielmann*', *Grillparzer Forum Forchtenstein*, 1966, pp. 97–102.

Swales, M. W. 'The narrative perspective in Grillparzer's *Der arme Spielmann*', *German Life and Letters*, N.S., XX (1967), 107–18.

Wiese, Benno von. 'Franz Grillparzer: *Der arme Spielmann*', in *Die deutsche Novelle*, I, 134–53.

KELLER: *Die drei gerechten Kammacher*

Jennings, Lee B. 'Gottfried Keller and the Grotesque', *Monatshefte*, L. (1958), 19–20.

Kayser, Wolfgang. *Das Groteske: Seine Gestaltung in Malerei und Dichtung*. Oldenburg, 1957.

Pregel, Dietrich. 'Das Kuriose, Komische und Groteske in Kellers Novelle *Die drei gerechten Kammacher*', *Wirkendes Wort*, XIII (1963), 331–45.

STORM: *Der Schimmelreiter*

Artiss, David S. 'Bird Motif and Myth in Theodor Storm's *Schimmelreiter*', *Seminar: A Journal of Germanic Studies*, IV (1968), 1–16.

Bernd, Clifford A. 'Das Verhältnis von erlittenem und überwundenem

217

Vergänglichkeitsgefühl in Theodor Storms Erzählhaltung', *Schriften der Theodor Storm Gesellschaft*, X (1961), 32–8.

Blankenagel, John C. 'Tragic Guilt in Storm's *Schimmelreiter*', *German Quarterly*, XXV (1952), 170–81.

Burchard, Annemarie. 'Theodor Storms *Schimmelreiter*. Ein Mythos im Werden', *Antaios*, II (1960–1), 456–69.

Ellis, J. M. 'Narration in Storm's *Der Schimmelreiter*', *Germanic Review*, XLIV (1969), 21–30.

Hermand, Jost. 'Hauke Haien. – Kritik oder Ideal des gründerzeitlichen Übermenschen?', *Wirkendes Wort*, XV (1965), 40–50.

Loeb, Ernst. 'Faust ohne Transzendenz: Theodor Storms *Schimmelreiter*', *Studies in Germanic Languages and Literatures. In memory of Fred O. Nolte*. St. Louis, 1963, pp. 121–32.

Silz, Walter. 'Theodor Storm's *Der Schimmelreiter*', *Publications of the Modern Language Association of America*, LXI (1946), 762–83; partly reprinted as: 'Storm, *Der Schimmelreiter*', in *Realism and Reality*, pp. 117–36.

Wittmann, Lothar. 'Theodor Storm: *Der Schimmelreiter*', in *Deutsche Novellen des 19. Jahrhunderts. Interpretationen zu Storm und Keller*. Frankfurt a. M., 1961, pp. 50–92.

HAUPTMANN: *Bahnwärter Thiel*

Martini, Fritz. 'Gerhart Hauptmann: *Bahnwärter Thiel*', in *Das Wagnis der Sprache*. Stuttgart, 1954, pp. 56–98.

Ordon, Marianne. 'Unconscious Contents in *Bahnwärter Thiel*', *Germanic Review*, XXVI (1951), 223–9.

Requadt, P. 'Die Bilderwelt in Gerhart Hauptmanns *Bahnwärter Thiel*', in *Minotaurus. Dichtung unter den Hufen von Staat und Industrie*, ed. A. Döblin. Wiesbaden, 1953.

Silz, Walter. 'Hauptmann, *Bahnwärter Thiel*', in *Realism and Reality*, pp. 137–52.

Wiese, Benno von. 'Gerhart Hauptmann: *Bahnwärter Thiel*', in *Die deutsche Novelle*, I, 268–83.

Zimmermann, Werner. 'Gerhart Hauptmann: *Bahnwärter Thiel*', in *Deutsche Prosadichtungen unseres Jahrhunderts*, I, 69–87; identical with: *Deutsche Prosadichtungen der Gegenwart*, I, 39–61.

KAFKA: *Das Urteil*

Beissner, Friedrich. 'Kafka the Artist', in *Kafka. A Collection of Critical Essays*, ed. Ronald Gray. Englewood Cliffs, 1962, pp. 15–31. (Translation of his *Kafka der Dichter*, Stuttgart, 1958.)

Edel, Edmund. 'Franz Kafka: *Das Urteil*', *Wirkendes Wort*, IX (1959), 216–55.

Politzer, Heinz. *Franz Kafka, der Künstler*. Gütersloh, 1965.

Ruhleder, Karl H. 'Franz Kafka's *Das Urteil*. An Interpretation', *Monatshefte*, LV (1963), 13–22.

Sokel, Walter. *Franz Kafka: Tragik und Ironie*. Vienna/Munich, 1964, pp. 44–76.

White, John J. 'Franz Kafka's *Das Urteil* – An Interpretation', *Deutsche Vierteljahrsschrift für Literaturwissenschaft und Geistesgeschichte*, XXXVIII (1964), 208–29.

Zimmermann, Werner. 'Franz Kafka: *Das Urteil*', in *Deutsche Prosadichtungen unseres Jahrhunderts*, I, 189–208; revised version of: *Deutsche Prosadichtungen der Gegenwart*, III, 93–110.